# Industrial Policies:
# International
# Restructuring
# and Transnationals

# Industrial Policies: International Restructuring and Transnationals

**Jack N. Behrman**
The University of
North Carolina at Chapel Hill

**LexingtonBooks**
D.C. Heath and Company
Lexington, Massachusetts
Toronto

**Library of Congress Cataloging in Publication Data**

Behrman, Jack N.
  Industrial policies.

  Includes bibliographies and index.
  1. International economic integration.      2. International business enterprises. 3. Industry and state.   I. Title.
HF1418.5.B44   1984                     337.1                      83-49533
ISBN 0-669-08275-9 (alk. paper)

*Copyright © 1984 by D.C. Heath and Company*

Published simultaneously in Canada

Printed in the United States of America on acid-free paper

International Standard Book Number: 0-669-08275-9

Library of Congress Catalog Card Number: 83-49533

*To the Memory of My*
*Professors in International Political Economy*
*Frank D. Graham*
*Ervin Hexner*
*Jacob Viner*

*The words of my book nothing,*
*the drift everything.*

—Walt Whitman

# Contents

# Contents

# Preface

Over the last two decades, I have tried to remain an objective observer of international corporate strategies and governments' foreign economic policies in order to help each understand the other better. In recent years, these two groups have increasingly recognized their mutual interests, despite occasional conflicts and the assumption of fairly strident positions at times. Still, much remains to be done to regain a sufficient degree of order and balance in the world economy so that industrial progress may be accelerated and the benefits distributed widely.

In my discussions with both corporate and government officials, I have frequently been asked to take the next step into prescription, pointing the way as to what should be done to reach the asserted desirable goals. These goals relate to obtaining the advantages of international economic integration. This book is an attempt to answer that request. It emanates from earlier research (as my readers will quickly recognize) but more recently from a request by the Council on Foreign Relations to conduct a series of discussions on transnationals in U.S. foreign economic policy and from my participation in research by the National Academy of Engineering on U.S. international competitiveness. These exercises offered the opportunity to meld a number of ideas related to the multinational enterprise, trade and investment policies, economic integration in developing countries, and the experience of the NATO co-production agreements. Still more recently I have been engaged in an analysis of industrial policies as they are emerging in the advanced and developing countries. It has become evident that pursuit of international competitiveness on a sectoral basis has pulled nations into protectionist stances. Many analysts of the situation have urged a return to freer trade policies, but it does not appear that this will happen. However much we might prefer an open world economy, it will remain selectively closed for a number of justifiable reasons—including the fact that the world is not at peace and several other assumptions underlying free trade do not exist.

In responding to the request for new norms of behavior in the world economy, the proposals here are avowedly persuasive in advocating a redirection of U.S. foreign economic policy. The wrench to U.S. policy orientations in what is proposed here causes me to to assign a low probability to the likelihood of the government (essentially State Department) taking an initiative in seeking greater interdependence and integration in ways other than traditional. Yet these proposals indicate that there are ways of achieving industrial integration through modification of existing mechanisms and some new institutional arrangements, without sacrificing—and possibly even enhancing—efficiency. The thrust of my argument is that major problems will not be resolved unless we develop a closer community of interests to deal with problems of distributive justice. We must begin by enhancing government–business dialogues and cooperation, expanding corporate responsibilities, and restructuring international industrial patterns. Only with such communal interests and cooperative efforts can many of the requisite trade-offs be made.

Readers steeped in the classical or Keynesian traditions will disagree with the thrust of these chapters, but neither group has developed an appreciation of institutional change, and that is what we are now facing. Existing institutions are not satisfactory, and they *will* be changed. In what direction, to what new modes of cooperation, and under what new ordering principles remain to be seen. The suggestions made here are a response to present trends in world political economy and are achievable given its present institutional structure. My own preferences are presented in the final chapter, which carries the argument beyond industrial integration or economics.

Being essays in persuasion, the arguments stand or fall on their own validity and cannot be strengthened by appeals to authority. The ideas presented here are drawn from numerous authors amalgamated with ideas of my own, garnered from several different research projects over the past two decades. I have refrained from citing any but a few sources made necessary by quotation, though a bibliography of books that have influenced me directly is added at the end.

I acknowledge with thanks the permission of the National Science Foundation to publish the material in chapters 2 and 3, much of which was prepared at its request. Chapter 3 has appeared also in its essentials in a collection on national industrial policies, published here by permission of OG&H, Boston, Mass.

I am especially grateful for the continued encouragement of Helena Stalson and William Diebold, Jr., of the Council on Foreign Relations to proceed with many rewritings. My thanks go to Helena also for reading and rereading several of the drafts, and to my colleagues Nancy Hyer and Monty Graham; they have prevented me from making serious errors or leaving even more substantial gaps than still remain in the argument. Those that do remain reflect my own stubbornness as to the content and mode of presentation.

# 1 Introduction

The past thousand years have seen the creation of increasingly large groups of communal units, integrated both politically and economically. The process has moved from family units to tribes, to city-states, to federations of city-states, to nations, and, most recently, to regional association of nations. World federation is still some decades or centuries away. During the past centuries, there have been long periods of relatively static relationships, and periods of dis-integration. But the evolution of mankind appears to hold within it a process of coalescing peoples into larger groupings, leading to closer social and political association and greater economic specialization.

Presently, there are strong simultaneous counter movements—one toward economic nationalism and another toward international interdependence. The nation-state is seen as an obstacle to, rather than a building block for, closer worldwide cooperation. In addition, a new protectionism is arising in which national governments are turning inward to focus on problems of economic growth and stability. At the same time, pressures continue to mount, forcing nations together in the pursuit of mutual goals or the resolution of international problems. Closer economic ties at the regional and global levels are asserted by many government officials as desirable policy goals, and numerous intergovernmental efforts are being made toward economic cooperation, both bilaterally and multilaterally. Some observers recommend and hope for a jump to world federalism over the grave of the nation-state. But when world federation comes, it will more likely be *through* the state system, representing their citizens, with regional federation yet to come in the interim.

Currently, many national economic policies are directed at greater self-reliance, which in the application of some policies means a pulling away from international specialization toward economic independence, at least in basic agriculture and industry. Some nations have gone so far as to select priority industries for promotion or protection by measures denominated as industrial policies. Some observers argue that this trend is so strong that it is likely to reshape completely the nature and role of transnational corporations (TNCs), splitting them and destroying the structure of international production that has arisen over the past twenty years through their activities. If this occurs, the nature and extent of international economic integration will change significantly in a direction that will reduce the specialization among nations, thereby altering the composition and rate of economic growth.

This may be the way in which the world is moving. But it is highly unlikely that *national* industrial policies can be implemented without their clashing. The most advanced countries are all currently stressing the buildup of the high- and sophisticated-technology sectors, without regard for what the others are doing. Nor are those national industrial policies that are structured to strengthen later bargaining positions in negotiating integration arrangements likely to produce the most effective or equitable results. Therefore, current consideration of international economic integration is desirable before national policies are locked into a mode of protectionism. There are ways in which it can be pursued more effectively than we have in the recent past, without complete government withdrawal. But a restructuring of industry internationally or regionally will be required.

For most of the time, after World War II, international integration—which is another name for the concept of international specialization or division of labor—was achieved by the reduction of barriers to trade, inducing each country to produce according to its comparative or competitive advantage, based on its resource endowment and its market size and composition.

In the past twenty years, integration through trade has been supplemented by integration based on international production rising from an expansion of direct foreign investment. International trade has been increasingly tied to and based on the spread of international production, which has shifted the nature of specialization. It did so through the movement of factors of production (labor, management, technology, and capital), increasing the duplication of industry sectors but enhancing specialization in components. Thus more and more countries have established production in the major industrial sectors, but product lines within that sector have been specialized, or specialization has occurred in subunits, parts, components, and even through variations in volume of production, with some nations both producing and importing similar products. Specialization has also occurred based on different product characteristics: mass consumption versus high fashion, or low quality versus high quality, or generic verses trademarked goods.

The benefits of specialization include a greater production from given resources and greater efficiency through exchange of materials, components, and final products. It is in the process of exchange that the question of the gains from production and trade arises. Much of the questioning of economic dependence or independence currently arises from policymakers' doubts as to the appropriateness of gains from the present and emerging structure of international production and trade and leads to their demands for restructuring. The question of benefits has largely been swept under the rug at policy levels in the past three decades. The question of the gains has always underlain international negotiations or deliberations, but its resolution has been so difficult that even economists have tended to disregard it. It will not go away.

It is in fact brought to the fore in the various resolutions in the United Nations concerning the construction of a New International Economic Order (NIEO). The Charter of Economic Rights and Duties and the developing countries have sought to gain acceptance of the need to redistribute not only current gains from production and trade but also wealth, which is the basis of these gains, and even to induce reparations for past inequities in the distribution of benefits. It is not likely that any of these will occur in the ways in which the developing countries assert that they wish, but the problem remains. The issues can be couched in terms of (1) the degree of international economic integration desired; (2) the underlying specialization in the determination of the location of industrial activity; and (3) an acceptable distribution of benefits for all nations involved.

None of these have been faced frontally and collectively by nations since the Bretton Woods Agreements. In an effort to make certain that there is an acceptable distribution of the costs and benefits of international industrial development, a number of governments have turned toward national economic protectionism through complex non-tariff barriers, increased barter, exchange rate interference, creation of state-enterprises, constraints on private investment, and guidelines for transitional company operations. These moves reduce the *total* economic benefits (as compared to those available under greater economic interdependence) as well as the absolute and relative benefits received by some individual nations.

At the same time that greater economic nationalism is arising in OECD countries, we are faced with demands by less developed countries (LDCs) to restructure the world economy so as to make it more equitable and to increase their participation in industrial production. We have on hand mechanisms by which economic interdependence can be made both effective and equitable—that is, efficient in achieving production objectives and a distribution of benefits and costs that is acceptable to governments involved. Yet we have not formulated policies that would use these new mechanisms, because to do so would lead to a restructuring of international industry, and the advanced countries do not yet see that need. The reason for this is that they (both government and corporate officials) are still bound by the growth paradigm—that is, that more rapid growth is all that is needed to solve the world's economic problems. Not only does growth not solve some of the critical problems, it creates new ones (as is well recognized, for example, in the environmental area). Another effect of growth is to sharpen recognition of inequities in distribution of rewards. These inequities are evident not only in income itself but also in location of income-generating industry—that is, wealth. The mechanisms for helping to resolve the problem are institutional and require focused policies. Policies that would employ these mechanisms would include the formation of industrial strategies, focusing on sectoral and structural problems rather than economic aggregates, such as in the monetary and fiscal areas. But these cannot help resolve the issue of distribution if they are based solely on national interests; international (at least binational) cooperation would also be necessary.

This is a completely different approach from that proposing a "GATT for International Investment." But such a new GATT is much too broad and all-encompassing for present governmental concerns. Consequently it would be too vague and irrelevant for specific sectors. Contrarily, many governments at present see their responsibilities in maintaining and encouraging key sectors of industry and commerce, not in merely maintaining desired growth rates. This orientation will push us toward quite specific arrangements on industry sectors, probably bilaterally and regionally rather than worldwide. We are, therefore, in a phase of developing sufficient cooperative experience, sector-by-sector, so that we can move to a larger community of interest with greater mutual trust.

A shift to international *sectoral* cooperation has been opposed by economists and many policymakers because it does not fit with the classical economic scheme and does not have a generally accepted theory of its own, at least as yet. To develop a theory will require moving beyond economics into politics and probably into ethics, both of which economists of all persuasions have historically recognized as necessary to support the social philosophy of a capitalist system but are overlooked by most present-day economists. The first shift that is needed is a conceptual one—substituting the classical, atomistic, competitive market, equilibrium paradigm with one recognizing the role of large corporate entities, governmental and oligopoly interferences in the market, diverse social changes, and disturbances from innovations. This would place process over status: a process of cooperative competition within a structure and under rules that provide a place for all participants without yielding significantly the kind of flexibility needed to permit creative changes around the world. Creative destruction is, of course, necessary for human evolution, but an objective is not to waste resources and denigrate people in the process.

We have not yet put into practice the recognitions that we are all legitimate passengers on spaceship earth, that the evolution of any one of us depends on our treatment of others, and that the evolution of mankind depends on the elevation of each person. There is a fundamental interdependence of each with all, all with each, and all with the environment.

When we actively recognize these principles, we will place a higher priority on the roles offered to each individual and on a more equitable (not equal) distribution of the benefits of progress—economic, social, and cultural— among nations. We have means at hand for addressing the concerns over distribution; to use them would be to our benefit in the enhancement of the dignity of individuals and the progress of mankind.

Within the advanced (OECD) countries, the problem of reindustrialization (or restructuring of industry or industrial policy) is being raised to a high priority in government policies. In the United States, reindustrialization means a reorientation of priorities, a redirection of capital, rededication to productivity, and a reassessment of government-business relations. Internationally, it means an effort to shift into high-technology sectors, exporting these products to other OECD countries and some LDCs. Of course, other OECD members have the same goals. Therefore, any effort to restructure industry at the national level implies a restructuring internationally. Not to take the international implications into account will lead to greater protectionism, as governments attempt to overcome or cover over their mistakes (in the form of duplication of capacities aimed at the same world markets).

One major instrument for implementation of international (or binational or regional) sectoral cooperation is the transnational corporation (TNC). TNCs have become pervasive internationally and are widely criticized; yet they can be used effectively in the restructuring of industry internationally. The major problem of TNCs is not how to reshape their social or commercial behavior (e.g., through intergovernmental or national codes of conduct), but how to make certain that their capabilities are directed toward solving some of the pressing problems in the international economy. They have been asked to help solve a number in which they are directly or indirectly involved: hunger and nutrition, disease and health, environmental protection, energy conservation and development, mass-consumption products, transportation and communication, community development, population, application of science and technology to basic human needs, and so on. But they have not been used as a major instrument in achieving international economic integration, despite the repeated assertions by governments that this objective has a high priority. If they were so used, and if observers became convinced that the activities of TNCs were supporting major policy objectives, concerns over their behavior would be mitigated, for TNCs' operations would be seen as both more effective and equitable.

The first step toward restructuring industry internationally is willingness on the parts of both business and governments to alter their policy orientations jointly and severally. The second step is a reorientation behavior on the part of TNCs—away from short-term profitability toward longer-term contributions, both economically and socially. This shift involves acceptance of a larger and wider responsibility on the part of the TNCs to make certain that their operations and behavior benefit the various communities that have a stake in the processes of production and the distribution of rewards. Acceptance of a more responsive role does not imply greater rigidity. Contrarily, corporations should be a means of maintaining flexibility and a desirable mobility of factors. Innovation would still be a major responsibility of private industry.

There have been many calls for a more cooperative world economy, but few governments have been willing to make the institutional changes necessary. A restructuring is required, but with the TNC as a major actor, both in policy formation and implementation. LDC governments have previously sought to exclude TNCs, but they are recently actively courting TNCs for national development objectives. LDCs need next to recognize that an international restructuring that undercuts or bypasses (and thereby destroys) TNCs is likely to lead to a dis-integration of the world economy, bringing to a halt desirable moves toward the integration and interdependence which are needed to meet the pressing socioeconomic problems of the rich and poor.[1]

The third step is toward a governmental approach that attempts to use the capabilities of the TNCs so as to achieve economic and social goals rather than merely issuing prohibitions. This requires an institutional shift in the ties between private companies and governments, without undercutting desirable decision-making freedom at operating levels within individual firms.

The following chapters examine means of restructuring international industry toward greater integration and the role of the transnational corporations therein as alternatives to a competitive and adversarial system. The objective is a form of competitive cooperation or cooperative competition. Cooperation alone would not give sufficient opportunity for testing of new ideas or respond rapidly enough to changes in the composition of demand (as population and tastes change). Competition alone tends to be destructive, not only of physical and social assets but also ethical values and even destructive of competition itself. We should therefore seek as many new ways of forming coorperative arrangements as possible, without creating deadening bureaucracies or losing the bracing and change-oriented contribution of competition within rules laid down to assure that the competitive process does in fact lead to progress for all. It is in the formation and acceptance of the rules that the greatest cooperation takes place.

These chapters are related to the search for rules under a New International Economic Order, but they start from an assumption that we will not be able to redesign rules for the entire system as under the Bretton Woods Agreements. New rules will have to be reached in a step-by-step determination of the nature and extent of integration permitted—that is, determining who produces what, where and who trades what with whom— decisions that U.S. policy has assigned to market forces, reflecting supply and demand.

Governments and peoples now realize that the conditions of supply and demand can be readily altered, either at the hands of single or collective governments or at the will of single or collective companies, since the latter have become large and economically powerful. Given these abilities to interfere in the market, either directly by setting prices or quantities or indirectly by altering the comparative advantages, the major questions of distribution and the use of power come to the fore. Power is now employed through both exclusive decision-making mechanisms and control over resources, which is why the developing countries seek to restructure the decision-making processes to increase their participation and why they seek to redistribute the ownership and control over resources, including technology. Governments can exercise such power, and they will be induced to do so because of their assumption of responsibility for economic and social growth. The problem is to find internationally acceptable limits for the exercise of government power in corporate activities.

Not all of the aspects of the world economy subject to restructuring are examined here (for example, the questions of the international monetary system, the UN codes on transnationals, technology, and world-wide problems of food and hunger are left aside). The issues addressed here are related to one of the prime movers in a restructuring of world industry—the transnational corporations—and to the ordering principles that will guide international industrialization within a New International Economic Order. These principles will be derived neither by a reversion to the processes of the free market nor by relying solely on governments for decisions. There are too many actors involved; the private sector and the TNCs will remain on the scene along with governments as primary actors indefinitely. We are faced, therefore, with a necessity to guide the international economy through cooperative efforts on the part of business and government, with the supporting cooperation of labor and a variety of other interest groups making their voices heard essentially through governments and to TNCs themselves. This effort would lead to a cooperative restructuring of the location of industry sectors and the reorganization and control of enterprise.

The United States is ill-prepared to engage in such cooperative efforts, having based its government-business relations on an adversarial concept that tends to separate the two parties and keep them at a distance. Government-business dialogues tend to be over conflicts rather than how to move cooperatively towards mutual goals, much less how to determine mutual interests, nationally or internationally.

The Executive Branch in the United States, represented especially by the State Department, finds the world economy not operating to its liking; it seeks a classical market economy, without distortions in trade and investment flows. But the officials recognize the probable continued interference by governments and therefore remain in a dilemma as to how to move to form their desired economy. What they do not seem to realize is that the ability of the United States to enunciate and enforce the rules of behavior has declined to a point where it must seriously consider how to operate by different, internationally agreed-upon rules. Other countries' rules are much more nationalistically oriented than those aimed at international economic integration under the classical system. But new means of achieving the desired integration can be found, and in ways that balance national interests.

TNCs, as presently constituted, have unique capabilities to accelerate specialization and international industrial integration (though different in structure from classical integration), which we should seek to utilize as a basis for the inevitable restructuring of industry rather than let them atrophy under the pressures of increasing national regulation. These regulations are forming the new industrial policies which are aimed also at stimulating nationally based companies, as discussed in part I. How the TNCs might be used in different settings is examined in the subsequent chapters (part II), beginning with an assessment of the emerging patterns of dis-integration in the absence of policy coordination, followed by a characterization of TNCs and their potential roles. Application of their capabilities is then directed (part III) to restructured integration within the OECD region, between the East and the West, between the North and the South, and among countries of the South. A concluding chapter looks at the obstacles to restructuring industrial integration as suggested in these chapters, emphasizing the increased responsibility of government and the close ties between TNCs and governments that would be required. If such ties are deemed undesirable, some alternative modes of cooperation still remain and are imperative in the long run. But they appear even less likely in the present world. All of us need to recognize that the objective of mankind is to evolve, individually and collectively, to higher levels of understanding and behavior; recognition must then be followed by an act of greater will, in recognition of the power that high purpose provides.

**Note**

1. One can conceive a world built on the concepts of "Small Is Beautiful," as expounded by E.F. Schumacher and his supporters, and there are undoubtedly advantages to a decentralization of both decision-making and

operations. However, some operations are more efficiently done on large scale (petroleum refining and petro-chemicals, for example, and auto assembly). There is a place for both, and the precise size and structure yields to sound analysis of trade-offs. The thesis expounded here does not depend on size—rather it relates to the meshing on constituent elements, whether owned or under contract, into an integrated system, both within and across national boundaries.

## Selected Readings for the Introduction

Belassa, B. *The Theory of Economic Integration.* London: Geo. Allen and Unwin, 1965.

Machlup, F. (ed.) *Economic Integration: Worldwide, Regional, Sectoral.* London: Macmillan, 1976.

Meade, J.E. *The Theory of Customs Union.* Amsterdam: North-Holland, 1975.

Röpke, W. *International Economic Disintegration.* N.Y.: Macmillan, 1942.

Staley, E. *World Economic Development.* Montreal; International Labor Office, 1944.

Viner, J. *The Customs Union Issue.* N.Y.: Stevens & Sons, 1950.

# Part I
# Industrial Policies

Industrial policies, which focus on specific sectors, originated in the period of Mercantilism (fifteenth to eighteenth centuries) and have never fully closed in Europe. But they have been thrust to the fore in the post–World War II decades by their perceived success in France and Japan. These policies have shifted significantly in the past thirty years, with sectors that were stimulated in the 1950s now being supported in their declining years. Japan, which gave incentives to the auto industry in the 1930s and 1950s, is now prepared to see that sector decline. Sectors such as textiles, steel, and shipbuilding have largely shifted to the newly industrialized countries, such as Taiwan, Singapore, South Korea, Mexico, Brazil, and India.

The major nations of the world have progressively shifted both trade and investment policies toward attention to specific industry sectors rather than to industrialization as a whole. Governments have long protected different sectors differentially under tariff schedules, but even these industry supports were directed more at products than at the survival of the sector as such and were certainly not instituted simply for the protection of a major company. More recently, a series of sector-specific, and even company-specific, supports have been employed by a number of countries. The supports are frequently aimed at the same sectors, especially among the advanced countries, leading to a new form of protectionism.

Moves to the new protectionism are marked by the adoption of industrial policies for the promotion of sectors that seem to be advancing, the maintenance of mature sectors, and either the protection or the easing of adjustments in the declining sectors. The declining sectors are those that are under strong competitive pressure from both imports and foreign direct investment. Advancing sectors are identified as those with high technology, new innovations in product lines, and potentials for reaching into the world markets. Among these, some sectors are assisted purely for national-security reasons, and others obtain assistance through aggregate industrial development stimuli.

To set the stage for discussion of problems of international industrial integration, it is desirable to survey briefly the activities of three industrialized and three newly industrialized countries as to their industrial policies. The purpose here is to show the problems arising from nationally oriented policies, pointing toward the emerging conflicts. Those familiar with comparative national industrial policies can move quickly through these two chapters to the examination of the potential role of the transnationals in reducing sectoral conflicts and the trade and investment wars envisioned by some observers.

Industrial policies reflect a governmental desire to mitigate a number of economic and political pressures. Nations have continued to build specific industrial structures, which satisfy their political-social-economic-security objectives. But they have also pursued policies of reducing barriers to trade, so that there has been increasing competitive pressure across the board on industrial sectors. This pressure has been buttressed by the increasing significance of economies of scale in achieving competitiveness in key sectors, the increasing cost of R&D and innovation in key sectors, increasingly long lead time for development of new products, and the instabilities of foreign exchange rates—all of which have raised barriers to entry in a number of industrial sectors and have increased the significance of developing an appropriate corporate strategy. In addition, given the socioeconomic-military objectives of governments in certain sectors, market signals would sometimes cause an undesirable contraction in a key sector.

The following chapters give in broad outline the industrial policy orientations of selected advanced and developing countries, making some comparisons among them. All such policies are directed to national industrial structures, with little regard to what others are doing, thereby raising significant problems for international industrial development.

The debates on industrial policies have so far taken the approach that they can be assessed from the standpoint of the national interest in isolation. Despite the fact that each of the countries has had an objective of enhancing international competitiveness, even their own views as to the implications of the policies are focused on national economies rather than the international economy. Nevertheless, the fundamental problem that is being addressed is that of international specialization or the division of labor. Each of the industrial policies seeks to retain or to expand within the national economy an industrial activity that would otherwise not occur in the same fashion. This altering of the location and structure of production affects the ability of other countries to industrialize, changing both the structure and the rate of industrialization. This effect occurs not only between the advanced and the developing countries but among the advanced countries themselves.

What countries are saying is that they do not like the structure of international specialization and the resulting trade that would occur under a more hands-off posture. They are, in effect, saying that the market has serious limitations in permitting the country to seek its national objectives. The market does, in fact, have serious limitations in two directions: It does not provide adequate signals for the future, and it does not take into account social (extramarket) objectives. We do not even have a theory to explain or a process to achieve the reconciliation of a self-equilibrating mechanism with socially acceptable results.

Although the market is not expected to cover all social objectives (and governments assume the responsibility for pursuing these through their own procedures), the lack of a future orientation of the market is not always understood adequately. The signals in a market are only those that are generated at the moment; the market cannot embody future signals (only present expectations as to the future), nor can it *currently* dictate future decisions. What the market does is signal current decisions that have future implications and impacts or current decisions on what the future may be. These decisions can, of course, be retaken or revised in the future, though at a cost to someone. It is the role of managers to try to estimate, extrapolate, or guess what future demands will be; and it is up to the government to determine what future needs or socially acceptable desires should be met. These are not two separate realms, and they therefore require some degree of coordination. The greater the degree of concern for social acceptability, the greater will be the government intervention.

To pursue the objectives of economic growth and stability while at the same time achieving socially acceptable results for various interests, groups, and regions within the country through aggregate techniques has not proven sufficiently effective in achieving the ends sought. Therefore more attention has been paid recently to the micro-sectoral approach, seeking to alter the structure and level of production within each country, thereby affecting trade patterns. This concern is identical with the concept of specialization.

Where specialization is altered in line with objectives sought through present industrial policies, the result can only be greater protection in trade relations. In fact, national industrial policies are inherently protectionist unless developed under international agreements, subject to agreed rules, and seeking coordinated objectives. Recent efforts to reduce national subsidies through negotiation under the GATT have been frustrated by the fact that there can be little agreement on the techniques unless there is an agreement on how the problem that gave rise to the restrictive measures is itself to be met. The Bretton Woods Agreements did set up for the post–World War II period a group of institutions to implement newly agreed-upon rules on how industrial activity would be located around the world—under market signals, with nondiscrimination and multilateral freeing of trade and payments. The continued priority given to *national* employment and economic growth and to noneconomic objectives in the development of key industrial sectors has ruptured these agreements, and no new ordering principle has been substituted. Consequently, governments are increasingly turning to protectionist or nationally oriented solutions. If the world is to be led away from this neo-mercantilist orientation, international economic policies will have to give priority concern to the structure and criteria for international specialization, to the agreed procedures for implementation, and to a more acceptable distribution of benefits of industrial development.

# 2 Policies of Three Advanced and Three Newly Industrialized Countries

Industrial policies are more significant in the economic orientations of some OECD countries than in the newly industrialized countries. Each of those examined in this chapter shows numerous shifts in objectives and techniques; but for both advanced countries (ACs) and newly industrialized countries (NICs) the shifts do not indicate a lessening of government intervention, in favor of greater reliance on market signals, save in a few minor instances. Rather, each is attempting to find more effective means to achieve changing goals and meet new sectoral priorities. France has experimented more than most, though Japan has shifted its sectoral priorities without significantly altering its policy goals, techniques, or orientations. West Germany has not altered its strategies or mechanisms significantly, once it cut loose from the extreme free market orientation of the 1950s and early 1960s.

The newly industrialized countries have not faced the same pressures for the creation of industrial policies that the advanced countries have, and their objectives and institutional mechanisms are different. They are still more in the phase of supporting infant industries or overcoming the disadvantage of a late start through a variety of measures that protect the domestic market so as to stimulate local production. Still, it is just these measures to expand their participation in worldwide industrial production that raise problems of restructuring on the part of the advanced countries as well. Many of these countries, however, have industrialization policies, rather than industrial policies, and are simply stimulating the industrial sector compared to agriculture. They are often willing to accept any industry that arrives, though in some of these countries there is an increasing focus on specific types of industry, especially the high technology sectors. The policies in the three NICs—Brazil, South Korea, and Taiwan—demonstrate that, although they differ in their degree of openness to the world economy, they are similar in providing specific stimuli to industrial sectors under a set of guidelines emanating from the government.

## Japanese Policy

Japanese business-government cooperation began in the mid-nineteenth century with the Meiji revolution to industrialize the country. The government sold state enterprises to the private sector (composed largely of merchants and former *Samurai*) who felt a responsibility for growth and security of the country. Following the post–World War II breakup of the Zaibatsu, the companies formerly associated regrouped into Keiretsu. (The Keiretsu are not holding companies, as were the Zaibatsu, but are separate companies, commonly held, with their own boards of directors but using the same tradename; the heads of each of the operating companies meet periodically to form strategy.) This concentration and the connection of each Keiretsu with one of the major banks make coordination with the government easy compared with other countries.

In the late 1950s, Japan had established a list of priority sectors— including textiles, shipbuilding, steel, autos, and chemicals—for which it restricted imports, prohibited foreign investment (except as minority partners), and encouraged imports of foreign technology. Automobiles were supported as early as the 1930s, but they began their post-war expansion with a boost from the Korean War; parts manufacturers were consolidated and modernized. Electronics, telecommunications, and other sectors were encouraged.

Presently, Japan constructs a national industrial plan (really a vision of the future), in which it identifies sectors that it considers to have the best prospects for technological advance and international competitiveness and then adopts supporting techniques. At the same time, Japan attempts to shift workers out of declining industries into those with better prospects. This process is conducted under a consensus approach that involves several stages of consultation between the government and all other interested parties.

Recent guidelines emerged from a document entitled "Industrial Policy Vision of the 1980s" published by the Ministry of International Trade and Industry (MITI) in April 1980. This document sets priorities, and industry sectors are expected to respond appropriately. Each company is in principle free to respond in its own way, but industry officials were members of an advisory board (the Industrial Structure Council), composed of more than fifty representatives of government, business, and academia. The council meets frequently and is composed of individuals personally known to each other in many other contexts so that they were able and willing to make compromises. Government industrial responsibilities are centered in divisions of MITI, and company interests are represented in MITI by industry associations through standing and ad hoc committees, which are often attended by labor officials as well. The mutual concern is to achieve consensus, if feasible, without endangering company survival. Agreement is not always reached, but the process is a continuing one.

The mechanisms of coordination are completed through the ties among Japanese industry and banks. Industry has four major associations, with multiple subgroupings related to industry sectors and policy issues, and the banks are linked to both the government and the Keiretsu, as shown in table 2-1.

**Table 2-1**
**Japanese Mechanisms of Coordination**

| | |
|---|---|
| Ministry of International Trade and Industry (MITI) | Tax incentives, antitrust, lending, price and capacity controls, export-import measures, environmental regulations, raw material price setting and procurement, technology subsidies, dislocation subsidies, and regional policies, *anything* affecting the sector or firm, judged on a differential basis according to priorities |
| Ministry of Finance | Tax incentives, low-cost loans, subsidies, tariffs, foreign exchange rate changes |
| Research Development Corporation | Subsidy for R&D, joint private/government research, licensing of technology |
| Ministry of Post and Telecommunications | Guidance to telecommunications sector |
| Ministry of Health and Welfare | Guidance to pharmaceutical sector |
| Keidanren (Federation of Economic Organizations) | Coordination of industry views on industry policies |
| Shoko Kaigesho (Chamber of Commerce and Industry) | Coordination of the views of industry, including medium- and small-sized companies, commerce, and banking |
| Keizai Doyukai (Committee on Economic Development) | Position papers on economic and industrial policies by companies |
| Nikkeiren (Federation of Employers Associations) | Coordination of industrial relations among industries and companies |
| Zaikai (Friday Club) | Small group of chief executive officers, close to prime minister and parties |
| Industry associations | Coordination with MITI on specific sectoral policies and formation of industry cartels as desired |
| City banks | Linked with Keiretsu (conglomerate enterprises) as financial sources and directors; linked with Bank of Japan and other government banks (Industrial Bank, Development Bank) |

*Growing Sectors*

The objective of industrial policy in the growing sectors is to anticipate and accelerate signals from the market; consequently, the Japanese government supports R&D activities, capital expenditures, and export efforts but maintains a highly unrestrained competition for market share among the companies within the domestic market. Financial assistance is provided both by MITI and the Ministry of Finance and through the Japan Development Bank, and Industrial Bank of Japan, and indirectly through commercial banks. In addition, MITI will support a selected group of R&D projects and technologies proposed by key companies in these sectors, and it is currently funding (in whole or in part) nine group projects for the development of high-technology breakthroughs in steel, jet engines, robotics, and various energy sources. This support is frequently in the hundreds of millions of dollars for a given project over a several-year period. Participating companies share in the development work and in the rights to innovation. The government also provides tax incentives and low-cost financing, plus accelerated depreciation to encourage R&D activities of any qualifying firms.

The industrial sectors to be emphasized in the 1980s are so-called knowledge-intensive industries. The industry sectors added to those already picked in the 1970s include the following: ultra-high-speed computers, oceanic and space development, aircraft, optical fibers, ceramics, amorphous materials, high-efficiency resins, and a group of energy producers including coal liquefaction and gasification, nuclear and solar energy, and deep geothermal generation of energy. Adding these twelve to those already selected for the 1970s makes a total of around twenty-four specific sectors to be given governmental support.

In industrial machinery, the government has moved the sector from the mere production of mechanical components and machine assembly in the 1950s to the construction of entire plants, with all of the components of machinery and assembly therein. As its companies have become more competitive, the government has shifted its support from financial aid and specific guidance to a looser form of support, responding to strategic initiatives of different companies. The government has assisted this sector with a wide range of techniques in over 100 programs during the past three decades, including funds for modernization and development, rationalization cartels, establishment of standards, preferential tax rates, consolidation of enterprises, and the establishment of joint ventures. The emphasis has shifted from the improvement of individual company efficiency in the later 1950s to a consolidation of the sector during the early 1960s, and, in the late 1960s and 1970s, to the encouragement of greater specialization and economies of scale. In the early 1970s, it shifted toward R&D assistance and sales of entire plants abroad. Some 60 percent of Export-Import Bank loans are now directed to exports of entire plants. A number of Japanese institutions work together to promote these exports: MITI has published a 400-page book on how to make such sales in particular markets overseas; industry associations and trading companies cooperate: the banks cooperate with all three groups in support of the cartels which have been formed under MITI guidance.

Japanese financial support for industrial policies comes through the Ministry of Finance, the Bank of Japan, several specialized government banks, and the city banks. The budget procedure of the Ministry of Finance sets the limits on the scope of industrial policy and approves the financial packages. Senior officials of the ministry examine industrial policy proposals at several stages and at several levels within the ministry. Each of the ministry's seven bureaus—budget, tax, financial, banking, international finance, customs, and tariffs and securities—has a role to play. The Financial Bureau manages the Fiscal Investment and Loan Plan (FILP), through which trust funds are channeled into specific sectors via public financial corporations such as the Japan Development Bank, the Export Import Bank, Japan Industrial Bank and others; this trust fund is equal to one-half of the government's general-account budget. Thus resources of the FILP are a major stimulus (or constraint) on cash flows to specific sectors. In addition, the International Finance Bureau employs exchange rate changes as an instrument of industrial policy by altering comparative advantages at the margin and thereby forcing specific industrial restructuring.

Thirteen city banks are large enough to extend one-quarter of all loans and discounts made by financial institutions (both public and private) in Japan. They are principally tied to large corporations (Keiretsu). Each Keiretsu has a principal bank on which it relies for funding advice on investment and operating positions; this bank is not the only source of funding but also is the one to which the company turns in time of expansion or need. This relationship is so important that one Keiretsu, which refused to adopt such a close relationship, lost significant market position when it got into difficulties and could not obtain adequate financing.

Traditionally, the Keiretsu have relied on loans rather than equity, increasing the ties to the banks; this is shifting somewhat currently with increasing self-financing by the companies. The governmental ministries and the banks discuss industrial objectives together, setting up ad hoc committees to examine specific proposals and issues. These banks are linked with the Bank of Japan, which is in turn supervised by the Ministry of Finance, and which lends to the thirteen city banks for industrial expansion. Further, they can be encouraged to press out funds through industrial sectors as guided by the Ministry of Finance. Finally, these city banks have officers sitting on the board of directors of various companies of the Keiretsu and are therefore able to help in the balancing of operations or shifting the emphasis among the companies of the Keiretsu or of a sector.

Direct government R&D activities are small in Japan; rather, the major

effort is made under contracts with the Keiretsu, usually formed into consortia for large-scale projects. MITI has formed sixteen associated research
institutes for such long-range, large-scale projects, developing systems for
commercial use. They are engaged in projects on very large scale integrated
(VLSI) semiconductors, high-performance jet engines for aircraft, water
desalination, and natural resource recycling. In addition, R&D support is
provided in tax credits, grants, low-cost loans, accelerated depreciation,
and sponsorship of R&D consortia for both large and small companies.

Information electronics is supported through substantial R&D subsidization such as the VLSI circuit development project and the special assistance given to software development. MITI has used government funds to
create consortia among firms to conduct joint R&D activities; but it has
been unsuccessful in consolidating companies to achieve greater economies.
The companies continue to be independent in production and sales of the
resulting products and systems.

On the marketing side, the government has aided those companies purchasing computers, expanding the national market. It offers financial assistance and established a joint venture with private enterprise to lease computers. The government also reserves about 90 percent of its purchases of
computers for Japanese producers. In semiconductors, much of the private
market is closed to foreigners, and in telecommunications, it has been
extremely difficult to open up purchasing to foreign bids. Nippon Telephone and Telegraph Corporation (NTT) not only has given a preference to
Japanese suppliers, but it has directly supported R&D of the major telecommunications equipment suppliers and has helped to finance their exports.

As a result of these trilateral cooperative efforts among the government, private enterprises, and financing institutions, the Japanese companies have a high degree of flexibility in pricing and in competitive efforts
both domestically and internationally.


*Declining Industries*

Aluminum, fertilizers, ferro-alloys, plywood, sugar refining, synthetic textile fibers, shipbuilding, and other sectors have been classified as declining
(increasingly less competitive internationally) by MITI officials. If the
sector is declared structurally depressed, it will receive reconstruction measures; to be so classified, an industry must have substantial overcapacity, be
in serious financial difficulty, and two-thirds of the firms must sign a petition for such designation. MITI then develops a stabilization plan, fore-
casting supply and demand; it calculates excess capacity, and it identifies
marginal plants and ones to be cut back or eliminated. During this process,

MITI consults with the industry, and labor unions are given a voice. A workable plan is agreed upon, and measures are then put into effect. To date, some forty industries have been so classified; these industries have accepted MITI guidance so that the government approves the process that it is funding. This assistance is given regardless of the *origin* of the difficulty; that is, it is not dependent on injury from imports.

One of the sectors so classified has been aluminum smelting, but the industry and the government have not been able to agree on a plan. The companies do not wish to rationalize or regroup or even to cut capacity significantly on any permanent basis; but MITI is seeking a permanent structural shift and does not want to provide any protection to sustain existing capacity. Similar difficulties were faced in rationalizing electric-furnace steel production.

The government has also supported and guided the shipbuilding industry over its rise and decline within the past three decades. In the first decade, the Ministry of Transport and the Ministry of Finance assisted the introduction of new technology and encouraged rationalization, providing tax benefits financing, price subsidies, and consumer financing. Government assistance virtually disappeared in the late 1960s and early 1970s, but after the tanker boom faded in the mid-1970s, Japan's launchings fell to less than 50 percent of prior levels. As the industry has progressively shifted to lower-wage countries, an advisory commission has recommended significant cutbacks in capacity. Again, however, not all of the firms in the industry have agreed as to the specific measures to be taken to bring about rationalization, not wanting to cut capacity permanently and looking for strong temporary financial support. The standoff had to eventually be broken by a direct order from the prime minister, who commanded that a solution be found. Even so, no final agreement has been found on how the cutbacks are to be distributed among the producers.

This experience in Japan indicates the relative difficulty of gaining consensus on measures to adjust a declining sector, as distinct from the ease of distributing benefits in a growing sector.

**French Policy**

Prior to the mid-1970s, French industrial policy was aimed at preventing the takeover of French industry by foreign firms and at strengthening it through consolidation, in order to compete more effectively with European firms in anticipation of further European integration. Even during the 1950s and early 1960s, the French government used a wide variety of techniques to stimulate industry, encompassing virtually all that are used currently. It selected certain sectors for encouragement, through R&D assistance; support of mergers and consolidation; creation of investment-banking facilities to provide risk capital; and protection of industry from international competition. It deliberately exposed some sectors to international and domestic competition to force efficiency and competitiveness, encouraging them to cut their losses short when competitive forces were overwhelming. In others, it allowed cartel-like groupings of industry in order to attempt to achieve competitiveness. Its policy has been highly selective, pragmatically shifting between market and nonmarket approaches to meet whatever pressures seemed to need countering. In addition, it has sought to promote high-technology industries through government investment in national champions (sometimes a state-owned company) and through the selective admittance of foreign firms that could accelerate technological innovation in cooperation with French companies.

During the late 1970s, crises in steel, oil refining, and petrochemicals led to government support for cartels in these sectors, followed by a partial nationalization of the steel industry. Efforts were also made to maintain employment in steel, shipbuilding, autos, and machine tool sectors through subsidies and low-interest loans plus several efforts at export promotion, such as loan guarantees, export credits to foreign customers, and direct assistance in sales of aircraft and nuclear power units to foreign governments. Under the regime of Raymond Barre, industries were left more to the free market, with price controls removed so as to stimulate investment; bankruptcies were permitted to eliminate marginal firms; mergers were slowed and competition encouraged; and subsidies were reduced. Even so, promotion efforts were directed at high-technology sectors, including nuclear energy, aircraft and aerospace, energy conservation, electronic data processing, and telecommunications, through a variety of techniques including government purchasing, R&D support, tax incentives and direct financial assistance, and special funds for distressed regions. In addition, consultations between companies and labor were encouraged, and capital markets were bolstered.

One major departure from pre-1976 policy was that the criterion of success was to be that of achieving international competitiveness, preferably without, but if necessary with, technological assistance from abroad, even so far as accepting joint ventures with foreign firms. Also, the techniques shifted somewhat from *direct* guidance by the government to specific sectors and firms toward greater reliance on market signals, enterprise strategy, and government stimulus to growing enterprises, so as to hasten market processes. These moves brought French policy in the late 1970s closer to both West German and Japanese practice.

The planning structure for guidance of a sector may be either fairly simple or complex. In the case of computers, there are four separate plans: the Plan Calcul, for the mainframe computers; the Plan Composants, for microelectronic components; Plan Peripherique, for EDP peripheral equipment; and the Plan Software. In addition, there is a Plan Electronique Civile; and a Plan Mechanique for the entire mechanical industry. All of these are formulated in close cooperation with industry. (See table 2-2).

**Table 2-2**
**French Mechanisms of Coordination**

| | |
|---|---|
| Planning Mechanisms | |
| Commisariat du Plan | Interministerial Planning Agency of Federal Government: selects priority sectors, determines techniques of stimulation; selects national champions, provides directives to ministries for application of techniques |
| Plan Calcul | Planning for the mainframe computer sector |
| Plan Composants | Planning for microelectronic components |
| Plan Peripherique | Planning for EDP peripheral equipment |
| Plan Software | Assistance for a creation of appropriate software |
| Plan Electronic Civile | Planning for the civilian electronic sector |
| Plan Mechanique | Planning for the entire mechanical industry |
| Ministry of Industry | Bureaus and divisions related specifically to industries (as under Japanese MITI) in continuing dialogue with specific sectors |
| Caisse dés Depôts et des Designations | Largest French bank, it is state-owned but independent. It dominates the bond market, utilizing all small postal savings and funds in savings banks, holding pension funds of state-enterprises and municipalities, as well as government accounts and other funds. Ministry of Finance and Fonds de Development Economique et Social (FDES), it has reponsibility for financing large projects in the plan. |
| Banks | Channels for capital provided by the state for priority sectors and national champions |
| Nationalized Firms | Both leaders in specific sectors and purchasers of equipment on a preferential basis |
| Patronat | National Association of Industry Associations, coordinating representation to the federal government. (French industry has a large number of weaker firms in each sector, though it has attempted to merge and concentrate them for easier coordination, without much success.) |

French financial assistance for industrial objectives is channeled through government controlled institutions—namely, the Caisse and Postal Savings, which are the savings and loans institutions that mobilize individual and small company savings of the economy. These funds are agglomerated and passed out through the Bank of France and now state-owned banks. The control of the government over access to credit has restricted the commercial banks' ability to lend and has permitted the government to direct the ultimate recipients of loan funds. The French banks are not, however, tied directly to private companies as they are in Japan and West Germany. In addition, the government has created state-owned, venture-capital institutions.

Coordination in France is made easier by the fact that its leaders in government and industry are (in large majority) members of an elite, having graduated from one or more of the *grands écoles* of the country. The top graduates go into the top ministries or companies and maintain their old-school ties throughout life; on retirement, a government official will join a company as a board member or top official. Personal requests for information, consultation, or cooperation are therefore responded to more readily than in the United States or West Germany.

Despite these efforts, France has not been able to gain a strong position in electronics. Its policy has shifted several times, but market share has not increased, and it remains dependent on foreign technology.

In other growing sectors, efforts in the nuclear industry raised employment by the end of the 1970s, to a level equal that in the French steel industry. It gave direct support to the takeover of Citroën's management. The rise of the French auto industry to the third largest (after the United States and Japan) appeared to validate its efforts in that sector. R&D grants to the aircraft industry plus government purchasing and state-supplied risk capital helped regain commercial aircraft markets as well as some in aircraft engines. Exports in many sectors were substantially increased, more than might have been expected given relative price movements between France and its major customers.

In the declining industries, France continued the sectoral investment programs in steel, obtained sanction for a crisis cartel in steel, and ensured trade protection from EEC members. It was also a strong proponent of tightening the Multi-Fiber Agreement on textiles during 1977, and it retarded the shrinking of its clothing industry that would have otherwise taken place. French policy toward textiles illustrates its reluctance to accept adjustments that cause severe unemployment. It has not cut its facilities in this sector as much as have West Germany or Britain, partly because of the structure of the industry, which is greatly fragmented and therefore difficult to guide. Sweeping policies of admitting foreign competition would damage too many areas of the country and make assistance difficult in the government's view. The government has established an interministerial committee for restructuring of industry, which gives direct assistance to a number of firms about to go under. But recently it has allowed a number of bankruptcies in declining sectors.

Despite the liberal measures adopted in the latter part of the 1970s, France has not given up its historical orientation of state intervention. Only France and Japan have publicly announced the selection of target industries for government support in the 1980s, and the lists are virtually identical. To encourage competitive efforts in these sectors, tax deductions have been offered to individuals who purchase shares on the stock exchange, and mergers are being restricted. Business-government discussions have been refocused on raw material and energy needs. And a five-year, five-billion-franc support program for electronic data processing and telecommunications equipment is in place. In 1982, President Mitterrand announced a 33 percent increase in spending by the Ministry of Research and Technology and expects to raise total research spending from 1.8 percent of GNP to 2.5 percent by 1985. These moves are expected to assist French businesses in achieving greater international competitiveness, especially in the selected industries.

French policy is also critically dependent on the existence of state enterprises in key sectors—particularly petroleum, computers, and aerospace. These enterprises are used to subsidize customer companies (through lower prices) and supplier companies (through preferential orders). Five of the ten largest corporations in France are state-owned, including Electricité de France and Renault, each employing more than 100,000 workers. The French government holds monopolies in telecommunications, electricity, gas, railroads, seaports and airports, potash, lignite and coal, banking, and aerospace. It holds more than 40 percent of the sectors of shipping, shipbuilding, insurance, and trucking and over 20 percent of the machine tools, automotive, and petrochemical sectors. Where such enterprises are state-owned, their purchases take on the coloration of government purchasing and therefore are potentially politically guided. In banking, the four largest French banks, encompassing 80 percent of banking activities in the country, have been nationalized; savings institutions and insurance companies have also undergone nationalization. President Mitterrand undertook the nationalization of all but the smallest banks in the early 1980s. In steel, the government controls private companies through price and investment guidance, supplies coal to the industry through its monopoly companies, and is the major customer. In aircraft, the government owns the major companies, holding between 50 and 100 percent of equity. In addition, it is a joint-venture partner in a number of companies manufacturing specialized aircraft equipment. All of these activities give it a strong influence, if not complete control, over the relevant sectors.

In 1982 France expanded the scope of industrial policy by the adoption of the *filière* concept, referring to vertical lines of production which are intimately tied. Four large industrial sectors have been identified, with government policy extending beyond these sectors to the support elements and secondary and tertiary industry related to them. These four—chemicals, electronics, health, and materials—have within them the five large state-owned complexes. Thus state enterprises are relied upon to lead in these four priority areas. The government's objective in each is to consolidate enterprises, particularly the state-owned ones, so that they will be stronger, better integrated in terms of raw materials, and have more effective control over their markets. Given the ties among state companies, it is feasible to accelerate the use of electronics, for example, in other sectors and to maintain a fairly secure pattern of demand. Even the use of materials developed by the state enterprises can be channeled into other sectors in a more controlled fashion. Despite these governmentally directed activities, the Minister of Industry has asserted that once the groups have been launched effectively, they must then be managed so as to gain profits sufficient to ensure the continued development of the companies and produce a normal return on investment.

Accomplishing these objectives has been made exceedingly difficult in the last couple of years by the low value of the franc on exchange markets and the reliance on the world markets to make French plans successful. The government has not been able to close off the French economy sufficiently to be in control to the extent desired, given the adverse impacts on growth from such isolation.

### West German Policy

Prior to the mid-1970s, the West German economy progressed under its free-market miracle, but this did not preclude substantial government assistance. A new science and technology ministry was created to provide federal R&D funding; some industries were rationalized through the promotion of mergers; preference was given in government purchasing to West German industries in the high-technology sectors, and West Germany participated in European-wide projects in nuclear energy and aerospace. In addition, the states (Länder) provided regional development aid; and substantial federal aid was given through grants, low cost loans, and tax concessions.

In the mid-1970s, the government emphasized export promotion with substantial increases in the financing of capital goods exports and export-insurance facilities. It offered an innovation premium tied to the labor costs of R&D and set up some special programs for distressed areas.

In the late 1970s and early 1980s, the government increased federal funding for R&D, especially in aerospace ventures in cooperation with other European countries and in the West German microelectronics industry. It helped finance firms buying data-processing equipment and provided additional funds for R&D in energy-related projects.

Throughout all three periods from the 1960s into the 1980s, subsidies were given to the shipbuilding industry, and loan guarantees were provided to ship owners to help them to purchase West German-built ships. In addition, the government cushioned the decline of the coal industry through protection, consolidation of enterprises, subsidies, and an extensive program for the relief of distress in the Ruhr.

In contrast to the Japanese system of consensus, in which the government offers strong guidance, the system of consensus developed in West Germany since World War II lets the individual companies lead. They respond essentially to market signals, but with guidance from the banks with which the companies are associated and governmental support from several ministries. The primary responsibility for industrial planning has, since 1972, been divided between the Economic Ministry and that for Research and Technology; later the Education Ministry and the Postal Ministry entered the picture through research support and preferential purchasing, respectively. A major thrust has been to move the country into the high-technology sectors— fire chemicals, polyester, filaments, specialty steels, industrial electronics, environmental control, advanced medicine, and so forth. In addition, labor makes a significant input through the system of co-determination under which it has representation on the supervisory boards of major companies. Consequently, there is a degree of concerted action (called concertation) involving three-way dialogues among business, government, and labor. These dialogues led in the 1960s and into the 1970s to an agreement that labor will contain its wage demands within the level of productivity increases, and to a framework for investment—but no *plan*.

The system of dialogues and co-determination means that information is fairly widely spread and adjustments to perceived changes are more readily made. These adjustments are not made under a system of direct planning, where goals are projected, but simply under collegial decisions to adjust to market changes, sometimes supported with tax and other incentives. The initiating group under this system is the enterprises themselves through their strategic planning, which are, in turn, guided informally to respond with alacrity to market signals. West Germany's process of concertation was partly a response to the success of French indicative planning in the late 1950s and early 1960s. Economics Minister Erhard saw a need for developing greater competitiveness of the economy but doubted that it could be done through the large corporate agglomerations that existed in the country at that time. Accordingly, he reinforced his economic policies by developing more cooperation among the major actors in the economy, hoping to reduce conflicts of interest through a coordinated assumption of responsibility for economic growth.

This concept of an enlightened market economy was pursued by the succeeding economics minister in the late 1960s in an effort to reconcile national problems with the philosophy of economic freedom and with the necessity to become competitive internationally. Minister Schiller considered that the government had to provide a continuous forum with organized interest groups in order to make the government's economic policy effective; he hoped to meld the interests of enterprise and the government so that enterprise led in the direction that the government wanted to go and only intermittent support would be needed. The government was to hold the reins but not to provide the driving force.

Mergers and consolidations had been promoted in coal, aerospace, and aircraft in the late 1960s and throughout industry generally. In petroleum, loans and subsidies were given to various enterprises, and one company was turned into a partly state-owned oil company. During the early 1970s, it was recognized that if West German industry were to remain competitive internationally, it had to shift out of the low-skill, low-value-added products that were being undertaken by the developing countries. The Ministry of Industry essentially forced coal mines, steel, shipbuilding, and textiles to rationalize themselves and offered regional development policies to ease the adjustment. At the same time, it increased government support to the high-technology sectors, so that by the late 1970s the West German programs and techniques employed were not significantly different from those of France.

German financial assistance for industrial objectives is channeled through the Bundesbank into the major banks, of which three are predominant—the Deutsche Bank, Dresdner Bank, and the Commerzbank. These and other banks have officers who sit on the supervisory board of major companies, and since West German industry is highly concentrated, it only requires that they be on the boards of the larger companies in order to control significantly the finances available to any given sector. The bank official may even be the chairman or deputy chairman of the board of the company and therefore regard as part of his responsibility to apprise the management of new ideas, opportunities, or techniques that have been developed in other companies with which he is familiar (through a similar seat on the board). He even may organize formal or informal exchanges among companies on matters that would improve their productivity or competitiveness. Being a member of the bank that has many officials sitting on different boards, each bank official—while maintaining precise confidentiality on company operations and decisions—will discuss the future of the sector and which companies should be leading in which areas. For example, in the case of the steel industry, the Deutsche Bank itself had a director or member of the senior staff on the board of nearly every one of the dozen largest steel companies. When the industry got into difficulty, it was easy for them to develop an approach of coordination that dissuaded two of the largest companies from going ahead with expansion and helped to alter the investment structure, concentration, and product lines of the companies. The banks were also the key to maintenance of viability in the auto sector, offering a moratorium on Volkswagen debt in 1975, which permitted V.W. to make the necessary investments to replace the Beetle.

This coordination has been eased by the concentration of West German industry, but this is not the sole basis, for it arises out of a long-term habit of close cooperation between industry and government, the responsibility of the Unternehmer for maintenance of the private enterprise system. Being thus oriented toward togetherness, the banks are ready leaders or channels for organizing cartels or other cooperative arrangements. The banks themselves take a long-run view of their role, seeing themselves as the grand strategists of industry, but with no desire to lose money in the process. Therefore, they look carefully to market signals and to long-run competitiveness of the companies to which they lend. (The mechanisms are outlined in table 2–3).

Another influence given to the banks if through the fact that subsidies (usually low-cost loans) offered by the Central Government are channeled through the banks, which assist in choosing particular recipients. In fact, each project proposed to the Ministry of Economics for a subsidy must be approved by the applicants, which in turn must oversee the use and repayment of the loan.

Being free-market oriented, state-owned enterprises are less significant in West Germany than in France; still a few are important. Government ownership was sold off immediately after World War II in a large number of state-owned enterprises, but governments still retain a substantial participation in numerous public and private enterprises. The largest are Salzgitter, Saarberwerke, Vereinigte Industries, IVG, and Prakia-Seismos. The government has over a 30 percent participation in shipbuilding, 28 percent in auto production, and 17 percent in electricity supply. Except for those companies providing infrastructure services, each is operated as a profit center and by commercial criteria. Companies owned by the government carry out the government's purchasing policies and give preference to West German industry. In addition, a government industrial equipment company holds shares in several mechanical engineering companies in order to supply them with needed financing. Also, the extractive companies owned by the government have been used to subsidize manufacturing; for example, the government owns 80 percent of West German output of iron ore, which can be sold at low prices to the steel companies, and state-owned enterprises in the materials-input sectors. State-owned enterprises comprised 50 percent

**Table 2-3**
**West German Mechanisms of Coordination**

| | |
|---|---|
| Planning mechanisms | No central agency; industrial policy begun in 1960s in response to the French success |
| Banks | Central Bank coordinates government policy through three major banks: Deutscher Bank, Dresdner bank, Commerzbank, plus smaller banks |
| | Banks own or control two-thirds of the hundred largest firms; bank loans are venture capital, since their directors influence management through sitting on the board of directors of companies; banks provide strategic direction and insist on competitive returns from industry; each bank sits on the board of numerous companies having the right through direct ownership of shares and representation of shares deposited with it by individuals |
| Ministry of Finance | Backs the banks and companies through tax incentives, loans, and so on |
| Ministry of Economy | Support through R&D funding, funds for training, et cetera; national champions are selected for discriminatory assistance; industry is concentrated in a few substantial firms in a number of sectors, making coordination relatively easy |
| Ministry of Research and Technology | Funds research and development by companies in priority sectors, in concert with Ministry of Economy |
| Ministry of Science and Technology | Provides direct and indirect support to R&D of selected companies |
| Bundesverband der Deutschen Industrie (BDI) | Federation of West German Industry; coordinates views of industry associations on government policies; officials of industry associations are on Standing Advisory Committees to each ministry dealing with economic policies |

of production in aluminum but less than 10 percent in steel. The government is heavily in aircraft and aerospace sectors, supporting or directly owning VFW, Fokker, and MBB, the last of which is owned by a state (Länder) government.

Presently, West Germany is increasing federal support for R&D in microelectronics and aerospace, including support of the client firms for investing in computerized capital equipment. Their priority list is heavy with high-technology sectors to be supported by the government, but in an amalgam of guidance and response that leaves the initiative for expansion to industry itself.

The West German experience is characterized by a degree of schizophrenia because the Ministry of Economy remained market-oriented during the control of the Social Democratic Party (SPD), while others (including the Ministry of Science and Technology) were oriented more toward planning. No policy decision resolved this split over the past few decades.

## Comparison of Three ACs

The differences in approaches of these three countries are shown by a comparison of policies toward autos, telecommunications, and semiconductors and an evaluation of their success.

### Sectoral Policies

In *autos*, France has been the most involved of the three countries, having fostered the growth and international penetration of two multinational companies: one state-owned (Renault, ranked eighth in the world) and a family firm (Peugeot, ranked sixth). It has strengthened these companies through subsidies for their expansion and assistance in consolidation and has provided protection against imports of Japanese cars. These efforts were successful until the early 1980s in maintaining production, expanding employment, expanding exports, and increasing the presence of the French companies in international investment. The companies fell into serious trouble by 1983, and the period of recovery is in doubt.

The West German government has been only slightly involved in supporting the automotive industry. Mercedes has not really needed such assistance. Volkswagen needed financial aid only in the mid-1970s when it went through a change of models; the government achieved a consensus among banks, private stockholders, labor, and other interested parties to support Volkswagen (held in a minority share of the government). The banks have blocked some capital investment by other auto companies which was deemed misdirected; they thereby altered the structure of the industry.

Automobiles were supported as early as the 1930s by the Japanese government, and again in the post–World War II period, when the companies were bankrupt. The growth of the industry in Japan was boosted by the Korean War and by the fact that the government discouraged foreign investment and encouraged imports of foreign technology through licenses.

The government also provided tax benefits and attempted to rationalize the component suppliers as well as the major manufacturers, but neither of these efforts met the government's objectives. The government has continued to provide export credits and assistance in foreign market research and distribution facilities.

The *telecommunications* sector has been seen by all three governments as one that would expand employment, meet increasing international competition, and require support to guarantee a strong participant nationally. This sector also is seen as intimately tied with the computer industry and as supportable through development of a strong national entity in electronics.

In France and West Germany, telecommunications is nationalized within the post-telephone-telegraph (PTT) system, and support to manufacturers of telecommunications equipment comes through government procurement mainly but also through some subsidies for R&D projects. In addition, the PTTs are encouraging competition in microelectronic development to reduce costs and accelerate the application of advanced technology. France has also encouraged the consolidation of manufacturing in telecommunication and has subsidized exports to developing countries so as to expand production and maintain employment. It has not been as successful in these efforts as have Japan or the Netherlands, both of which have used fewer intervening techniques.

In Japan, the Nippon Telegraph and Telephone Public Corporation (NTT) not only influences the development of the communications manufacturing through its procurement but also funds some university research programs as well as those of its chosen suppliers. NTT is a national monopoly; by law, it can manufacture nothing. Consequently, it has developed very close ties with its suppliers and has, in practice, bought virtually nothing from overseas, thereby providing an effectively protected domestic market in telecommunications equipment. Nearly half of NTT's equipment and supplies purchases in 1980 went to four companies in Japan, effectively concentrating competitive strength. This strength has catapulted several of the companies into the international markets, where they are successfully outbidding U.S. and European suppliers. However, in view of some manufacturers, Japanese telecommunications is lagging in the technology of digital switching because of the purchasing practices of NTT.

In *semiconductors,* the major countries and firms have been locked in worldwide competition. Both France and West Germany consider that they had too few firms and too great a technological gap in electronics and that they had to support the industry, which they did from the mid-1960s to the mid-1970s. When in the mid-1970s semiconductors became highly important, both countries offered R&D grants to stimulate the advance of technology. Although West Germany made no move to change the structure of its industry, France sought structural consolidation to enlarge the capabilities of particular firms and to stimulate new firms entering the sector;

France also nationalized some of the producers and helped to guide the activities of private firms. Military and government procurement has also been important in France. In addition, France has sought to bargain access to its markets against some inflows of technology or establishment of joint ventures or even the establishment of local R&D facilities.

Despite apparent differences, the basic policies of both France and West Germany are relatively similar in that both have taken the position that supporting the strategies of the more advanced semiconductor firms was good for the national interest as well. The relative success of the West German approach was due more to the fact that the companies were better placed and could utilize R&D support more effectively than could the French companies; the imitative lag of West German industries appears to be shorter than that of the French. Both countries were successful in maintaining a foothold in the sector, though only the West German companies are within the larger worldwide grouping. However, the French companies appear to be strengthening, having been chosen as national champions and encouraged through new technology imports from U.S. companies.

The Japanese have surpassed European technology in the sector under policies of prohibition of foreign direct investment and controls over imports. Instead of letting foreigners come in, it promoted technology imports, designated common technological targets among companies, distributed technical information to *all* firms in the sector, and sponsored a number of cooperative research projects among the companies. It fostered intensive competition domestically and helped remove structural constraints that would reduce profitability of the companies. Consequently, its policies essentially followed a competitive company strategy both domestically and internationally, accelerating the growth of this sector.

*Evaluation*

In evaluating success of these policies, attention must be given to differences in degree of intervention in industrial structure and development. West Germany has intervened less than either Japan or France. Yet Japan and West Germany have been more successful than France in cutting declining sectors, in accelerating high-technology sectors, in shifting some resources and industrial activity toward the high-technology sectors, and in increasing their international competitiveness. The keys to these successes appear to lie in the following:

a widespread acceptance of the rules of the game;

a loyalty to and concern for company objectives on the part of both workers and the government;

self-imposed restraint by labor to keep wages in line with productivity;

continuing dialogues among government, business, and labor;

the absence of a need for legislation or control to achieve enterprise performance;

a flexibility and willingness to respond to shifting pressures and environmental conditions, rather than insisting on application of fixed policies or plans; and

an identification of the interests of management with national interests in which management feels a responsibility for maintaining the socio-economic-political system.

*A necessary condition for a successful long-term industrial policy therefore is social consensus on goals derived from continuing dialog among leaders in government, business, and labor and exercising statesmanship.* Consensus also makes implementation more effective; adversarial positions obstruct it.

Japan and West Germany add a governmental (and banking) assessment of future trends to industrial strategies and then employ government resources to *accelerate* those trends. These countries are committed to helping industry but to move it in ways they see as appropriate to *future* needs and competitive pressures. France, on the other hand, appears more likely to try to counter undesirable market signals with government interference and consequently has had little success in phasing out declining industries or even in accelerating some of the advancing sectors. It faces some differential obstacles in its pursuit of industrial policies in that the sectors under consideration remain dispersed rather than concentrated, as in Japan and West Germany, making it difficult to achieve coordination of a large portion of the industry. Finally, while there is a desire for authoritarian structures in France, there is an equal reluctance on the part of individuals or companies to abide by directives from the center—unless there are strong personal ties through membership of the elite. Thus only a portion of the French economy marches to the same drummer.

Despite the apparent *overall* success in Japan and West Germany, however, it should be noted that there have been some significant failures of efforts by Japan to provide industrial support or stimulation. These failures have resulted from an aggressive response on the part of other countries or an inability to come to an agreement among the companies involved.

Strategies relative to construction equipment, chain saws, plate heat exchangers, and marine engines were frustrated by aggressive responses in the United States and Europe in meeting Japanese competition both in the world and in Japan itself. Sectoral policies were not successfully mounted in aluminum smelting, plywood, sugar refining, ferro-alloys, and synthetic textile fibers because of lack of agreement between business and governments.

Conversely, there have been some resounding successes; most notable are the industrial machinery and electronic sectors in Japan. But a number of others have been at least credible successes; these include automobiles in Japan, electronics and automobiles in France, aircraft in West Germany and France, and semiconductors in West Germany. In addition, there have been some notable successes as well as failures in easing the decline of specific sectors—shipbuilding, steel, and textiles—though problems in these sectors do remain.

Although successes or failures are broadly discernible, what is less easily determined is whether or not the results were a direct response to particular government signals or incentives. Usually, there are too many variables (quantitative and nonquantitative), resulting from the employment of several different techniques, to allow determination as to whether or not any given result occurred because of a specific influence. In addition, we find a number of sectors that had become competitive internationally *without* being the subject of a concerted industrial policy (e.g., tires and selected industrial machinery in France, autos and chemicals in West Germany, motorcycles and photographic equipment in Japan). This list could be enlarged substantially, indicating that market criteria are socially acceptable in the development of numerous industrial sectors, and an adequate response is obtained from industry to these signals. However, if conditions or results change adversely in any sector, the view of social acceptability will change according to how critical the sector is perceived. The most critical problem of social acceptability is that of the distribution of benefits; again, this is a problem for which we have no adequate economic theory or political process of resolution.

The difficulty of evaluating specific techniques is seen further in the fact that there is frequently no direct link between a given incentive and the result desired. For example, support of R&D activities by industry is not linked directly to the goal of innovation and commercialization of products. Many decisions are made in between, and the desired result can be frustrated by other conditions. Even if one tries to assess the effectiveness of a single technique—such as subsidization—the results are equivocal. There are too many forms of subsidization (direct and indirect, open and hidden, federal and local, generalized and discriminatory) to be able to determine which sectors are subsidized in fact and which are not. Further, a subsidy to one sector can become a subsidy to another through reduced prices of raw materials or capital equipment.

Comparisons across countries are made difficult by the fact that data on subsidies are not comparable either in terms of definition or scope.

Given these differences, and given the differences in industrial structure and the responses of managers to similar or varying conditions, a similar set of subsidies in two or more countries will have differential effects in causing industry to move from one country to another.

Consequently, recent attempts to negotiate reciprocal reduction or elimination of subsidies have run into serious obstacles of inability to agree on what are in fact subsidies and what specific (undesirable) results are obtained. When negotiations are complicated by the existence of a number of different incentives and disincentives, direct negotiation on specific techniques is likely to be unsuccessful. A different approach is required to meet the problems raised by national industrial policies among OECD countries.

## Brazilian Policy

Brazil does not yet have an overall industrial policy within which specific industrial sectors are stimulated. Rather, it has a policy of supporting industrial development through a number of decentralized institutions. Overall directives for economic policy, including those relative to industrial development, are the responsibility of the Council for Economic Development (CDE), composed of the economic ministers and the president. The Industrial Development Commission (CDI) is responsible for implementation of any industrial policies. Principally it grants fiscal incentives (including reduction of import duties on capital equipment), which trigger the grant of incentives by other agencies in the government as well. Sectoral agencies provide assistance to shipbuilding, steel and metal manufacturing, communications equipment, and mining. Several other agencies grant fiscal incentives to induce specific industries to locate in selected regions of the country. Finally, a number of financial institutions (e.g., the National Bank for Economic Development (BNDE) and its subsidiaries) provide significant funding for specific industrial projects. Other funding sources support technological development and R&D activities, and still others finance infrastructure needs.

Support of supplier sectors is given through prohibitions of imports of capital equipment if similar products are available domestically. These determinations are made by the Foreign Trade Department of the Banco do Brasil, which also provides incentives for exports and stimulates participation of domestic firms in industrial and infrastructure projects. Conversely, the Commission for Tariff Policy reduces duties on imports of specific products needed for desired industrial projects and also provides tariff protection selectively.

In addition, other institutions have responsibilities related to price controls, the entrance of foreign technology or capital, permissions for mergers, and so on, that can be used to support given sectors, although this is not their main purpose.

The multiplicity of institutions involved in industrial development objectives permits contradictory or inconsistent moves to occur, under-cutting any embryonic effort toward policy. Even the CDE, whose respon-sibilities include the implementation of a coordinated industrial policy, is not an executive institution and cannot, therefore, bring about the imple-mentation of the policies it recommends.

*Policy Instruments*

The policy instruments employed by Brazil include fiscal incentives to imports of capital goods; funding for exports of manufactures; specific incentives to selected sectors (notably shipbuilding, petrochemicals, and steel), capital funding for industry in general; infrastructure generation; and promotion of state enterprises in specific sectors (including energy, mining, metallurgy, and chemicals).

It was not until the mid-1970s that industrial policy goals were estab-lished sufficiently well to focus the use of these instruments. The criteria for application of industry assistance then included the following:

production to substitute for imports;

potential expansion of exports;

regional decentralization of location of the industry;

adequate Brazilian ownership of equity capital;

adequate capitalization to meet fixed and working capital needs;

intensive use of domestic inputs and materials;

use of appropriate technological processes to foster sectoral and regional development;

a scale of production compatible with competitive costs and prices; and

fulfillment of environmental protection requirements.

In addition, affiliates of foreign enterprises were subjected to require-ments that the operations have a positive balance of payments effect on the country, that sufficient financing is provided to pay for imports of capital equipment, that the domestic market was sufficiently unsatisfied to require additional capacity of production, and that purchases of domestically pro-duced equipment and supplies would be expanded.

*Objectives*

The broad objectives of industrial development policy in Brazil include an improvement in the balance of payments and trade, especially through import substitution and export promotion, the acquisition of recently developed technology, matching the scale of projects with the potential size of the domestic market, directing demand for capital goods and engineering services to locally owned firms. This last objective was to be implemented by constraints imposed through the banking system, various regulatory agencies, and through projects with government participation insisting on local participation even if the major private sector participant was foreign. The participation of local private firms was given priority as a means of catalyzing an effective absorption of technology by these companies.

The problems that Brazil has faced in the late 1970s and early 1980s with its international balance of payments have, however, been detrimental to creating a longer-term, comprehensive industrial policy.

Despite the problems in the formation of Brazilian industrial policy, the discussion at official levels is toward developing means of formulating a more comprehensive and coordinated policy as well as the mechanisms for carrying this out. Key officials consider that a more unified policy would accelerate Brazilian entry into the world economy and make its enterprises more competitive with transnationals.

**Industrial Policy of South Korea**

Since the first five-year economic development plan in 1962, South Korea has tied its industrial progress to expansion of exports of manufacturers. This has required careful attention to the industrial structure of the country, accelerating the transition from an agricultural society into a newly industrialized one. Its success raised the share of industry in GNP from 14 percent in 1962 to nearly 30 percent in 1980.

The necessity to shift economic activity from agriculture was part of an industrialization policy aimed merely at stimulating whatever industry was feasible. Only more lately has South Korea focused attention on specific industrial sectors. In the process of industrialization, specific activities were chosen for emphasis—steelmaking, shipbuilding, metalworking, and so forth—but these were essentially for the building of an industrial base.

Only after the mid-1970s did South Korea begin to shift from a general industrialization policy to a sectoral industrial policy. Prior to that time, South Korea was mostly following an import-substitution policy in the early 1960s and a policy of export-lead development in the decade following 1965.

During the export-lead period, government incursions were focused mainly on textiles, clothing, and electronics, with supports offered in the forms of credit subsidies, tax exemption, and a continuing supply of capital as needed.

During the period from 1973–1979, South Korea concentrated on heavy equipment and chemical sectors to develop the capital goods industry and inputs of intermediate products. Investments in these sectors were induced through preferential tax and credit incentives offered by a newly established National Investment Fund (NIF). These funds supported purchase of land, provided fixed and working capital, and permitted the extension of long-term export credits. NIF funding is made available at preferential rates and is subsidized by the government. In addition, the government has supported or constructed infrastructure related to the priority sectors. Tax incentives included complete exemption from corporate and income tax for three years followed by taxation at 50 percent of normal rates for the subsequent two years. These incentives were offered to petrochemicals, shipbuilding, machinery, electronics, steel, nonferrous metals, fertilizer, defense industry, electric power plants, aircraft, and mining activities. As a consequence, investments in the desired sectors doubled in real terms during the last three years of the 1970s, while investment in light industry increased by only 50 percent. In fact, investment exceeded the targets of the fourth plan, creating some structural adjustment difficulties in the economy and contributing to high rates of inflation in the late 1970s. The previous priority on export competitiveness was thereby somewhat undercut.

The establishment of these priorities and overfulfillment of objectives created some problems other than inflation. These included an unbalanced growth among industry sectors so that the secondary and tertiary sectors could not keep up, adding further to the inflation; also, workers were able to demand higher wages. Both of these factors reduced export competitiveness. Further, export competitiveness was reduced by the protection given to the priority sectors, which permitted them to raise costs higher than would be acceptable in export markets.

The fifth five-year plan began in 1980 and was the first to incorporate the concepts of an industrial policy. It focuses on the structural imbalances in the economy. In order to let competitive markets signal the priorities for investment, the government has backed away from determining the strategic industries for promotion. But it will still establish broad guidelines within which investment is to take place. To guide this approach, an Industrial Policy Council consisting of the various economic ministers was established. It is charged with coordinating the policies coming from these ministries so as to achieve a more efficient allocation of investment, a more advanced industrial structure, an improved agri-industry sector, and a rationalized energy sector.

Within these policies, highest priority will be given to energy conservation, technology acquisition and development, and manpower training. The focus, therefore, is on support of industrialization, with an emphasis on skill-intensive sectors, again looking toward international competitiveness.

The development or acquisition of key technologies receives government support through new tax and financial incentives. The priority sectors in this regard include electronics, fine chemicals, machinery, industrial safety technology, and systems development. In addition, more attention is to be paid to the import and proper assimilation of foreign technologies through the provision of technical information services, overseas training opportunities, and the employment of foreign engineers and technicians.

For industry as a whole, investments are made by the government in social infrastructure to provide adequate living conditions, communications, sanitation, and environmental protection.

Within specific sectors, target objectives have been delineated, such as expansion of capacity in both the automotive and shipbuilding sectors and high utilization of capacity through economies of scale gained by specialization and export promotion. The electronics industry is focused on technological innovation and new products in the industrial electronic machinery area (rather than consumer electronics), relying on foreign technologies if necessary, to meet the expanded domestic needs in telecommunications and computer needs in manufacturing and service sectors. Under the plan, the machinery sector will be assisted in the development of components and parts suppliers. The steel industry is also to be expanded so as to reduce import needs, as will the nonferrous metal industry. Given the problems of petroleum supply, prior emphasis on petrochemical complexes is to be reduced.

The light manufacturing sector and small and medium industries are also considered critical. This sector is to be expanded significantly and remain the backbone of South Korean industry. To help improve the efficiency of small and medium industries, governmental assistance will be given for management and technical extension services. Also, training opportunities will be offered to managers in overseas programs, and small and medium companies will receive financial support for modernization of their capacities. Finally, financial sources will give priority to venture capital and modernization projects in the small and medium sector.

The government expects as a consequence of these efforts to increase the share of exports out of total industrial production, thereby permitting greater imports of capital equipment, intermediaries, and technology. In order to stimulate domestic production, the government will provide tariff protection at high levels while the industry is in infancy and then gradually reduce them as competitive positions are attained. Further, priority will be given to obtaining advanced technologies directly and through joint ventures, and, if necessary, through foreign direct investment. Greater attention will be given to sources of technology and investment other than the United States and Japan, which have been the primary suppliers in the past. This promotion will, however, be guided by the sectoral priorities already mentioned. Foreign investment will be given specific incentives if in a group of encouraged industries including machinery, metals, electronics, energy, food processing, pharmaceuticals, and various of the service sectors deemed important in supporting these priority industries.

## Industrial Incentives in Taiwan

Under a policy of industrialization, Taiwan raised its per capita GNP ten times in the period from 1965 to 1981, as industry share of total production rose from 18 percent to 45 percent. Economic planning has been a characteristic of the entire period of post war development for the Republic of China. The first plan was formulated in 1953; four-year, six-year, and ten-year plans have been carried out successively to stimulate agriculture, create import substitution, and stimulate high-technology sectors.

The Council for Economic Planning and Development (CEPD) has overall responsibility for policy formulation and coordinating the plans submitted by various ministries, who receive inputs from the academic and business sectors. The CEPD also follows up on the implementation of the plans and evaluates them for modifying future plans. The resulting plans are indicative, so that the private sector is largely independent. However, the government offers a number of incentives and inducements to achieve fulfillment of the plan objectives. Some state-controlled enterprises are under more direct guidance, but the private sector also seeks to cooperate to a high degree. This cooperation has been so effective that plan fulfillment has reached or exceeded 100 percent in virtually every period, with overfulfillment occurring in industrial production and exports.

In the early plans, priorities were given to labor intensive, import-substituting industries, whereas in the plans during the 1960s, more emphasis was given to exports and export-oriented industries to raise skill levels and gain foreign exchange. Through the 1970s, the priorities were shifted to infrastructure investment to support key industries (those which were capital- and technology-intensive) and to support backward integration through intermediate-goods sectors. The upgrading of the industrial structure was also facilitated by the establishment of a complete science and technology complex and a science-based industrial part.

Industrial priorities for the 1980s include the following:

the development of capital-intensive high-technology sectors that will increase the value added by industry;

restructuring of industrial balance, with emphasis on investment in the private sector;

intensification of R&D activities and the support of science and technology in general;

manpower training and productivity improvement through automation;

modernization of light manufacturing and expansion of capacity;

diversification of export markets; and

emphasis on balanced economic and social development.

To achieve these objectives, the ten-year plan (1980–1989) focuses less on industry sectors than on means of achieving economic stability and a more equitable distribution of income among the various claimants in the country. Per capita income is to be raised three times by the end of the planning period. In this process, Taiwan intends to become a virtually advanced country through an industrial structure that includes high value-added, capital-intensive sectors, with an annual rate of industrial growth set at 10 percent throughout the period, and high-technology sectors growing even more rapidly so as to rise from 24 percent of industrial production to 35 percent in 1989.

Although Taiwan's economic planning is macro in extent, it is also applied at the micro level with strong emphasis on industrial production, as evidenced by the fact that between 1952 and 1980 industrial output rose more than 40 times. During this time, emphasis shifted from primary products import-substitution to promotion of exports in the 1960s and afterwards again toward import substitution but at more sophisticated ends of the industrial classification. During the 1950s, in order to gain rapid industrial advance, emphasis was given to light industrial consumer industries, which were largely labor-intensive. During the 1960s, attention was given to the intermediate products sectors—that is, textile mill products, chemicals, electrical machinery, petroleum products, and coal mining. By the end of the 1960s, greater attention was being paid to the more capital-intensive industries requiring higher skills in labor. The decade of the 1970s saw Taiwan attempting to hold its own in a worldwide recession and able to do little to alter its industrial structure significantly by focusing on machinery, electrical equipment, transportation, electronics, and information processing as priority sectors to receive special support. These sectors are expected to grow at twice the rate for nonpriority sectors.

To support these priority industries, the CEPD will facilitate the exploration and exploitation of materials inputs, and the conclusion of technical assistance agreements with foreign companies, promote inward foreign investment, constrain the expansion of industries relying on high inputs of energy so as to conserve that resource, and facilitate the consolidation of medium- and small-sized companies into more efficient manufacturing and exporting complexes. Throughout all of these, attention will be paid to possibilities of automation and ways of streamlining operations so as to become more internationally competitive and mitigate the damage from protectionist policies in advanced countries. Rationalization of industry will be focused particularly on the sectors including steel, aluminum, zinc, lead, and petrochemicals, to ensure that they will meet domestic industrial needs at reasonable costs.

In guiding industrial development, state enterprise in Taiwan has historically been significant, reaching over 50 percent of industrial production in the 1950s. But its proportion has dropped continuously to less than 20 percent in 1980, and further reductions are anticipated in the present decade.

Given the necessity to maintain foreign-exchange earnings, attention will be paid also to international competitiveness, and especially to the declining strength in textiles, electronics, and footwear. Although these will be prevented from declining too rapidly, the sectors that are seen as having growth potential and are therefore priorities for the future include the following: sophisticated electronic instruments, systems and components, including telecommunications equipment; machine tools and precision instruments; vehicles of all weight; heavy industrial equipment; chemicals of all types; steel; and nonferrous metals.

To facilitate the growth of these sectors, the government will induce foreign investment as appropriate and assist in the acquisition and utilization of foreign technology as well as in the generation of science and technology domestically and its dissemination. A number of techniques will be employed to achieve these objectives in cooperation between government and the private sector. To facilitate these transfers, the Republic of China has signed technical cooperation agreements with Japan, Singapore, and Saudi Arabia providing for increasing contacts among scientists, engineers, and technicians and for exchanges of information and promotion of private agreements.

Finally, in support of the priority sectors Taiwan will increase its attention to manpower development so that the skilled and technically trained workers will increase at twice the rate of increase in overall employment during the coming decade. Since the government anticipates shortages of skills, labor, and engineers, it places a high priority on providing educational opportunities and training programs. These will be coordinated with the priority sectors so that shortages are removed there as rapidly as possible.

**Comparison of NICs**

These three newly industrialized countries display some similarities among themselves and with the advanced countries in their pursuit of industrial policies. However, the NICs first had to proceed from agriculturally oriented countries to industrially based through a process of raising agricultural productivity. Rather than shrinking the agricultural sector, the process in NICs was similar to that in advanced countries; that is, agricultural productivity was raised and a flow of workers into the industrial sectors was permitted. The first stages were simply those of promoting industry itself— generally labor-intensive and import substituting—so as to industrialize with less capital costs and as rapidly as possible. Only recently have the NICs turned to the structure of industry and to assigning priorities to given sectors. As they have done so, emphasis has been placed on meeting an expanded domestic demand and moving into export markets so as to accelerate overall growth through higher value-added production. This has led each of the NICs into similar industrial sectors, which are primarily competing with the advanced countries.

The industrial orientations of each of these countries is, therefore, adding to the problems of accommodations of industrial policies and structure and will add to the new protectionism unless more acceptable means are found of coordinating industrial development, at least in these key sectors.

**Note**

The author wishes to acknowledge the discussions in the "Symposium on National Industrial Policies and International Restructuring of Industry," held at Mount Kisco, New York, in March 1982. For information on Brazil, the author is grateful to Luiz A. Correa do Lago; on South Korea, to Young Yoo; and on Taiwan, to Tai-Ying Liu and Yie-Lang Chan. The proceedings of the symposium are to be published in *National Industrial Policies* (Boston: OG&H, 1984).

# 3 Industrial Strategies in the United States

The United States officially avoids any semblance of an industrial policy. Even public discussion tends to avoid the word *policy,* substituting the terms *industrial strategies* or *reindustrialization.* This rewording makes it more comfortable to analyze rationally several alternatives rather than to define a policy that implies a context of national economic planning. This orientation signals a clear rejection of what is perceived to be the content of industrial policies employed by other countries. However, numerous activities of the government do help shape the industrial structure of the United States, as a considered industrial policy would, though in different directions and with different techniques. Further, the U.S. government is taking tentative steps in the direction of guidance of some industrial development through its examination of the role of technology in U.S. exports; its concern for international competitiveness of U.S. industry; its examination of the potential disadvantages of locating U.S. industrial activity overseas; and its support of individual segments of U.S. industry in the face of strong foreign competition. Still the government officially eschews any mention of a U.S. industrial strategy.

## Principles of U.S. Policy

Industrial policies, whether explicit (as in some countries) or implicit (as in the United States), are a response to the question of *where* industrial activities should be located (that is, the determination of the international division of labor). The U.S. government is still, in principle, wedded to the concept that international location decisions should be made by TNCs and other (private) corporations in response only to market signals, with governments merely setting the broad rules of the game. This policy is readily inferred from an official document, which comments on the effects of investment performance requirements imposed by other countries, and states that these requirements are "an economic detriment to the extent that they create economic behavior inconsistent with market-dictated forces."[1]

However, the United States finds it hard to hold to its principles in the face of low growth rates, continued high-level unemployment, inflation, and shifts in exchange rates and international competitive conditions. All of these factors in turn are reflected in four major developments: the increased difficulties of moving any further toward liberalized trade through the GATT; the inadequacy of the IMF in maintaining free and stable exchange rates; the growth of and concerns over the roles of TNCs in international industrial integration; and the efforts to handle problems of specific industrial sectors through bilateral or multilateral agreements, such as in so-called orderly marketing arrangements. Orderly marketing arrangements translates to prevention or dampening of shifts in the location of industry. This interference constitutes an industrial policy (at least for one sector), even though not adopted with the full consideration of the final objectives or of the best mechanisms for industrial change. The U.S. government, therefore, is applying strategies that are normal under industrial policies, but which it does not want considered as constituting either an industrial strategy or policy. These are considered aberrations, which it deplores.[2]

The U.S. Congress is also generally in accord with these open-market principles, but it is frequently pressed to take differential action with reference to specific sectors. It also does not relish such ad hoc policy making. In the words of the staff director of the Congressional Subcommittee on International Economic Policy and Trade of the House Foreign Affairs Committee, "Congress has exhausted—and is increasingly exhausted with—*ad hoc* 'fixes' for industries suffering from foreign competition, and cannot relish the prospect of having to pass judgment on what could be a long procession of troubled industries seeking government help." The director goes on to argue that a national industrial policy might well become infused with political rather than economic considerations and, therefore, could well "perpetuate diseconomies rather than eliminate them." Without more extensive economic analysis and planning, he argues, any attempt to address the problems of specific sectors would lead to only partial and inadequate solutions: "Only through such a comparative analysis of the shortcomings and potentials of all sectors, and the full range of possible government and private means of enhancing the performance of each sector, will a selective plan constitute an improvement over *ad hoc* measures." He argues further that ". . . to be operational and effective, whatever its precise format and content, a national industrial plan must be specific in proposing adjustments in existing government policies and programs. A conscious review of all such policies and programs directly or indirectly affecting industrial performance must be a part of the planning process, and of the final planning document." None of these suggestions are operative, in his view, however, since the U.S. government does not have a planning mechanism and therefore does not have the ability to fit industrial policies into any larger scheme.[3]

Of course, neither the Department of Commerce, nor the Federal Trade

Commission, nor the Congress formulates the foreign economic policy of the U.S. government, but all have significant inputs. What is said here is that the decisions are best left to the market. But if we are going to move to assistance to specific sectors, it must be done in the context of much wider national economic planning, which is, of course, rejected. The U.S. government is certainly not ready philosophically for such a move. Therefore it has, despite its distaste, addressed specific problems in distressed sectors, including textiles, footwear, autos, steel, citizens-band radios (transreceivers), color televisions, and a variety of agricultural products, plus a series of other products that have been given safeguards under the Escape Clause provision of the GATT. These, plus its protective responses to industrial policies in Europe, Japan, and the NICs are exacerbating the problems of moving toward closer international integration under more cooperative arrangements.

The basic principles underlying U.S. policy toward international integration are still, therefore, those embodied in the Bretton Woods Agreements. Despite the fact that the underlying principle of these agreements—multilateral, nondiscriminatory trade and payments—government is to provide a stimulus to overall economic growth, within which industry is a key, but not sole, part. The role of the government is that of stimulating aggregate investment and employment, without much attention to where either occurs geographically or sectorally. There is, therefore, no policy on a desired mix between agriculture and industry or between industry and service sectors. The shift of employment from agriculture into industry and from industry into the service sector has not been guided in any sense directly by the government, and no preference is shown for one or the other, save in exceptional circumstances (e.g., a distressed area). Nor is there any policy preference shown as to the distribution of activities between rural and urban areas or among particular regions of the country. Although support is at times given to specific agricultural activities (wheat, tobacco) and to particular service sectors (shipping), these aberrations are a response to political and strategic pressures. Far less likely is any guidance as to the degree of concentration or the particular conglomerate structure of industry, to its sectoral composition (even as between high-wage and low-wage industries), or to the location of specific sectors within the country or abroad.

Even purchases by the military establishment and R&D support have not been conducted for the purposes of supporting international industrial competitiveness of the industrial sectors involved. Rather, they seek to meet the national security needs of the United States in the most efficient manner. In fact, the tie of the high-technology sectors to the military interests of the United States has been a reason for limiting or prohibiting the export of goods and services (including the licensing of technology) to countries considered to be undesirable recipients, thereby limiting the market as compared to what would have been the case under more open orientations.

The significance of military purchasing can be illustrated by the fact that since its first purchases of semiconductors in mid-1950s, Department of Defense (DOD) purchasing accounted for over 25 percent of the total market, declining thereafter. In addition, the armed forces have imposed high standards and required close quality control in the production of these items, raising repeatedly their requirements and opening up the competition to new suppliers. In the first years of its purchasing of integrated circuits (in the early 1960s) the DOD bought 100 percent of U.S. production, at prices averaging $50 per circuit. As the learning curve was traced, prices dropped by 90 percent and commercial demand rose to over two-thirds of total production. Military demand, therefore, has stimulated the acceleration of technological advances and the entrance of new companies into the sector and reduced costs by pushing companies along the learning curve. International competitiveness followed, but this was not the objective of DOD's policy.

In the area of R&D support, the DOD has contracted directly for R&D projects in a number of fields, including electronics, aerospace, aerodynamics, food preservation and supply, fabrics, metals and metallurgy, and so on. It has also financed production refinement programs to assist in improving industrial preparedness and the ability to produce higher-quality products. Again, there is a diffusion of results into commercial competitiveness, but these results are not taken into account in the selection of industries to be supported by the DOD.

Support for R&D throughout U.S. industry has been generalized, rather than targeted at specific sectors, except where the sectors have a domestic purpose such as maintaining national security or in solving particular problems that have a pressing need in a socio-political sense. Thus, support for medical research (including that on tobacco as a cause of cancer), research on toxicity of pesticides, on natural means of controlling varmints and pests, on lasers, telecommunications, and so on result from specific demands in meeting general social needs rather than from international competitivenes. There is obviously some throw-off of the R&D assistance into the commercial sector, but again that is not its primary purpose. Nor are additional funds made available in order to make the translation from the original purpose into commercially viable innovations, in contrast to Japan's R&D support objectives.

The conclusion to be drawn is that the U.S. government has not seen itself as an appropriate decision-maker on the location or activities of industries but rather as a supporter of industrial growth and competitiveness in general. *In principle* only, the government stands ready to see the United States develop industrially in whatever ways the international markets and the transnational companies decide. The principle is violated whenever it begins to hurt seriously, and political hurt is more likely to catalyze interference than is economic hurt. In addition, if state governments wish to operate on different principles, they are permitted to do so, so long as they do not violate national law or international treaties to which the United States is a party.

## State-Government Incentives

Companies are incorporated within the United States by each of the several fifty states. There is no federal incorporation law, but companies operate across state boundaries under federal laws prohibiting restraint of trade among the fifty states, and they invest nationally under principles of comity. A corporation headquartered in one state can operate in any others; or, incorporated in one state, a corporation can locate its headquarters in another. Corporations have been wooed by states just to get them incorporated within that state jurisdiction for purposes of taxation, even if the manufacturing or headquarters activities are located elsewhere. Other states have sought corporate investment for the purpose of increasing employment opportunities or expanding port activities through foreign trade.

Probably none of the states has developed a coordinated set of tactics that could be called a strategy in the sense of determining precisely what sectors it would like to have enter it although several have sought to establish biogenetic or microelectronic centers in specific areas of their state. Most of the states are simply interested in larger payrolls and higher tax bases. However, some few of them have sought to shift the structure of economic activity away from agriculture into industry and, within industry, to the higher-wage jobs associated with high-technology industries. In others, industrial diversification is sought so as to reduce dependence on a dominant industry or a few sectors that might be hit hard by economic recession or by obsolescence of product lines. Some also seek a dispersion of job opportunities throughout the state so as to prevent concentration in a few urban areas and to reduce the infrastructure costs of such agglomerations. A few states have selected specific industry sectors they would like to promote and have established industrial parks to attract them: for example, the Research Triangle Park in North Carolina, where high technology industries are attracted by the limitations on polluting kinds of manufacturing, the requirements for a high percentage of R&D operations within the facilities located in the Park, and the ambiance of the three university communities in which there is the highest per capita concentration of Ph.D.'s in the world.

The techniques for attracting industry have ranged from low-cost loans to grants, the donation of land, low-cost leases of manufacturing facilities, tax waivers or credits, and the training of the workforce or technical personnel needed by the company.

Particular states that have chosen specific industrial segments to sponsor have sometimes been exceptionally successful: Massachusetts with the electronics industry (after the loss of the textile and shoe manufacturing sectors to southern states); California with Silicon Valley; Texas with aerospace; and several states are now interested in promoting biotechnology centers. These efforts do not reflect a search for a high degree of specialization nor any concerted or coordinated industrial policy looking to the future structure of industry within the state. Rather, they demonstrate only a high priority given to *one* sector in the total economic development of the state. In some instances, the efforts of one state have conflicted with the objectives of another, leading to some competitive extension of incentives, which probably did not significantly alter the decisions of the companies as to locations or product lines. Municipalities also have offered tax and loan incentives, with the probable result of simply reducing the tax revenues to both local and state governments.

In the absence of federal government coordination of these activities, or even any prohibition of the use of incentives to attract foreign industry, foreign investors benefit equally with U.S. investors and share in the resultant market distortions. These activities of states and cities are an embarrassment to the federal government in its efforts to encourage other countries to eliminate their national incentives for investors.

### National Interventions

The federal government has rejected any active role in establishing the *pattern* of industrial development in the United States and is supported in this by both business and labor. Neither of the latter sees it as desirable for the government to adopt a *policy* of stimulation of specific sectors in order to increase their competitiveness or to alter the market forces determining the location of activities in that sector. Yet there is significant government guidance (stimulation or preclusion) in the national security, communication, transportation, utility, and shipbuilding sectors. In each of these, a variety of direct and indirect subsidies and constraints are provided, and foreign firms are precluded from some of these. But a policy is different from a specific sectoral problem, and both management and labor have called for help in specific sectors (e.g., machine tools and electronics). Also, stimulation is different from protection, and both labor and business have urged government to *protect* existing interests when they are threatened.

National policies, therefore, tend to be ad hoc and essentially political in purpose rather than economic. This view is illustrated in the manner in which assistance has been given to specific sectors and by the extension of safeguards and adjustment assistance for labor, firms, and communities threatened by imports.

However, within the past few years, the government has begun to see the desirability of stimulating industry but has done so under the commonly designated policy of reindustrialization. It is a policy of nondiscriminating encouragement to industrialization, increased productivity, and improved competitiveness, without priority or emphasis given to specific sectors. The stimulation is through aggregate tax incentives of accelerated depreciation, investment credits, reduced taxes on capital gains, and provisions that encourage leasing of capital equipment. All are aimed to accelerate investment in new facilities, thereby hoping to improve productivity and competitive position as well as increasing employment through a larger volume of sales.

In addition, a stimulus to reduce costs and, therefore, to raise productivity is sought through deregulation of industry, which has been assessed as too costly in terms not only of the regulations themselves but also in relation to the administrative burdens of compliance and in terms of constraining the decisions of industry.

Further, the government has recently adopted a policy stance of weakening, or at least not strengthening, the bargaining position of labor unions, in the hopes of reducing wage pressure and, therefore, increasing the cost-effectiveness of manufacturing in major segments of industry. The government has also examined ways in which it might provide a stimulus to R&D activities of companies so as to accelerate innovation and thereby increase sales at home and abroad. These investigations have not led to any specific encouragements; for example, there are no new grants or subsidies to R&D activities, and no sectors have been singled out as those to be encouraged on a priority basis. The major effort on the part of the government is through vocal persuasion to companies to undertake more R&D and to raise productivity.

In terms of the international location of industry, the government has not significantly altered its prior positions of noninterference as between exports, licensing of technology, or foreign direct investment. The present administration is not pushing foreign direct investment as prior ones have save in its Caribbean Initiative; it has given no new stimulation to exports, and has, in fact, cut back on the resources of the Export-Import Bank. It has reduced the burden of taxation on placement of Americans abroad in foreign subsidiaries, but, again, this is nondiscriminatory among countries or sectors.

*Sectoral Programs*

The closest that the U.S. government has come to sectoral priorities is its consideration that the future of U.S. industry rests with the high-technology sectors. The government is hoping that U.S. industry will find ways to move more extensively into electronics, chemicals, energy substitutes for petroleum, aerospace, telecommunications, informatics, biophysics, genetics, and medical specialties—each with the purpose of expanding markets at home and abroad. But it has not sought the entrance of foreign high-technology companies into the United States to bolster this development. Despite its *preference* for the development of certain industrial sectors, the U.S. government has no policy for the stimulation of science and technology for these sectors, although it recognizes that their growth will depend heavily on R&D expenditures. Rather, its attention is drawn to key sectors, which are those having sufficient political power to command governmental support (shipbuilding, national-security industries, chemicals, petroleum and petrochemicals, steel, textiles, automobiles, aircraft, and a variety of industries that are seen as injured from time to time).

In between, there is a list of sectors that are seen as neither preferential nor as critical in the political sense; these include pharmaceuticals, rubber products, wood products, paper and pulp, metals and metal products, a wide range of instruments and instrumentation, electrical and other machinery, agricultural and construction vehicles and equipment, transport equipment, optical and photographic products, and so forth. From its present and historical stances, it would appear that the U.S. government would permit the demise of any one of these sectors or at least of major producers therein, thereby reducing significantly U.S. participation in any given sector.

It was assumed, of course, that the reduction of barriers to trade, as accomplished in several GATT negotiations since 1945, would cut into U.S. industry only at the margins, eliminating the inefficient producers and thereby raising the gains from trade. Obviously, as with all countries, the United States has availed itself of the Escape Clause provisions of the GATT when imports threatened a given sector more than marginally. The use of such safeguards is merely to save what exists rather than to develop any overt industrial strategy.

Outside of the usual safeguard procedures, the U.S. government has provided support or protection of a quite special nature to six different sectors or companies within them: textiles and apparel, footwear, color televisions, steel, aircraft, and automobiles.

**Multi-Fiber Agreement.** The textile industry has long been protected by a fairly high level of tariffs covering a large portion of the products and imposed against all suppliers. In addition, quantitative restrictions are imposed on most of the leading foreign exporters. The latter were applied under a procedure known as voluntary export restraints, whereby the U.S. government persuaded several of the exporting countries to limit their exports voluntarily. These negotiations produced bilateral agreements that established annual quantitative limits for textile products, defined in a very specific manner so as to prevent circumvention of the restraints. These agreements cover a period of three to five years, but allow for an annual increase in the ceiling for particular product categories, with greater flexibility built in through a carry-forward or carry-back of a country's quota and a permission to swing a certain percentage of one product category's entitlement to another category for a given year.

These limitations, imposed through bilateral agreements, are sanctioned by a multilateral agreement entitled the Multi-Fiber Arrangement (MFA), which was concluded under the auspices of the GATT, and to which nearly all major textile importing and exporting countries are signatory. The MFA includes not only cotton textiles but also man-made fiber and wool textile products. The agreement has been extended in various forms since the inception of the bilateral agreements in 1961.

These restraints were literally imposed on many of the developing countries by the U.S. government under threat of extensive and prohibitive import quotas, which the Kennedy Administration did not want to employ. The agreement therefore maintained the charade that the U.S. government is in principle in favor of freer trade and does not itself impose barriers to that trade.

**Footwear.** From the mid-1960s the footwear industry in the United States has been in decline. This trend in evidenced by a reduction of the number of plants, declining production, and reduced employment, accelerated by an increase in imports from about 13 percent in mid-1960 to nearly 50 percent of total consumption in recent years. In the early 1960s, the source of imports was Italy and Japan; in the latter part of that decade and the early 1970s, imports surged from South Korea and Taiwan, followed later by Brazil.

After the surge in 1977 from the Far East, the International Trade Commission determined that serious injury had occurred as a result of the imports and recommended application of a tariff-quota. President Carter chose instead to negotiate an orderly marketing arrangement with Taiwan and South Korea on rubber footwear. Each supplier nation agreed to cut back its exports by between 15 and 20 percent, with a growth factor built in for subsequent years.

These agreements have not arrested the decline of the footwear industry, which is faced with increased imports from other suppliers.

**Color Television.** Also in 1977, an orderly marketing agreement was negotiated with Japan on its exports of color television to the United States. This
agreement was in response to a petition from a group of labor unions and
some smaller firms in the electronics industry to the International Trade
Commission to prevent continued injury from such imports. The ITC
recommended multistage tariff relief, over a five year period, but the president again opted for restraint by the exporting nation. Japan agreed to limit
its exports to around 60 percent of its most recent level. Despite a drop of
over one million sets per year from Japan, imports of color television were
increased substantially—ninefold from South Korea and twofold from
Taiwan. There also was a dramatic rise in imports of incomplete color
television receivers from Taiwan and Mexico, many of which were produced by subsidiaries of U.S. companies abroad. In addition, Japanese
companies established or expanded production facilities in the U.S. for television sets and components.

The result has been a concentration of production in fewer manufacturers within the United States and a reduction of worker man-hours due to
the import of incomplete television sets and components.

Consequently, orderly marketing arrangements (OMAs) were negotiated also with South Korea and Taiwan in order to maintain U.S. production, which has increasingly been shifted to the control of foreign-
owned subsidiaries.

**Steel.** In the face of rapidly increasing imports in the 1970s from both
Europe and Japan, and strong pleas from steel companies for import
quotas, the U.S. government has devised and imposed a trigger-price mechanism. Under it, the duties on steel rise if the foreign price falls below the
U.S. price by a specified amount. The purpose of the protection was to give
the U.S. steel industry the opportunity to begin the modernization of its
investment and to institute other programs to raise its productivity. The
industry responded that it was, in fact, as productive as foreign companies,
but that the latter were subsidized by their governments and were dumping
in the U.S. markets.

Since the mechanism did not work adequately in the view of the companies, pressure to impose quotas or to obtain voluntary export limitations
on the part of the foreign countries—notably Japan and some in Europe—
resulted in such agreements in 1983. Once again, the onus is placed on the
foreigner, thereby keeping the reputation of the United States clean, at least
in its own eyes, through maintaining the principle of freer, open-market
trade.

The lack of an industrial policy for this sector is demonstrated by the
fact that, in the face of no significant acceleration of capital investment in
the sector, the U.S. government is taking no action to make certain that the

sector survives or is competitive. Even the U.S. Steel Corporation is seeking to diversify (*vide,* the acquisition of Marathon Oil Company) rather than spend those hundreds of millions of dollars in modernizing steel production. Several billions of dollars will be needed over the next decade to return this sector to a position of international competitiveness, and these funds are not yet forthcoming. But the steel industry seems to have read the administrations' policy correctly, for the government apparently does not care if U.S. production falls and some producers fail or cut back on capacity. Efficiency rather than capacity appears to be the goal. Also, government aid would probably *not* have been forthcoming but for the threat of greater unemployment in an area critical to presidential electoral strength and at a time of widespread unemployment. Again, the government's action appears to have greater political than economic justification.

**Aircraft.** Another example of the ad hoc approach of the U.S. government to industry development is the support for Lockheed; it demonstrates that the role assumed by the U.S. government is that of aid for ailing manufacturers, not for the promotion of a given sector. Lockheed had difficulty in meeting its obligations because of inadequate sales of the L-1011. A $200 million loan was requested from Congress, which it eventually guaranteed. (This action became a precedent for the Chrysler loan.) One of the significant arguments in favor of governmental support was the depressed employment condition in the area and in the industry itself. Lockheed was able to regain its footing, largely through success in sales of planes other than the L-1011, which it phased out. Some analysts consider that this plane should have been scrapped earlier, as it would have been if the loan guarantee had not been supplied. Despite the general distress of the industry and incursions of foreign suppliers in world markets for commercial aircraft, the U.S. government offered no long-term program. The Lockheed loan was considered strictly as a bail-out. Although the potential failure of Lockheed had little political implications, there was fear that Lockheed's commercial losses would drag down its defense capacities as well, although, in retrospect, the termination of the L-1011 appears to have strengthened Lockheed as a defense contractor.

**Automobiles.** The automotive industry has had more attention from government in the past two decades than any other, with the exception of textiles, and without the government itself taking the initiative. There are four phases of government involvement in the sector: the U.S.-Canadian Auto Agreement; the negotiation of an orderly marketing arrangement with Japan; support to Chrysler; and attempts at persuading Japanese companies to establish manufacturing facilities in the United States. All of these were in response to external conditions affecting the industry, which has historically been in favor of free trade with the full support of both management and labor. Only recently has this orientation shifted, essentially under the thrust of Japanese competition into the U.S. market itself. Each of the four aspects are themselves efforts to resolve the question of the location of industrial activity and to maintain high levels of production and employment in the United States. They help to indicate the way in which the United States is likely to respond to problems of international industrial integration, when pressed to take some formal action.

The Canada–U.S. Automotive Agreement of 1965 was initiated by the U.S. government, but it was in response to a Canadian threat of imposition of barriers to both investment and trade resulting from Canada's desire to shift location of production more into Canada so as to reduce a large balance-of-payments deficit in automotive trade. The Canadian government had proposed quietly to a number of U.S. companies manufacturing in Canada that they shift some of their manufacturing facilities into Canada, thereby eliminating the need to import from the United States. It offered encouragements to export through a permission to import at lower duties those components that would remain supplied from the United States. When the U.S. government heard of the proposals, it responded that it would involve subsidization of Canadian exports and would trigger countervailing duties on its part. It appeared that trade in automobiles and automotive components between the two countries was heading for numerous restraints.

Consequently, though the special arrangement would be in violation of the GATT, an intergovernmental agreement was negotiated providing for duty-free trade between the two countries in most new vehicles and those parts to be used as original equipment. Tires, tubes, and some specialty vehicles and chassis were not included in the agreement. Since duty-free treatment was restricted only to Canada, the United States was in technical violation of the GATT and required a waiver, which was granted later in 1965. In order for Canada not to become a passthrough for imports of components or automobiles from other countries, imports from Canada required a minimum of 50 percent North American content to be given duty-free treatment. Canada also imposed local-content requirements so as to raise the value-added in vehicles production in Canada. Though the agreement did not guarantee it, an objective of the Canadian government was to gain a significant increase in Canadian automotive production by the end of 1968.

This agreement was an attempt to alter the location of production through a requirement of local production-to-sales ratio, which in effect prevented the industry from relocating on the United States side if it became more attractive to do so either economically or commercially.

In the operation of the agreement, neither the United States nor Canada has been wholly satisfied, and both have sought renegotiation.

Analyses of the effects of the agreement indicate that by 1969 even, value added in the Canadian parts industry had been raised twofold over what it would have been in the absence of the agreement, and value added in the assembly portion was 100 percent larger. The agreement also raised Canadian hourly earnings, employment, industry profits, and exports by substantial factors. Vehicle exports to the United States after the agreement were increased nearly twenty times, and imports were substantially increased as well. Canada's parts exports to the United States were raised nine times and its imports by a factor of two. Increasing intraindustry specialization occurred as a result of the agreement.

One study has concluded that the stimulus to the overall Canadian economy was profound: Gross national expenditure rose by 1969 by nearly 5 percent in real terms; exports of total goods and services rose by over 20 percent; and total employment rose over 2.8 percent above the levels that would have occurred in the absence of the agreement or of compensatory government actions.[4]

In the late 1970s, under the pressure of imports of automobiles from Japan rising to 30 percent of U.S. sales, the auto industry (both management and labor) turned to the U.S. government for import restrictions, specifically requesting quotas. Rather than impose such quantitative limitations, the administration once again turned to an orderly marketing arrangement, requesting the Japanese to undertake voluntary export restraint. The Japanese government was reluctant to provide evidence of such close ties between the government and industry as would be indicated by a ready acceptance of a governmental request, so the automotive industry itself decided to reduce shipments. This was done company-by-company under procedures not made public.

The U.S. government had still not made any determination as to the desirable size of U.S. automotive capacity or production, nor as to how the industry should be structured or what ownership pattern would be acceptable. Thus it had readily permitted, without any observation pro or con, American Motors to be bought on a minority basis by a French company. Also, Chrysler, Ford, and GM have instituted joint ventures with Japanese counterparts that include a shipment of components and vehicles from the joint venture into the U.S. market. In the absence of Japanese export restraint, Ford Motor Company threatened to move more of its production facilities overseas and to import back into the United States.

In an attempt to retain production capacities inside of the United States, and thereby to maintain employment in the auto industry, the U.S. government has sent delegations to Japan to encourage direct foreign investment by its auto companies in the United States—not only in final vehicle production and assembly but also in production of components and replacement parts. It has also encouraged Japanese companies to buy some of their original equipment components in the United States so as to achieve greater intracompany specialization among the two countries and thereby reduce the import bill in automobile trade. In this effort, the U.S. initiative is similar to that undertaken by Canada in the mid-1960s, but the United States is not presently considering any such free-trade agreement with Japan in this sector. In fact, it seems not to have any particular view as to the desired structure or scope of this industry. Again, if it were not for the high level of unemployment and the depressed nature of the economy in general, it appears unlikely that any serious attention would be given to the automotive industry at present. It is only because of generalized unemployment and the industry's employment problems are so concentrated in a specific area that it is receiving attention.

* * *

All four sectoral experiences—textiles, steel, autos, and airplanes—demonstrate that the U.S. government assists a sector or company differentially only when it faces difficulties that raise concerns for broader economic policies and political objectives of the U.S. government. A textile industry in decline would have meant considerable unemployment in the South in a period when President Kennedy was trying to get the country moving again, and in a region that he required for political support. Little was done to stimulate the industry; rather, a series of signals were given to it that it required readjustment and redirection of its product lines to become viable internationally. This was done over a period of several years, and the industry is relatively viable under the present arrangements.

The threatened cutback in steel employment and the possibility of failure of some companies was also considered serious by the U.S. government. The Lockheed and Chrysler situations, wherein the U.S. government showed itself willing to prevent a firm from failing but not to encourage its expansion or an improved position once shown it is able to survive, were similar. In fact, it *appears* that the U.S. government would let the U.S. auto companies gradually go out of business if they found a way to do so without damage to U.S. employment and incomes (for example, by encouraging foreign companies to come in). If there were low levels of unemployment in the United States, which permitted a rapid move of workers out of the auto industry into electronics or other high-technology sectors, it appears that the U.S. government would let the auto industry itself atrophy somewhat; this attitude is also true for steel, although it is not necessarily so for the airplanes, aerospace, and munitions sectors. However, the government is willing to see some *companies* in these industries fail.

But there is no public evidence that the government has considered the question of how *far* it would let any sector die out before it determined to stop or reverse the situation. That is, there seems to be no policy position that the United States ought to have a given amount of steel production, or of textiles, autos, or any industry within its borders. It appears certain that there *is* such a figure and that the U.S. Congress, if not the administration, would react if production fell to near that level. But there seems to be little anticipation as to what those levels would be in the absence of a clear and present danger nor of the portion of any sector that should be retained under U.S. ownership. Both questions have been finessed because the condition of key sectors has been one of continued growth, and ownership has been safely in U.S. hands. Close examination would undoubtedly be given them officially, however, if conditions worsened significantly.

## Safeguards and Adjustments

Although the Escape Clause provision of the GATT have not been used by the U.S. government to structure any specific sector under a national strategy, they have been used to maintain production in the United States, and therefore alter the location of economic activity from what would occur under freer trade. For example, in an action on citizens-band radio transceivers, the International Trade Commission recommended that duties be raised as a remedy for the pressure of imports from South Korea and Taiwan or that trade adjustment assistance be provided to qualifying workers' firms and communities. The president decided to raise duties for three years by an additional 15 percentage points in the first year, decreasing the three percentage points in each of the next two years; further, the preferential (GSP) rates applied to South Korea and Taiwan were removed. The tariff route was used probably because of its more immediate effect and the general dissatisfaction of labor and some companies with the provisions of trade adjustment assistance.

Trade adjustment assistance was first provided under the Trade Expansion Act of 1962 essentially to obtain the support of labor for the tariff reduction provisions of the act. The act provided that labor, firms, and communities would receive various forms of assistance if the company involved had been injured in major parts as the result of imports increasing because of a negotiated reduction in duties. Thus it must be shown that the increased imports were the major cause of the difficulties faced by the company, that the workers were harmed as a result of these difficulties, and that the imports were a direct result of the reduction of duties through an international agreement.

Given these conditions, assistance would be given to the company to improve its position by enhancing productivity in the existing product line, or to help it move out of that particular line into another. Assistance would also be given to workers who were declared redundant through retraining, moving expenses, or direct compensation for the loss of their job. In later amendments of the act, communities were included; they would receive some support to attract new economic activities.

All of these measures have been aimed at facilitating market-dictated adjustments under conditions moving toward freer trade. Thus the U.S. government has maintained that the structure of industry required by the working of competitive forces is the structure that is desired, and marginal companies will simply have to move out. In order to buy their acquiescence, and therefore to reduce opposition to freer trade, trade adjustment programs have been provided. They are, however, reactive and cannot be considered part of an overall industrial policy save that they are an integral part of a policy that indicates that the structure of industry should be whatever is determined by the market.


*Evaluation*

The details above have been emphasized in order to demonstrate that the United States—despite its open-economy principles—will employ numerous techniques of industrial policy when deemed in its interest. It has been able to hold to the myth of an open world economy because it was so dominant in the world for twenty-five years after World War II. The U.S.'s GNP was about 45 percent of free-world production even into the mid-1960s, its foreign direct investment accounted for half the world total, and its percentage of world trade was over one-third of the total for some years— though all three of these began to decline in the 1970s toward present proportions nearly half their 1950s levels.

In principle, the United States was willing to recognize that open trading channels would constrain the increase of wages in the United States, determine the level of specific product prices, alter product lines through competition and determine the types of technology which are appropriate or required. However, operating in a *relatively* closed national market, some industries were able to raise wages far above international levels and still remain competitive simply because of the weakness of international competition. With the growing competitiveness of other countries, and the interests of governments in shaping industrial structures, U.S. competitiveness has declined, thereby constraining the growth of key U.S. industrial sectors, both at home and abroad.

Many government and business officials in the United States have not yet fully realized that industrial development in other countries will *significantly* alter the pattern of U.S. industrial growth and its international position. New entrants into a sector are more readily accepted when it is growing rapidly and marginally inefficient producers can move into other sectors. A wide and expanding international market permits growth to be diversified enough to accommodate a large number of entrants in a variety of countries. But when a number of advanced countries seek to stimulate growth in the same sectors and export to each other—as has occurred in shipbuilding, steel, autos and in projects in the high-technology sectors— and world market growth does not match production capacities, the problem of the distribution of the burden of adjustments comes acute.

State Department officials are, however, beginning to recognize that the world of the 1980s is not the world of the 1950s and 1960s. They see considerably greater government involvement in decisions as to the location of economic activity and the nature and direction of trade and investment. Yet any move toward formation of an industrial strategy would require a considerable shift in economic policy. Such development faces several obstacles: First, many of the policymakers in the U.S. government are imbued with classical economic precepts, which they find difficult to discard; as evidenced only partly but continuously by their use of the concept of market distortions they are unable to abandon the *principles* of Bretton Woods and to seek an alternative ordering principle. They react almost emotionally against any proposals that start from different precepts. They appear not even to know how to begin to determine new criteria for decision-making as to the process and nature of international industrial integration. Consequently, they remain frustrated with the moves that are occurring toward industrial disintegration under the new protectionism. Not knowing where to go, they cannot leave where they are. Second, the legal officers in the U.S. government have grown up on an orientation of adversarial relationships, based on win or lose postures in court and conflict attitudes toward business motives. Third, U.S. business has had a historical orientation of private motives, which makes it difficult to take into consideration socioeconomic-political problems of the system as a whole. Many U.S. business managers still consider that the society's major purpose is to support business activities, which prevents them from accepting readily a role of cooperation with other elements in the society relative to business decisions. Fourth, there has been a lack of leadership within the U.S. government in the international economic realm since the mid-1960s; it has remained bent toward a perpetuation and enhancement of the precepts of the Bretton Woods Agreements, save for its violation of U.S. perpetrated rules of stable exchange rates, when it became in its interest to permit floating rates. These agreements were based on free-market determinations, which, in a critical sense, remove the necessity for business or government to assume responsibility for decisions that affect the life and development of the community. The *impersonal* forces of the market are supposed to be determinative in major decisions in social and economic welfare, both affecting and effecting the evolution of *persons*.

The major force that has changed the ability of the United States to hold to this paradigm is the decline in its *relative* economic significance in the world. Although U.S. growth will continue in absolute terms (however changed in composition), the rest of the world will be growing faster, and the relative influence of the United States will decline still further. As a consequence, the policy orientations of other nations (few of which have grown up and remained in the Anglo-Saxon, classical economic tradition) will have to be given more weight and accommodation through a change in U.S. policies. This shift is exceedingly difficult for the U.S. government to accept even if it perceives the change; a similar reticence exists for U.S. companies, which have been used to negotiating from the background of the strength of the U.S. economy and the influence of the U.S. government.

Given these obstacles to change on the part of the U.S. government, there is a strong likelihood that the United States itself will turn inward either in pique or frustration in not being able to persuade others to adopt its liberal policy stance. Not seeing an alternative way of maintaining high levels of international economic integration and seeking to cut off perceived interferences of other economies, it will likely remain ambivalent in policy prescription and implementation.

If the United States were to decide to adopt an industrial policy, it would still be missing a few of the techniques and a more fundamental practice—that of planning or strategy formation. There is no planning agency and no industrial strategy. Nor do sectoral plans arise even on an ad hoc basis. Missing also is a widespread dialog between the government, the banking system, and enterprises, such as is found in the other OECD countries examined in chapter 2. Therefore, investment financing could be done directly only after some new institutional arrangements were put in place. In addition, differential taxation would require congressional authority, as would direct subsidies to a sector or a leading company. Discrimination among companies is not an acceptable approach in U.S. economic policy, and it would also require congressional authority for the government to pick an industrial champion.

However, a number of other possible techniques for stimulation or guidance of specific sectors are in place: government procurement, export credits, assistance in marketing overseas, encouragement to standardization of products, joint-venture research projects and consolidation of industry under antitrust exemption, coordination of aid to distressed regions, provision of infrastructure, trade adjustment assistance, mitigation or intensification of foreign competitive pressures to help or ease the demise of marginal producers, assistance in manpower training, and, in conjunction with state governments, aid in relocation of facilities to become more competitive. However, these available techniques are not meshed into a plan giving priority to individual sectors, and no coordinating mechanism is in place.

The U.S. response tends, therefore, to focus more on declining industries or those under ad hoc pressure and is, consequently, decidedly protectionist. This feeds the widely held cynicism that the United States talks one way and acts another. If it cannot lead the way out of this impasse, the initiative will fall to others or be taken by no one until the pressures for change are inexorable.

**Notes**

1. The statement continues:

"In particular, trade-related performance requirements can lead to distortions in trade and investment flows and in the uneconomic use of resources. For example, local content requirements mandate the use of domestic factors of production irrespective of relative costs. Similarly, export requirements force a firm to export a certain amount of its production, irrespective of comparative advantage. Such exports can cause trade diversion through displacement of another country's exports to the third country markets or through increased imports in another country from the firm complying with the export requirements. Possible losses incurred in such exports can be made up by exploiting what are often monopoly-like positions in the host country. These requirements have effects similar to trade protection or subsidies in altering international trade flows and adversely affecting other countries. Trade distortion is most severe when two or more requirements are used in conjunction with each other (e.g., local content and export requirements in the same industry) or when they are used in conjunction with other restrictive practices (e.g., tariffs) or incentives." (*The Use of Investment Incentives and Performance Requirements by Foreign Governments,* Office of International Investment, U.S. Department of Commerce, October 1981, p. 7.)

2. In a Staff Report of the Bureau of Economics the Federal Trade Commission in June 1980 argued that orderly marketing arrangements as applied by the United States, have operated significantly to the net detriment of consumer interests and have imposed an (in)efficiency cost on the economy several times any calculable benefits; this loss occurs largely through passing to the foreigner the scarcity rents from the restriction of imports into the United States. The report recommends the elimination of such barriers rather than their adjustment to shift the locus of the scarcity rents to the United States. (Morris E. Morkre and David G. Tarr, *Staff Report on Effects of Restrictions of United State Imports: Five Cases Studies in Theory.* Washington, D.C.: Federal Trade Commission, June 1980. Pp. 196–200.) Although this is a staff report and not necessarily

reflective of the policy positions of the Trade Commission itself, it does in fact accord with the pronouncements of top government officials of the principles underlying U.S. policies.

3. R. Roger Majak, "When All Else Fails, National Industrial Planning?" in Mark B. Winchester (ed.), *The International Essays for Business Decision Makers,* Vol. V. New York: AMACOM, 1980, pp. 7–17.

4. David L. Emerson, *Production, Location, and the Automotive Agreement.* Ottawa: The Economic Council of Canada, 1975. See also Carl E. Beigie, *The Canada–U.S. Automotive Agreement: An Evaluation.* Montreal: Canadian–American Committee, 1970.

## Selected Readings for Part I

The Business Week Team. *The Reindustrialization of America.* New York: McGraw-Hill, 1982.

Diebold, Jr., William. *Industrial Policy as an International Issue.* New York: McGraw-Hill, 1980.

Dosi, Giovanni. "Technical Change and Survival: Europe's Semiconductor Industry." *Industrial Adjustment and Policy I.* Sussex European Papers No. 9, University of Sussex European Research Center, 1981.

Driscoll, R.E. and Behrman, J.N. (eds.). *National Industrial Policies.* Boston: Oelgeschlager, Gunn & Hain, 1984.

Duchene, Francois and Shepherd, Geoffrey. *Industrial Adjustment and Government Intervention in Western Europe.* Sussex: University of Sussex European Research Center, October 1980.

Franko, Lawrence. *European Industrial Policy: Past, Present, and Future.* Brussels: The Conference Board in Europe, European Research Report, February 1980.

Granstrand, Ove and Sigurdson, Jon (eds.). *Technological and Industrial Policy in China and Europe.* Lund, Sweden: Research Policy Institute, Occasional Report Series, No. 3, 1981.

Helleiner, G.K.; Franko, Lawrence G.; Junz, Helen B.; and Dreyer, Peter. *Protectionism or Industrial Adjustment?* Paris: The Atlantic Institute for International Affairs, 1980.

Jones, Daniel T. "Maturity and Crisis in the European Car Industry: Structural Change in Public Policy." *Industrial Adjustment and Policy: I.* Sussex European Papers, No. 8, University of Sussex European Research Center, 1981.

Magaziner, Ira C. and Hout, Thomas N. *Japanese Industrial Policy.* London: Policy Studies Institute, No. 585, January 1980.

OECD. *The Industrial Policies of 14 Member Countries.* Paris: Organization for Economic Cooperation and Development, 1971.

————. *The Industrial Policy of Japan*. Paris: Organization for Economic Cooperation and Development, 1972.

————. *Selected Industrial Policy Instruments*. Paris: OECD, 1978.

————. *The Case for Positive Adjustment Policies: A Compendium of OECD Documents, 1978/79*. Paris: OECD, June 1979.

Reich, Robert and Magaziner, I. *Minding America's Business*. New York: Harcourt Brace Jovanovich, 1982.

Roman, Zoltán, (ed.). *Industrial Development and Industrial Policy*. Budapest: Akademiai Kiado, 1979.

Subcommittee on Oversight and Investigation. *Capital Formation and Industrial Policy: A Compendium*. U.S. House of Representatives, Committee on Energy and Commerce, July 1981.

Trilateral Commission. *Industrial Policy and the International Economy*. New York: Report of the Trilateral Task Force on Industrial Policy, 1979.

Warnecke, S.J. *International Trade and Industrial Policies*. New York: Holmes and Meier, 1978.

# Part II
# International Integration and Transnationals

The new protectionism outlined in the previous chapters is not a way in which the United States anticipated that the postwar world would be organized. That world, based on the Bretton Woods Agreements, was fractured in the early 1970s, and we have for the past decade operated without an agreed-upon ordering principle for the world economy.

The next two chapters address the problems of creating a new international economic order and examine the factors that are presently at work in determining the questions of where industry should be located and the distribution of benefits.

The uncertain situation in which we find ourselves has significantly different impacts on different industrial sectors, raising diverse policy issues for governments. It is these distinctive effects that have buttressed the formation of sectional industrial policies.

Within this situation, the transnationals have played different roles, depending on their own market orientations and responses to governments. They can play still different and more useful roles if governments will but provide them appropriate guidelines. The question of how to use TNCs to effectively integrate world production and trade is the subject of part III of this text, but the desirability or even necessity of relying on the TNCs to achieve integration objectives is understandable through the assessments in the following two chapters.

# 4 Toward International Industrial Integration or Dis-Integration?

**Introduction**

Any effort to restructure industry internationally should determine first the extent to which the new structure is to be integrated or dis-integrated and in what ways. Integration is the process of fitting together constituent parts of a system so as to form an effectively functioning whole. Dis-integration is the separation of those parts. Intermediate conditions usually exist—rather than complete integration or dis-integration—in which some elements are integrated and others are not. The process of economic integration is, therefore, usually partial; that is, a few parts at a time or only certain sectors or functions of the economy.

Economic integration fits together elements of the economic system so that they are consistent and work toward maximizing the effectiveness of the entire system in reaching desired goals. Such a condition is acceptable only to socioeconomic-political groups that conceive of themselves as a *community*. This goal is accomplished within a nation by mobility of goods, labor, money and capital, ownership and ideas (technology)—all constituting an open market for citizens, acting under a single political and juridical system. The objective has been the increase of national wealth and power through the most efficient allocation of resources (human and natural) to the desired goals.

International economic integration fits national economic systems together to create a working relationship that is more effective in achieving agreed-upon goals than wholly separated national systems. International integration is accomplished by the movement of goods and capital, ownership, technology, management, and, increasingly, labor. But a completely open market has not yet been formed internationally (not even regionally within the European Community or other groups); conflicts of national laws and regulations remain to prevent complete integration. Therefore, conscious decisions must be made at the intergovernmental level as to the nature and extent of economic integration desired. These decisions sometimes require trade-offs between national (or multinational) wealth and power, limiting the integration.

A major concern in determining the extent of international integration

69

is that over the distribution of benefits, which is evidenced not only in trade policies but also in decisions on the location and activities of TNCs. The problem of an acceptable distribution of benefits is seldom squarely faced but more normally is subsumed in other policies or approaches. When the problem is faced, it tends to be separated from the process of production itself and is met by transfer payments; even in labor negotiations, some unions seem to consider that certain levels of income are due its members regardless of production results, effecting a type of transfer payment.

The composition, location, volume, and efficiency of production are all part and parcel of the process of a distribution of benefits. They are really a single issue, for the production and distribution of income are inseparably linked, and efforts to unlink them raise serious problems of motivation at various levels of production. Manifestations of the concerns over the distribution of benefits rise in determination of the receipt of income, in the process of determining the level and types of employment available, in efforts to rectify imbalances of international payments, in constraints on technology flows, and in decisions on the geographic location of specific industrial activities.

Whether or not these industrial activities are integrated worldwide so as to achieve the benefits of economic specialization and the most effective division of labor is a policy question that has been answered in the affirmative in terms of prescription but rather inadequately implemented. On the contrary, mercantilism appears to be on the ascendency worldwide. Mercantilism views international trade as a kind of war, in which a nation wins by having an export surplus in trade and loses by having a deficit; in addition, the world economy is seen as a static pie to be divided as favorably as possible for one's own nation.

Despite a worldwide increase in international trade and direct investment, the concerns for improved *national* benefits appear now to be leading toward international industrial *dis*-integration, under the guise of self-reliance, economic independence, and the freedom offered by floating exchange rates.

The forces leading toward economic nationalism are fed by the increasing demands for greater governmental responsibility for economic growth and social welfare. Greater responsibility leads to greater governmental intervention, which in turn leads to attempts to attenuate disturbances from abroad or control foreign trade and investment activities. Each such effort means that domestic goals are given primacy over cooperative international objectives, and moves toward international integration are weakened, if not reversed.

Despite government intervention, both international trade and investment have risen rapidly, even as a percentage of domestic production (GDP). Production by foreign-owned affiliates of TNCs has become an important contributor to industrial growth around the world, to the expansion of trade in the last two decades, and to the redeployment of industry to LDCs. As a result of the activities of TNCs, a new type of international integration is occurring. Whereas economies were previously tied across national boundaries almost wholly by the movement of goods (with relatively small movements of people and capital for commercial purposes), in the past twenty-five years, major movements of capital (both portfolio and direct), managers, technicians, and technology have been stimulated by the TNCs. The result is a series of impacts on domestic economies that are sometimes seen as interference in governmental objectives but at other times are viewed as highly desirable support to those objectives. For still other countries, identical activities will often appear to have reverse effects, depending on their reaction to the distribution of the benefits. There is, therefore, little support for international industrial integration *apart from the specific benefits each nation perceives as accruing to it.* There is little willingness to sacrifice other objectives for purely *potential* rewards of integration or for a larger benefit for the world economy as a whole. Yet it is difficult to foresee the benefits of generalized economic integration.

A fundamental question, therefore, is whether governments really do want international economic (industrial) integration. Official pronouncements argue in favor of it, but many governmental regulations and practices move away from it. There are, of course, different types of integration, but all involve a degree of interdependence and specialization, leading to reliance of one country on another for its economic development. The basic argument in support of integration is the productivity that arises from the expansion of the market, permitting the application of economies of scale and specialization through the division of labor. This is an *efficiency* justification, of course, but it can be implemented in several different ways, leading to more or less equity among nations in sharing the benefits. (Equity does not imply equality.)

Historically, it was considered that the free movement of international trade in final products or components was sufficient to integrate the world economy, since such trade would be substitute for factor movements. Given the interferences in trade and the costs of movements of final goods, it has become apparent that efficiencies can be achieved through the movement of factors, leading to the phenomenon of international production (production by foreign-owned affiliates located around the world or by foreign licenses). International production leads to a different form of specialization, focused within sectors or even within a single transnational corporation that moves materials and components among affiliates. Intraindustry or intracompany specialization can exist even within a single product line, differentiating among qualities of a single product, each produced in or for markets seeking different qualities. Similar specialization can occur in product design or styles or even different trademarks of similar products. Specialization occurs also on the basis of technologies, labor skills, labor supply, managerial capabilities, and even managerial orientations and styles.

Obviously, such integration is not static but opens options for operating choices by both governments and TNCs. But specialization and interdependence also raise problems for governments that are responsible for the level and growth of economic activity in their country. The key question is how to balance off the desired international integration with domestic responsibilities. Only if the international system can assist in meeting domestic responsibilities will governments strongly support moves toward international integration.

## Regional Integration

If the world can move away from its predominant national orientations, it is more likely to advance, step-fashion, to international integration *through* regional integration. Distinct sets of rules for economic activity will arise for different regions, each reflecting different views as to the way in which the members should be related to each other and to outsiders. A variety of economic groups exist presently, each with different (more or less fixed) rules of economic behavior and with different degrees and modes of industrial integration: the Western countries' Organization for Economic Cooperation and Development (OECD); the European Community; the Eastern countries' Committee for Mutual Economic Assistance (COMECON); the Latin American Free Trade Association (LAFTA); the Andean Pact; the Association of Southeast Asian Nations (ASEAN); and several aborted African groupings. In none of these associations has integration been carried to the point of removing all barriers to the movement of goods, services, or funds—much less those of persons. Some important countries remain unaffiliated (People's Republic of China, South Africa, and Israel), but they are not significant enough internationally to alter the rules within the others or to dictate unilaterally the rules of economic exchange between themselves and members of any of the major groupings.

A still-different set of rules will characterize the ties between members of any two of these regional blocs and (eventually) among all such blocs. Thus, there are East-West ties between OECD countries and the COMECON members; there are North-South ties between the OECD and LAFTA members; there are South-South ties between the LAFTA and ASEAN countries; and some East-South ties exist between COMECON and various developing countries. Most of these ties are bilateral, that is, between nations within different regions. Full-fledged interregional integration has not yet been achieved. These regions are likely to become *more* cohesive, making common rules among members on treatment of outsiders still more desirable.

Agreeing on interregional rules will be difficult, especially since the closed intraregional rules will have been tediously hammered out, and modifications for outsiders will not come easily. For example, in establishing the post–World War II rules, it was recognized during the debate on the International Trade Organization that it was impossible to accommodate state-trading methods in the market orientations of the West. In practice, some accommodations have been made by East and West to the methods of the other. But in the area of direct investment, when the East has come into the West or the West has gone into the East, the accommodation has been into the established rules of the host country. The West is more open, permitting the East to enter almost at will (although it has not entered extensively even into Europe, probably for fear of criticism at home, where investible resources are scarce). On its part, the East is largely closed, restricting substantially the types of arrangements that can be developed there by the West. The OECD countries remain predominantly market-oriented in their rules, while the COMECON countries are almost wholly state-enterprise oriented. The groupings of developing countries have varying mixtures, depending on their perceptions as to the desirability of governmental control and guidance compared to private enterprise; many lean toward state control and still more to a mixed economy. The developing countries are unwilling to accept the principles underlying the OECD rules, especially as they are embodied in the GATT and in the international monetary system. The NIEO that they are demanding is essentially a new set of rules between the North (West) and South. They are not demanding that the OECD members alter their behavior with each other nor that the COMECON does so within its region; nor are they focusing on rules between themselves and COMECON or on rules for South-South industrial integration.

The regional groups are more concerned with closer economic integration *within* regions rather than *among* regions. Even this move has been slowed by the difficulty of achieving an acceptable distribution of the benefits. OECD members even are showing a concern for the distribution of the benefits and the location of industrial activity among themselves. A variety of protectionist moves, bilateral balancing of payments and trade, and the emergence of orderly marketing arrangements evidence a growing concern over location of economic activity or maintenance of particular industry sectors within the OECD countries for strategic, employment, financial, and balance of payments reasons.

The questions of the location of specific industrial activity and the distribution of the benefits have been critical in the formation of COMECON. The Central American Common Market (CACM) and LAFTA have both found it impossible to resolve these issues satisfactorily, preventing further moves toward the agreed-upon goal of integration. The ANDEAN and ASEAN groups also have found the location of specific industrial sectors among the members to be a stumbling block.

It is significant that each of the groups is facing quite similar concerns on the part of their members. If it is difficult to resolve these *within* a group of countries that have decided to integrate more closely, it will be even more difficult to establish clear and certain rules between the various regional groups, for any opening to the outside will require adjustments within and among members of each group. This is not to say that it cannot be done; it is merely to emphasize the difficulty and to reemphasize the probability that no NIEO is likely to be created in the near future. This likelihood is reinforced by the complexity of common problems faced by each of the groups and between them: location of specific industrial sectors; protection of sectors that are under competitive threat from other members or those outside the region; bearing of the costs of adjustment when segments move geographically; maintenance of employment; utilization of specific technologies and generation of new technologies; balancing of international payments; equitable distribution of tax revenues; and means of balancing the benefits among countries of the development in one sector against those in another. The difficulty is exacerbated by the fact that not all of the governments have recognized the shifts in the underlying criteria of acceptability of new arrangements (discussed in the section "Criteria for a Cooperative Solution") and the necessity to seek new arrangements for meeting them.

A key element in the success of any international grouping of states (regional or worldwide) is the existence of a country or countries willing to bear the burdens of making the system work. The United States bore these costs in the post–World War II period, while Britain bore them during the nineteenth century. One of the visible elements in the breakdown of the present order is the absence of any country willing to undertake these burdens; Japan considers its economy too small and precarious; West Germany considers itself too small; and Europe is not sufficiently cohesive to bear them collectively. Even within the European Community, there is no single country that can sustain the burden-bearing role for that region; and Britain has demonstrated the acuteness of the problem in the agonizing negotiations over the distribution of the burden among the national members.

Therefore, to make any of the regional groupings effective and economically successful will require willingness of either a single or a few key countries to bear the costs of adjustment and of assistance to less fortunate members. The absence of such a member in LAFTA was a singular factor in its stagnation, since many of the benefits went to Argentina, Brazil, and Mexico, and these countries were unwilling to redistribute the benefits to the others in an acceptable fashion. Given the fact that there are no countries able or willing to undertake this role for the international economy—or even within the nonsocialist world—it seems inevitable that *if* there is to be any significant move toward regional integration, it will occur around a few major countries who *can* and *will* undertake this role for a defined region.

Such a development would lead the world into spheres of influence along the lines proposed by Britain and Russia at the end of World War II. This approach to structuring the post-war order was rejected by the U.S. Secretary of State Cordell Hull, who persuaded President Roosevelt that there should be one world. This concept was feasible so long as the United States was able and willing to play a key role in leadership and burden-bearing, which it no longer is. The United States can accept a smaller, more equal role within the world economy, or it can accept a larger proportionate role within a region, such as the Western Hemisphere. Europe has a long-standing key role with Africa, which neither the United States nor The Soviet Union has developed, so those two areas could form a complementary union. The Soviet Union, with East Europe and South Asia (Afghanistan, Pakistan and India) form another substantial sphere. Japan could be the burden bearer for the Far East and Southeast Asia, excluding the People's Republic of China, which is able to be a region of its own save for the Middle-East, which has joined with virtually all other groups. One can visualize five spheres of influence, each centering around dominant countries, with the periphery containing countries in the third and fourth worlds. The strength of the key currencies argues for such a division of the world, as does the location of economic sources, market developments, and political wills. The result would be a greater acceleration of trade and investment *within* each of these groupings (North-South) than is likely to occur (East-West) *between* them.

This is not to say that such spheres of influence are necessary or even desirable. Obviously, it is conceivable that this stage could be jumped and we could move directly into a more integrated world economy. But such a leap would require a considerable effort to develop an international community of interests prior to there having been created a regional community of interests. The formation of regional groups is not necessarily a detour in the road to formation of a worldwide community any more than the formation of states or provinces is a detour in the development of a nation-state. It depends on how each is *used;* nationalism itself is a sufficient obstacle if seen as an end in itself, and even it may fracture on provincial disagreements, as evidenced in Belgium and Canada.

In fact, regional associations may be a necessary next step in order to weaken nationalism and to begin to develop wider communities of interest. But there is the danger that nationalism will be substituted by rigid, inward-looking regionalism, making it difficult to take the next steps to international cooperation. However, if the process is understood in the broader sweep of the development and evolution of mankind, it need not be feared or permitted to slow that evolution. On the contrary, the ability to resolve difficult trade-offs within a group of a smaller number of participants with fewer cultural and language barriers and with relatively closer historical ties makes these groupings appear as a logical next step in achieving the criteria of acceptability of any economic order.

The difficulties of even this stage of cooperation are not to be underestimated, but they are still substantially less than establishing a set of rules with a worldwide applicability. This stage would also help to develop the assumption of responsibilities, which we seem to be slow in accepting. The steps in the process of regional integration will also probably have to be made on a functional basis, isolating specific problems that can be addressed communally and regionally, and gradually building up the association, as has occurred in the European community. In the industrial field, this leads to a sectoral approach.

## Sectoral Integration

In the formation of worldwide or regional integration, some industrial sectors will be seen as more critical than others. The extractive sectors (mineral and agricultural) are given a high priority, and governments have injected themselves strongly into the location of production of specific product lines as well as in the processing stages. Similarly, many governments have reserved some of the service sector (e.g., finance, retailing, insurance, accounting, engineering consultants, legal) for nationals, restricting foreign investors; whereas the COMECON countries have reserved most of these sectors for state enterprise. Of course, the problems of various industry sectors do differ, requiring diverse government policies, if the government is to do more than keep its hands off.

Even within the manufacturing sector, there are at least three subsets that are likely to be treated differently under any new set of rules. One might be called the mobile industries, including textiles, numerous chemicals, automotive components, electronics, and so on. These can be produced in many locations and sold on a world market because of standardization of the products. The major influences on location for this group will be factor availability plus receptivity in the host country; although as technology changes it will cause further relocation. A second category might be called market-fixed (some foods, shelter, tourism, services, and a variety of products that are specific to a market because of tastes, high costs of transport, or trade barriers), located near the final customer and unlikely to shift among countries. Market demands and governmental policies toward this group in each of the regions, rather than technology, will be the primary influence on location decisions.

The third set includes those whose location is primarily determined by technology and economies of scale—such as sophisticated electronics, aircraft, heavy machinery, sophisticated chemicals—which require an advanced science community and a large and sophisticated market. Different product groups will be treated differently in each region, for they are considered key industries by many of the advanced countries, and governments will seek to ensure that they have an appropriate share of the production in these sectors. Consequently, the form and extent of integration in this set of industries will be substantially different from that in the other two and will be affected by the policies and decisions of the TNCs involved.

These differences point to the likely formation of sectoral industrial strategies by nations and regions related to different goals in each. The results of such policies at national or regional levels will be to reduce the potential for worldwide specialization and interdependence, although this too *could* be achieved by coordinated cross-regional policies.

But the integration and dis-integration that are emerging among specific industry sectors are occurring under the impact of the uncoordinated forces of government, markets, TNCs, and science and technology. The resulting patterns will show substantial differences among geographic regions.

### Emerging (Uncoordinated) Structure

The pattern of international industrial location that is emerging is without design or clear relation even to national goals, much less to regional objectives or international needs. It is, therefore, not likely to be seen by nations as equitable or as producing generally acceptable results. The question of where economic activity shall take place and the extent of international industrial integration is presently being answered indirectly and nationalistically as expressed in the new protectionism. Although questions are raised about existing economic dependence and self-reliance is urged, little concerted attention is directed to the nature and extent of industrial interdependence and the specific dependencies that would be acceptable. Presently, the developing countries are inveighing against the form and the degree of their dependence on the advanced countries, and the industrialized countries are not willing to give up any significant degree of their independence. Though both talk of a desirable *inter*dependence, neither seems comfortable discussing specific means of restructuring international industry and relocating industrial activity, especially between the North and South.

Despite these reluctant positions, policies are being formulated and actions taken that affect the nature and extent of industrial integration. They involve both a selection of industries to be supported, sponsored, or protected within national economies *and* for each sector, determination of the form of industrial organization, the degree of public and private owner-ship, and the extent to which control can be exercised by foreign companies through direct investment. The emerging patterns can be discerned by an examination of the actors involved and their positions, the underlying criteria of acceptability of any restructuring, and the prospective roles for the TNCs. Each is strongly affected by the priority given to greater eco-nomic interdependence or independence.

### Actors and Factors in International Industrial Location

Under classical criteria, factor (resources) endowments—land, labor, and capital—were the fundamental bases for the determination of the location of economic activity in each country and among nations. Markets were to be left free to respond to supply and demand for products so as to allocate these resources most efficiently.

But the institutional structure and objectives of industrialization have changed. And, given the resource endowments (which themselves can be changed or increased), four actors and factors can be identified as the most significant in determining the location of economic activity around the world: (1) *governments* and their policies; (2) customers, as reflected in *markets* of various size, sophistication, growth, and structure; (3) the *TNCs* and their decisions to invest in specific locations; and (4) the science com-munity, as seen in existing and emerging *technology*. Among these, only governments and TNCs are decision-makers who are conscious of their direct impacts on industrial location and who adopt specific policies toward that end. Both customers (in markets) and scientists (through technologies) act in ways that are nondirected as far as industrial location is concerned. Yet all four sources *directly* influence the location of industrial activity and the distribution of benefits, often in divergent ways, leading in some cases to greater industrial integration and in others to dis-integration.

A number of other actors and factors are indirectly influential, includ-ing national and international labor groups, intergovernmental organiza-tions, and various special interest groups. As regards the location of eco-nomic activity, labor tends to make its desires felt through governments or TNCs, although there is also an indirect effect on the adoption of technol-ogies in various sectors and countries. The intergovernmental organizations apply their influence to national governments, being unable to operate directly on the TNCs. Consumer and other groups often act outside of the market and on governments, or the TNCs, seeking to alter policies on safety, environmental protection, products offered in different markets, et cetera.

**Government Policies.** Governments are not waiting on an intergovernmental agreement to coordinate the location of specific economic activities
and determine the distribution of the gains. Rather, they are acting under
unilateral policies, modified by bilateral and multilateral negotiations. Governments are determining the international industrial structure by a series of
ad hoc measures attempting to alter resource availabilities, demand, and
production capabilities, uncoordinated both among countries and within
them. Absent a coordinated industrial strategy, the pattern of industry
around the world is being pieced together for national purposes with overlapping capacities in key sectors and with each government seeking to
exploit the national markets of others through export drives, as discussed in
part I. If national governments are not providing incentives for foreign
investors, their provincial or state governments are, attempting to pull
capital, managements, and technology from one location into another.

Efforts are being made to harmonize or unify such incentives among
OECD countries, but they cannot be *unified* without removing the incentive
to invest in one place rather than another, for identical incentives would
simply provide a stimulus to investment in general. Even if the incentives
are merely harmonized—that is, differences defined and accepted—top-
level agreement still must be reached on the distribution of industry and the
gains accruing from the expected relocation under the incentives. Such
agreement appears unlikely at present, so nations (and states) will proceed
to compete for industry with incentives. Some observers have charged that
the world could be pushed into a kind of investment war, rather than a trade
war, eventually requiring a GATT for investment, but this form of agreement also appears too complex at present.

Agreement on harmonized incentives or investment policy *in general* is
unlikely because the need for specific investments or aggregate investment is
differentially strong in each country, and the desire for or fear of foreign
investment varies considerably. Further, in each country, constraints (disincentives) are placed on the TNCs to guide their investment to desired
objectives such as local ownership, reduction of unemployment in depressed
areas, acquisition of modern technology, provision of a pole of development around which other industry is multiplied, increased demand for local
raw materials, import substitution, and exports. Each of these objectives
indicates that there is little desire for *inter*dependence among nations;
rather, each is seeking national interests often at the expense of others,
inducing shifts in supply and demand and producing pressures on international balances of payments.

These disincentives offset somewhat the impacts of the incentives in the
sense that companies have to balance off the attraction of the market or
location of the plant in a host country (plus the incentives offered) against

the restrictions on local content, import prohibitions on materials or components (said-to-be) available locally, repatriation of dividends and remittances of royalties, allocation of headquarters expenses, prices, patent rights, R&D activities, and so on.

The decisions of TNCs (and local companies) in response to these myriad and independent governmental policies directly shape the pattern of international industrial integration or dis-integration. The more recent pattern is one of dis-integration—that is, foreign direct investment under governmental aegis has tended to separate national markets (while developing them) and to generate duplication of industrial capabilities around the world, especially among the OECD countries. Trade occurs either at the margin or within TNCs themselves, and industrial activity in key sectors is less specialized among nations. Though the volume of international trade has increased substantially over the past few decades, little can be said a priori about the distribution of gains among nations, although few are satisfied with what they perceive as their part.

The myriad governmental policies (both advanced and developing) aimed at relocating economic activity and redistributing the gains could not possibly produce the results desired by each because of a lack of understanding of the intimate ties among the institutions involved and the opposing objectives sought. This misdirection of effort results partly from the lack of applicability of past theories, which in turn arises partly from academic disciplines that have refused to understand the interactions of thought and action that occur in the world of practice under a set of highly influential institutions, partly from conflicts inherent in bureaucratic decision-making, and partly from an unwillingness to recognize the extent to which we are *all* part of the same planetary system and tied together in inexorable ways.

Governmental policies affect directly the decisions of TNCs as to the location and scope of their activities around the world and, therefore, the pattern of world production and trade. But this takes place under no agreed-upon principle, and the policies affect also the characteristics of the *markets* that would attract or are served by industrial development. Further, these policies affect the development and transfer of *technologies* that might accelerate industrial development. Therefore, the four major actors and factors are dependent on each other; together, they are shaping the pattern of industrial integration, but without agreed-upon objectives.

**Markets.** Reflecting final and intermediate customers, markets affect the location of economic activity through their size, sophistication, structure, growth, and ease of entry. The effects of these characteristics differ at the national, regional, and international levels. If a company is restricted to serving a national market only, it will locate activities differently than if regional opportunities existed or national markets were open to international competition. If the market to be served is open worldwide, a company can potentially locate wherever it can successfully manufacture and readily deliver the product, depending on its own assessment of the resource availabilities and attributes of supply and demand. But governments are reluctant to permit such choice.

In addition to governmental constraints on market access or activities in structuring the market itself, there is a constraint on the location choice in the mere economic size of the country being considered—not its market, but its production possibilities. For example, Singapore is too small to absorb the diesel manufacturing operation proposed for it under the ASEAN agreement, given the present claims on its resources. It has been argued that Britain is too small economically (in population, skills availability, and resources) to sustain an aircraft industry; and it appears that any single country in Europe is too small to be either a supplier or an adequate national market for commercial aircraft. This industry must, therefore, be multinational and integrated across national boundaries; it can be otherwise only at unacceptable costs.

But even if economic and market sizes are sufficient to be attractive, companies will still examine growth rates, the sophistication of the market (that is, whether it matches the products made by the company), and its ease of entry. Some companies prefer to go into a closed national market; others prefer to enter only if that market and others are open enough to form a larger marketing area. But even if the market is regional in scope, it will attract only certain kinds of industrial activities, depending on its demand structure and factor endowments and also on the extent of integration of the stages of production that is feasible across national boundaries. Thus regional integration may be permitted through export of final products but not encouraged through the exchange of components; the resulting specialization among the member countries and distribution of benefits will differ if trade, but not production, is integrated and specialized.

The sophistication of the market determines the degree of technology that will be used, the quality standards that are appropriate, and the product mix. These in turn will attract certain TNCs in relevant industry sectors while repelling others. Similarly, competitive pressures within a national market or a regional grouping (whether from local or foreign supply) will alter the location of industrial activity.

If national or regional markets are open to worldwide competition, demand forces are merged will all others, and the companies can make their location choices based principally on supply factors. But the results will not necessarily be acceptable to national governments. Governments, therefore, make a decision as to the degree of openness (interdependence and specialization) that is acceptable and impose constraints on location within the country even if their borders are open. (For example, governments restrict bidding on governmental contracts or purchases *and* on the location of production to satisfy the contract, even if they let foreign companies bid.)

Although governments are trying to expand markets within their area of interest, they are not necessarily trying to open all industry sections or make them available to service from any location outside or by any company. Not all of them are interested in the highly sophisticated sectors, but many have downgraded the priority of and support for the low-technology sectors. As shown in chapter 2, many governments (particularly those in the OECD) are seeking to expand their activities in the sectors of sophisticated technology and hoping to export, virtually without regard to the activities of each other. These efforts are aimed at altering the location of specific activities in favor of each of the countries, based on an assessment of market opportunities and governmental objectives, without coordination among the several national industrial policies. It is a recipe for future frustration.

**Transnational Corporations.** TNCs determine the location of their operations according the external conditions and a variety of company characteristics and objectives. Each reacts to resource availabilities, to *governmental* constraints, to *market* opportunities, and to *technologies* available according to their own management style, their organizational structure, and their long-run objectives. Their approaches to various locations can be delineated according to what they are seeking abroad. Some are resource seekers, some market seekers, and some efficiency seekers.

If the *resource-seekers* are looking for natural or human resources, they obviously will have to locate exploration and development operations where those resources exist—that is, for minerals (below ground, agricultural, or oceanic) and for low-cost labor that is also sufficiently productive. This location factor swamps all other considerations unless there are ample alternative sites. Thus an extractive company will reject any given opportunity only if the *conditions* of development are exceedingly bad. Since many alternative sources of labor exist, the company can pick and choose, forcing LDC governments to offer relatively favorable conditions. Also, it will relocate into another country if a sufficient differential arises among labor costs. Such mobile companies exist in electronics, chemicals, and textiles, for example. In contrast, the specific location in extraction tends to be fixed, but location tends to be unstable in the search of low-cost labor.

The *market-seekers* have been stopped from exporting to that country for some reason and must locate within the host country to serve it. Once again, the location of economic activity is determined by relative attractiveness of market opportunities, governmental constraints, and environmental conditions. Activities such as banking, insurance, hotels, retailing, and locally oriented manufacture fall into the market-seeking category. (The seeker after a regional market will also generally have to locate within the region; some degrees of freedom usually exist as to specific sites within the region.) Once inside a host country, the market-seeker can make the decision to move the activity to another country only at the cost of giving up all or most of the market that has been developed. The negotiating parameters for this type of company in dealing with the host government are narrower than those surrounding human-resource seekers but wider than those of natural-resource seekers, thus permitting the market-seekers some leeway in determining location of their activities.

*Efficiency-seekers* are looking for the most economic sources of production to serve a worldwide, standardized market. These types of TNCs have tended to develop within the OECD countries, largely to serve the markets of that region. Such companies are highly integrated, both horizontally and vertically, in the sense that affiliates are relatively specialized either in product line or components, serving the markets of other affiliates through an exchange of products or components. The location of activity tends to be determined at headquarters, with a number of decision factors going into the final calculations: market of the host country (to reduce transport costs of final product), technological skills, science community, political stability, labor stability, managerial availabilities, and numerous others. The weights given to each of the factors are not necessarily those that would be assigned by interested governments, which leads to conflicts in negotiations between the two actors.

Among these three types of TNCs, the one most effective in achieving international industrial integration is the efficiency-seeker, followed by the human-resource seeker, and then the natural-resource seeker. Market-seekers tend toward dis-integration of the world economy in the sense that they separate national markets and reduce sectoral specialization in trade and production although they often lead to some specialization in *other* product lines or components. (This is not to condemn this dis-integrating result, but merely to describe it. Some degree of separation is good; whether this type is bad depends on the desired structure of the world economy, the costs and benefits, and the criteria of acceptability.)

The effects of the decisions of TNCs as to the location of their manufacturing activities have not always been acceptable to governments. These decisions alter the structure of production around the world from what it was previously, shifting items in the balance of payments of countries, altering basic comparative advantages, and demonstrating the ability of foreign corporate offices to administer decisions on industrial development. To reassert TNCs interests, some governments have adopted policies to guide the growth of specific sectors. The activities of TNCs have, therefore, stimulated governmental interference in the system in order to redirect TNC investment in ways that governments can accept in terms of location of industrial activity and the distribution of its benefits.

Since not all of the advanced countries (ACs) have TNCs headquartered therein that reflect these three types—and certainly not in similar patterns or similar significance—the attitudes of home governments to locational decisions of TNCs differ considerably. Europe lags behind the United States in formation of efficiency-seekers, and Japan lags behind Europe in both efficiency- and market-seekers. But European and Japanese TNCs are catching up, and even some newly industrializing countries (NICs) have TNCs, while some U.S. TNCs have been drawing back through divestments or at least reducing the level of new investment.

**Technology.** Technology application is, of course, somewhat dependent on TNC decisions, although science and technology are certainly not wholly within the command of TNCs. Nor is the development of technology wholly within governmental responsibility, although governmental policies directly affect it. Since applied industrial technology strongly responds to market pulls, it is tied most tightly to market stimuli, but its adoption (and therefore the determination of the location of types of industrial activity) is altered also by governmental and TNC decisions. The particular uses of technology, therefore, respond to diverse market opportunities, varying governmental incentives or constraints, and multiple TNC orientations.

Technology moves within industrial sectors, across them and among countries partly according to its degree of sophistication and specificity with reference to a given industry sector. Some technologies are too sophisticated to be used except by a few companies in an industry and some are too specific to be used outside of a small industry sector; others are more generalizable. A low-level technology is likely to be transferable among numerous locations and frequently requires only a relatively small national market, whereas a highly sophisticated technology is likely to be located in only a few of the advanced countries and requires an international or large multinational market to support its application. (Of course, in some instances a high technology can be adopted even if the market is exceedingly small—as in medical specialties—and if subsidized, as in military items.)

Technology also moves to where it is appropriate from the standpoint of commercial and economic conditions and objectives. Most companies will transfer technologies directly from one market to another, adapting it to different economic and commercial conditions but only if any activity would be unprofitable without the adaptations. These adaptations frequently have more to do with the scale of production (market size) than with the relative cost of capital and labor. Therefore, appropriate technology is determined frequently according to the nature and size of the market rather than with reference to government desires or to resource or factor endowments in the host country.

But even if a market exists for products of a given technology, the host country simply may not be able to employ it. It may not have the appropriate receptors (management and technically skilled labor), and indigenous support institutions may not exist. Thus the type of industry that can enter is limited by the scientific and technical infrastructure in the host country. Even if the host country can use some technologies, it may be able to absorb only do-how rather than know-how; that is, it cannot make any adaptations of its own since it does not really understand the fundamentals of the technology. This situation affects the relationship of the TNC to the host country and limits the types of ownership and control relations that are acceptable. Imposition of some constraints by a government, without regard to their impact in the technology area, will cause TNCs to avoid locating activities where the government might desire.

The ability to establish industrial activity in a particular sector depends on the availability of the technology that is needed, and this availability will depend on the origin of the technology (whether it is held privately or in the public domain or held by governments). Many governments seem to think that technologies held within the private sector should be made available freely or at low cost, that is, subsidized either by the companies or by advanced-country governments. Such attitudes tend to repel TNCs, causing them to locate operations elsewhere.

In addition, distinctions are being made by governments according to whether they *perceive* the technology needed as a stock or a flow. Most TNCs perceive technology as a flow, whether it is applicable to a high-technology sector or to low-technology sectors or even to the service sectors. Company perceptions as to what governments will do to stocks of technology once they are acquired, or to the products from that stock, will alter TNC willingness to invest or permit use of their technology, thereby affecting location of industrial activity.

The effect of technologies on industrial location is also dependent on the rate of diffusion within the economy and on the dissemination of scientific attitude. Pockets of technology-oriented industry, untied to other sectors in the economy, will not accelerate industrial development as rapidly as if the technology were diffused, opening the way to new industry sectors. Also, a scientific (applied, industrial) attitude is required to stimulate diffusion of technology.

* * *

The interworking of these four factors—governments, TNCs, markets, and technology—does not lead to a determined and stable solution for the question of where industry should be located nor the distribution of benefits. The motives of the actors are diverse, the active forces are multiple, and the probability of disorder is greater than that of achieving a stable and desirable order. Therefore, without some guidelines, these factors will continue to induce industry location under ad hoc determinations, thus making it more difficult later to achieve a more cooperative and mutually acceptable pattern of industrial location and operation.

### Expectations in Key Sectors

The forces analyzed above can be applied to key sectors—for example, automotive, food, pharmaceutical, services, extractive, electronic, aircraft, machine tools, nuclear reactors, textile, and aluminum—to anticipate the pattern of relations emerging, assuming no coordination of national policies to establish regional or international rules.

**Automotive.** Locational decisions in the automotive sector are dominated by considerations of *markets* and efficiency (economies of scale), by *TNC* structure and organization, and by *government* policies, rather than new *technology*. Even government policies are constrained by market factors and the necessity of cost reduction. The necessity of cost reduction in pursuit of worldwide markets has moved the industry toward standardization, so that operations have become increasingly transnational. (Differences, of course, exist among regions—e.g., Taiwan and South Korea have pursued closed national markets in autos—and recently even the U.S. auto companies has received some protection of the U.S. market.) National economies will find it necessary to permit specialization among affiliates of fewer and fewer parent companies as the industry continues to become concentrated.

It is likely that only six or eight of the major companies will survive worldwide over the next decade (though small specialists will remain), providing a virtual worldwide integration of the automotive industry under a concentrated, oligopolistic structure. Governments will not likely intervene to stop this trend, given their interests in low-cost transportation.

Some national aberrations will continue for a while, such as the South Korean auto industry, which has been built on a nationally closed market with effectively subsidized exports. Such new entrants are likely to be absorbed in the long run by the major companies. This can only be prevented by keeping the national (home) market closed off, but it is unlikely that other countries will permit their markets to be penetrated significantly from such a company. Rather, the future is with the cross-national company producing a world car from components made in several and cross-shipped for assembly, including some major facilities owned by companies of two or more nations such as those Peugot and Renault are building and those arising from cooperative purchasing by several European companies.

Given this oligopolistic structure worldwide, governments will seek to make certain that they have a share in the industry through production of some components (as with Chile) or some segment of the product line (as with South Korea), or they may simply try to attract the TNC affiliates to the extent feasible (as with Britain or Taiwan), even to the point of there being no national entry in the automotive sector.

The automotive sector will be as integrated worldwide as any in the proximate future, crossing even lines of regional associations, since the TNCs are established in several countries of the major regions. The policy concern will be over distribution of benefits.

**Food Processing.** Location in the food processing sector (excluding agriculture) is dominated by *market* considerations and *government* policies, not by *technology* or by the policies of *TNCs*. The food companies have organized in a dispersed and decentralized fashion, but this was in response to the dispersion of markets, which are largely local. This sector is characterized by market seekers, with foreign investment placed close to the local market. To this dispersion is added governmental concerns that this sector be under *national* ownership and control, so that foreign-owned affiliates will be gradually pulled out from the control of the TNCs.

The only way that the food companies can retard or prevent this gradual dismemberment is by improving on export performance (which is exceedingly difficult) or demonstrating that R&D contributions to the food processing sector result in new technologies necessary to maintain low cost to meet mass needs, including the most nutritional foods. LDCs governments will interfere increasingly in the makeup of the food industry, creating a dis-integrated structure. For this reason, there will be fewer cross-company distribution agreements and greater efforts by each major company to market its own products worldwide, as some West German companies are doing in the United States.

Policies toward the food industry will be different according to the regional area under consideration. The OECD will remain relatively open although predominantly national-market oriented. Very little threat will arise from these countries to the present organizational structure of the industry or company ownership. However, if North-South spheres of influence were formed, greater integration in the sector would be likely, reducing the trend to dis-integration. Distribution of benefits is seen as resolved by intervention toward national control and market orientation.

**Pharmaceuticals.** Location of activities in pharmaceuticals is dominated by *markets, governmental policies,* and *technology.* No single *TNC* policy or approach is dominant; there are different company orientations in response to these three factors. Therefore TNC structure is not determinative but is, rather, responsive. LDC governments are pushing toward a national-market orientation of the companies, forcing a dis-aggregation and dis-integration of company activities by focusing on generic drug production at low cost for the local market. Markets themselves tend to be locally oriented, despite the fact that numerous diseases are prevalent among a large number of countries. Drug production does not require economies of scale reachable only through serving worldwide markets. But there are economies of scale in producing active ingredients (exported around the world), and the complexity of developing drugs (long-term R&D and high development costs) does require returns from worldwide sales to support the process. Research is also oriented toward market needs of several countries, rather than only one, especially if it is small in population or purchasing power.

Therefore, the pressure of governments to dis-integrate the industry is opposed somewhat by the necessity of worldwide integration to sustain substantial R&D expenditures. The conflict is not simply between company and government objectives but also between the necessities of technological advance and governmental desires for national-market products at low cost.

A resolution will require the splitting of product lines, market differentiation, and governmental support of R&D efforts. This will require a much closer cooperation between governments and companies than has existed in the past and a greater understanding of company limitations by organizations such as the World Health Organization and by national ministries of health.

The institutional arrangements that will evolve in this sector will differ substantially from those in other industrial sectors.

**Services.** The service sector includes some fifteen subsets, including banking, retailing, insurance, engineering consultation, entertainment, health care, shipping, hotels and tourism, and others. Location of services is denominated by *markets* and *governmental policies* rather than by *technology* or *TCN* orientations. The technology for services is seen by LDC governments largely as a stock: Once purchased, it is seen as sufficient to maintain the needed services. This view supports governmental policies aimed at localization and dispersion of ownership of the service sector. Foreign-owned affiliates will be increasingly pulled away from TNCs, who will have little bargaining power in retaining their ownership and control. Therefore, economic dis-integration is predictable.

Once again, there is a significant difference between the policies of LDCs and those of OECD countries, in that the latter are likely to remain fairly open. But even close regional cooperation is not likely to overcome the force of governmental desires for nationally controlled activities among the subsets of this sector. Constant conflict can be expected in a continuous tug over distribution of benefits.

**Extractive.** Location of extractive operations (petroleum, mineral, and agriculture) is dominated by the geographic location of the natural *resources,* economics of distribution (the *market*), and *governmental policies.* Although technology is significant, it is available from a variety of sources, and TNC orientations are not strong enough to stand against governmental control over resources. LDC governments, especially, but even some of the advanced countries, will continue to press for national sovereignty over all extractive sectors, demanding downstream processing of energy, minerals, metals, and foods. These demands will force a restructuring and relocation of the industry toward a new mode of integration, as compared to the recent past. The new mode would be significantly affected by any moves to regional cooperation.

The TNCs have little bargaining power in this situation, although their control of significant technology or market outlets provides some temporary negotiating strength. Closer cooperation between companies and governments will continue to emphasize consortia-type arrangements in which governments combine with various energy-producing companies (with a variety of market outlets and capital resources) to undertake vast projects largely oriented to national markets for energy and metals but increasingly seeking access to markets abroad. The distribution of benefits will move toward the producing countries as long as energy scarcity exists. The probability of repeated swings in demand and supply argues for institutionalizing a means of achieving equity.

**Computers.** Location of operations in mainframe computers is dominated by *technology* and *markets,* with *governments* taking a position behind the *TNCs.* National markets are insufficient to support the highly sophisticated computer industry, forcing companies to organize to meet regional and worldwide markets. Since the technology is sophisticated and proprietary, governments cannot command it, and they have not been able to penetrate the field effectively at the sophisticated end. In order to achieve low costs in the face of pervasive competition, production has to be on a large scale, again requiring world markets. Therefore, this sector will be highly integrated and centralized among a relatively small number of companies tied into a large number of suppliers and peripheral manufacturers, thus accentuating present trends. The sector will be integrated backwards and forwards (by contractual or ownership ties), welding variety of foreign sources of components and product models. Part of the industry, therefore, can be decentralized but still integrated, since pieces of the technology package can be separated for application at different locations.

To satisfy the desires of governments for equitable participation in this sector, the TNCs can be persuaded to locate various parts of production in numerous countries and to maintain an equitable level of exchange of components and final products, producing a type of TNC-controlled integration.

**Aircraft.** Location in the aircraft sector is also dominated by *technology* and *markets,* although *governmental policies* can alter significantly the organization of the companies and the way in which they meet the needs of production and distribution if the governments are willing to bear the costs (which they have not generally been willing to do save in military aircraft, and not all countries even are willing in that sector). Few countries have a sufficient national market to sustain the large production runs required in the aircraft industry, so that regional and worldwide markets are required. This reduces government influence, but governments are frequently major purchasers of commercial (as well as military) aircraft, so that they are able to demand a repartition of production in favor of local manufacturers of components.

Since the technology is quite expensive and sophisticated, it is again not possible for governments to develop the technology themselves so that they are unable to command localization of the industry. Regional groupings would permit greater local dispersion without substantial added costs.

Like large computers, the aircraft sector will be highly integrated and centralized, although there will be a sharing out of production geographically and a frequent combination of companies into consortia in order to share production and markets to the satisfaction of interested governments. The location of production in this sector is determined principally by market factors. National markets were dominant in the first instance, and government purchases have altered supplier locations. Therefore, location and the distribution of benefits will result from continuing negotiations among companies and governments as purchasers.

**Nuclear Reactors for Utilities.** Location of production of reactors is affected directly by each of the four actors and factors, making for a highly complex and difficult set of negotiations. This sector is strongly influenced by *market* factors simply because there are very few customers and they are frequently governments. Its location is determined also by *technologies* because it is highly sophisticated and costly and must be centralized in a few locations, thereby providing economies of scale. It is dominated by *governments* because of their interest as customers and because they use nuclear technology in other ways. Finally, the *TNCs* are important in location decisions because only a few of them have been able to develop effective technologies and penetrate the markets.

In the complex negotiations that have resulted, governments have been able to force local production of some elements (spin-off, or cost offset, or repartition), thereby acquiring some of the technical know-how as well. However, they are not able to acquire all technology, and the disagreements over the types of technologies that are appropriate remain critical, opening the way for continuing dialogues between governments and companies. The TNCs retain a strong bargaining position based on technology alone and also on the fact that only a few companies have entered the field.

This sector is likely to remain highly concentrated and integrated across national boundaries, largely forced by local production requirements of governments as customers. As the technological developments become more and more expensive, it is likely that consortia will be formed (including private and governmental interests) if the industry survives high costs and environmental objections.

**Textiles and Clothing.** Locational decisions in the textiles, cloth, and clothing sectors are dominated by *market* factors and by a cost structure that permits easy entry. *Governments* also retain a strong interest because of the high employment impact of the industry and its servicing basic needs, increasing their desire for local operations.

In the absence of sophisticated or proprietary *technology,* and with a proliferation of the number of companies involved, the *TNCs* have very little bargaining power in structuring the industry or setting the rules of operation. They will seek to add political power to competitive power. Since each national industry can play this game with its own government, the bargaining is elevated to that among governments, leading to intergovernmental agreements that attempt to balance a variety of interests. As a result of this bargaining, textiles tends to be predominantly local-market oriented and therefore dis-integrating in terms of the world economy. This is appropriate, given the diverse clothing needs, the lower cost of providing them from local sources, and the absence of economies of scale requiring worldwide markets. Despite the apparent large volume of world trade in fibers, mill products, and apparel, these exchanges remain a small percentage of consumption (and production) in virtually all countries.

Since this sector is among the mobile industries, it faces continuing adjustments and relocations, with pressure on governments to ease the burdens and to slow down the process of redeployment. Given the number of companies involved—seen in the lack of concentration in the industry—it is difficult for the TNCs to be a mechanism for sharing the burden for distributing the benefits among claimants. The TNCs in this sector are less likely to be able to help resolve the problems than they would be in other sectors such as automobiles. The difference lies, of course, in the number of companies and the extent of each company's penetration in numerous markets around the world.

**Aluminum Smelting and Processing.** Locational factors in aluminum smelting and processing are principally *technology* (the existence of cheap energy) and *markets*. It is less costly to transport bauxite to energy sources than vice versa and less costly to transport smelted aluminum to the fabricator (close to the market) than to transport the finished products long distances. *TNCs* will therefore locate operations so as to integrate them worldwide, shortening transport distances of finished goods where feasible.

*Governments* of bauxite producing countries will, however, move into smelting; and developing countries with surplus energy (petroleum or flared gas) will import bauxite to use their low-cost power sources. Such energy-surplus countries can smelt aluminum, obtaining by-products for use in desalination projects, thereby having three joint products: use of an otherwise-wasted resource, aluminum, and desalination materials. This joint result could permit dumping of aluminum on the world markets. TNCs would then be undercut by government policies, altering the location of industrial activity in this sector. The distribution of benefits in this sector will be determined in each (ad hoc) case between governments and TNCs; few agreed-upon rules are likely to emerge.

## Sectoral Conclusions

These brief analyses of specific sectors indicate that the solutions that are likely to arise in an effort to create regional (or worldwide) industrial integration will differ among the various sectors. Different patterns will be developed, with greater or less participation by the TNCs according to their orientations and the sophistication of the technology involved. Where the markets are extensive and attractive, the technology is proprietary and sophisticated, and the TNCs are relatively few, governmental policy will be less determinative. Where there are large numbers of companies involved in the sector and the markets are largely localized, the governments are dominant and will set the terms of reference locally. The result is likely to lead to dis-integration for the sector, for the objective is likely to be to slow down adjustments. In a setting of a regional community of interests such adjustments can be more easily accepted.

We come, therefore, to the conclusion that higher technologies, lower governmental power, and greater market concentration in an industry sector are likely to lead to greater international industrial integration. This integration is characterized both by a dispersion of the location of production and an increase in the volume of trade of specialized products or components, but not necessarily of the form or location desired by national governments. Regional integration can open up greater opportunities for TNCs and also for governments to achieve their goals with use of TNCs, as we shall see in subsequent chapters.

Conversely, where there is widespread competition and ease of entry, the increasing concerns of governments to control their national economies so as to meet their numerous responsibilities will encourage a dis-integration of the industry with a wide dispersion of production, less integrated through trade of products or components.

Consequently, without coordinated policies, greater industrial integration will arise in some regions than in others (the OECD as compared to ASEAN or ANDEAN), and greater integration will occur in some sectors than in others (automotives as compared to food). The degree to which this integration is desirable and feasible will be a subject of ad hoc negotitations among governments and, frequently, between governments and TNCs. But their success will be greatly hindered by the formation of *nationally* oriented industrial policies, which become an obstacle to international accommodations, for no government likes to give up activities in an industry sector it has so diligently built up. Such negotiations will likely lead to diverse rules of behavior, depending on negotiation skills in pursuing agreed-upon or conflicting objectives among several parties in different projects, thus making efforts at generalized rules irrelevant.

## Business–Government Cooperation

If this uncoordinated structure of industrialization is unacceptable to governments, they must begin to design a different future. But design of coordinated industrial strategies must begin with extensive dialogues between corporations and governments, not only on specific projects in which they are interested but also on the role of private companies and foreign investors in specific sectors, on the private sector's contribution to economic development, and on the relationship of science and technology to economic objectives in the host countries. An extension of technical dialogues will be needed on the trade-offs that will occur in meeting the objectives of both business and government. Dialogues are required on negotiating methods and procedures and on the potential effects of alternative policies. In order for companies to be well-received in initiating or engaging in such dialogues, they must first demonstrate their good faith by disclosing adequate information about their operations. They need to explain their policy orientations, objectives, and specific practices, detailing their contributions to host and home governments and the limitations on their response to governmental requests.

Pressure for information disclosure by companies is rising, and despite the fact that many governments have extensive control over the companies and require substantial reporting, what is wanted more than host-country information is an understanding of how the companies operate in *other* countries, so that each government feels that it is being treated equitably. With a background of an open dialogue (and an absence of illicit payments or corrupt practices), the companies would be more successful in explaining why many of the policies adopted by governments will not achieve the goals desired by governments themselves. They should be able to work out more readily the accommodations with governments as partners or with local participants so as to pursue the goals of economic integration, in those cases in which these are acceptable to host governments as well.

Formation and implementation of sectoral industrial strategies run into a second obstacle in those countries (particularly the Anglo-Saxon nations) that have developed under an adversarial relationship between business and government. Others have developed more cooperatively, and coordination is reflected in the attitudes and orientations of both parties. Such cooperation has the taint of economic planning in Anglo-Saxon countries. There it is seen as stifling dynamism and flexibility, leading to high-cost industry operations, although this is not the case in Japan and West Germany, and the French cost structure has other explanations.

The international mineral and petroleum companies should be able to explain more adequately than they have in the past what the costs are of moving rapidly toward a redeployment of refining activities into developing countries so as to aportion the costs of adjustment equitably. A variety of institutional arrangements are viable in these activities, ranging from host-government ownership and control with foreign contracting to foreign ownership and control with governmental surveillance. The precise arrangement within this range depends on the capital availabilities, the origins of technology, market experience and ties, transportation costs and facilities, distribution systems, size of the host country market for the relevant refined commodities, and so on. A variety of institutional arrangements would be suitable, and none is more or less integrative than another, since the existence of the *market* (world or regional) is the dominant factor affecting the structure of the industry, making it likely to be served in an integrated fashion, regardless of the institutional and contractual ties among TNCs and governments. However, TNC and government interests in the location of specific activities lead to coordination and cooperation in decisions.

One of the major questions in seeking accommodations for industrial restructuring is: Who will take appropriate initiatives? governments? or TNCs? Without a different concept of the world economy, TNCs are unlikely to take an initiative. Rather, TNCs will probably refuse even to disclose their operations and policies to begin dialogues at the technical level with government officials of national and regional bodies. To be most informative, these dialogues would need to be at the sectoral level with those in the national and regional agencies who are responsible for policies and their implementation. But if TNCs consider that LDCs need them more than they need LDCs, or if they consider that market criteria should be applied and that these criteria *will* be applied in time, they will sit back and wait.

The consequence is likely to be an increase in dis-integration of the world economy through national governments turning inward or forming tight regional associations, excluding the efficiency-seeker type of TNC in favor of the market-seeker. The eventual result will be the gradual takeover of affiliates of these companies through localization of ownership or even nationalization, leaving the international companies with fewer and fewer assets abroad. Unless halted by regional cooperation, these moves would result in a curtailment of investment in developing countries by TNCs, actual disinvestment of existing facilities, reduction of technology transfers and even trade ties, with an increased emphasis on activities within the OECD region.

In this scenario, TNCs would adopt more tentative attitudes toward LDCs, requiring greater certainty in any arrangements made with them, including the ability to escape with minimum loss and a higher front-end return. Higher thresholds would be required for investment projects, all of which would increase the distrust by host countries, who would then see themselves increasingly exploited, thereby providing the charges that have been made by socialist critics.

An alternative scenario would begin with two initiatives: one by the companies, as suggested above, and the other by host governments to determine whether or not they want international or regional economic integration, and if so, to what extent and in what sectors. Once the dialogues are opened up and the basic economic–social objectives of host countries determined, positive moves could be made to develop the appropriate organizational and institutional structure to provide the criteria of acceptability (discussed below), laying out all of the necessary trade-offs and deciding among them in an open and positive manner.

This more positive approach should appeal to many of the TNCs simply because some LDC markets and economies are proving relatively more profitable than some of the advanced-country markets, as the latter have failed to meet their growth objectives as a consequence of increasing costs for welfare, energy, and social–environmental protection. In both regions, however, there are increasing governmental constraints on business, and this requires a greater willingness to negotiate than previously. This willingness is being tested in many countries, and a number of companies are beginning to pull back—either out of managerial timidity, an unwillingness to see the rules changed, managerial inability to handle complex socio-political pressures, or simply a lack of desire to undertake difficult tasks when more palatable opportunities exist elsewhere.

The necessary (continued and repeated) negotiations with governments imply that specific problems will frequently be given quite distinct and different answers in various countries or regions. The Bretton Woods principle of nondiscrimination in trade and payments will be jettisoned both geographically and sectorally. That is, different regions and countries will be treated differently; and different sectors will be treated differently, simply because their impacts are disparate and the relationships among the various governments are dissimilar. The idea that only equal treatment is equitable has now been rejected, and equity is being sought over equality. This forces a discussion (negotiation) of what degrees of inequality will produce equity—that is, achieve an *acceptable* solution. This approach is not readily received by advanced country governments or TNCs. On the contrary, they will have to be forced virtually by circumstances to enter the game.

A more cooperative scenario could be achieved if TNCs and governments decided to give up their adversarial postures and to seek mutually advantageous solutions to the problems of the scarcities of raw materials and their processing and distribution, the location of energy-related industry, the expansion of agricultural production (requiring consortia of agricultural equipment manufacturers, pesticide and fertilizer manufacturers, and research on new plants and seeds, as well as new processing and distribution procedures), and the investment to meet the basic human needs of shelter, clothing, education, and employment. To move toward a cooperative restructuring of activity does not mean the elimination of competition, but it will alter the entrants and give rise to some handicapping so that the same players do not win all the time.

In many countries, a fairly close relationship exists among governments and financial institutions and the production and trading elements of industry (e.g., Japan and several European countries). To approximate such a relationship in the United States would require a substantial shift from the historical adversary posture between business and government that has continued to prevent a mutual focusing on the prospects for international industrial integration. U.S. government officials have been concerned with aggregate policies and are pushed only reluctantly to examining specific industry difficulties. Business managers, on the other hand, face specific problems that do not accord necessarily with the policies enunciated by the government. Therefore, policy resolution falls between the stools. In some cases, the nature of the problem is not adequately recognized or defined.

One reason we fail to recognize that acceptable solutions exist is that we tend to address problems for which we have appropriate tools—even if these are not the most significant problems. The chapters in this text seek to demonstrate that appropriate tools do exist for meeting the criteria for an acceptable restructuring of industrial integration, but that attitudes and orientations of both governments and TNCs will have to be changed.

The fundamental thesis of this text is that the TNCs themselves offer a structure for helping to resolve some of the problems of the composition of production and the collateral distribution of benefits around the world through the location of industry activity. However, it is questionable whether the companies will be or should be permitted to make the decisions as to location of their activities under criteria that are related *solely* to their profit or to free-market criteria, as evidenced by the continued intervention by governments through multiple incentives, subsidies, restrictions, cartels, guidelines, and negotiations concerning determination of foreign ownership. However, throughout the nonsocialist world, decisions as to industrial investment are made primarily by private enterprises, and therefore they will continue to play a significant role in the determination of the location of economic activities and the distribution of the benefits of industrial development.

TNCs have much more to gain than to lose by engaging in open negotiations on the issues and by exposing their activities to the public gaze for an objective analysis. The fear of an attack from biased sources is overdrawn, since these attacks have already arisen and will continue in any case. Positive contributions by the large majority of companies far outweigh the exploitive or illicit acts of a few, and these latter can be brought into line by a clearer picture of the socially acceptable and desirable activities expected of TNCs. If this candid discussion of objectives and procedures is followed by a willingness to examine new alternatives, TNCs will find a new reception in dialogues with governments.

In their turn, governments must be willing to seek to understand the roles which can be expected of TNCs and to learn how to use them in the pursuit of mutual objectives without destroying their flexible qualities and contributions of innovation, efficiency, and responsiveness to market demands. They can learn this only through continuing dialogue at the technical level in a variety of fora. What the new mechanisms and institutions might be awaits a close examination of ends and means in numerous specific cases. And new mechanisms for continuing dialogues between business (industry sectors) and governments will need to be constructed within the United States, within the OECD and other regional groups, and among them. Such institutional changes are not easy, but the issues require participation of several actors who have not yet been in effective communication.

**Criteria for a Cooperative Solution**

Before embarking on a program to restructure industry regionally or internationally, it is necessary to determine the criteria by which any agreement would be judged acceptable. That is, an ordering principle is needed. The principle of the Bretton Woods Agreements was multilateral, nondiscriminatory trade and payments as a means of achieving worldwide efficiency. But the criteria of acceptability have become more numerous and complex. These include at least six desiderata, some of which have been explicitly stated in UNCTAD proposals and others that can be delineated from the policy positions of governments. These criteria are sometimes mutually supporting and sometimes contradictory, and they do not have the same priority ranking by each government.

The criteria include concepts of efficiency, equity, participation, creativity, stability, and autonomy. *Efficiency* in some policy objectives means market efficiency (nondistortion of market decisions), but in others it means the most effective use of resources to achieve progress toward social and economic goals (market efficiency vs. allocative efficiency). Under classical concepts, allocative efficiency was to be sought for the entire world community; it would be achieved through permitting the market to determine the location of economic activity, acting under the law of comparative advantage. Given an acceptable worldwide community of interest, there is little doubt that the first-best solution under market efficiency criteria results from market determination of the use of resources and the location of economic activity. But there is no worldwide decision-making unit to establish such a procedure, and if there were, it would (like all political bodies) have to alter the efficiency results of market decisions by a host of adjustments, modifying the distribution of benefits from the market or the status of the entrants into the market. Efficiency, therefore, is an inadequate criterion by itself. Even the concept of the market must be carefully construed, constructed, and constrained if it is to be left free of specific governmental interference for efficiency's sake; otherwise, its results will not be deemed acceptable or equitable.

Classical precepts provided no resolution for the problem of *equity*— that is, the distribution of benefits. It was always stated that the efficiency solution permitted everyone to be better off; but it was also possible for one country to redistribute the gains in its favor if it were strong enough. The developing countries are now insisting on a redistribution of income and of wealth and even reparations for past inequities. Whether or not they will be able to achieve this depends on the receptiveness of the advanced countries to such redistribution, as well as on the negotiating position and persuasiveness of the developing countries. Equity, however, remains a significant criterion, as is shown by the concerns among the advanced countries in their dealings with each other and with developing countries in discussions in escape clauses and orderly marketing agreements. What constitutes equity is not easily determined and certainly not apart from the elements of each case; parties must negotiate what is acceptable (even at times negotiating the rules for negotiation). This is exceedingly difficult when the rules are to apply to *all* cases everywhere; some narrowing of scope is necessary for success.

The criterion of *participation* means that all countries concerned should be involved in the setting of rules as well as the determination of their application and in the negotiation of activities concerning their national interests. In the industrial sector, this criterion is illustrated by the Lima Declaration which asserts LDC claims for a 25 percent share in world industrial production by the end of the century, up from less than 10 percent prior to 1980. This would require a growth in LDC industrial production at a rate nearly three times that in the OECD countries. In the absence of such participation, they do not consider that the rules should apply to them. This is why the UNCTAD has sought to make the emerging codes on TNCs mandatory, thereby creating new international *law,* which they helped write. This activity is deemed important even if LDCs do not abide by the new rules. It is not merely a matter of self-respect but of the exercise of power, which they feel is (or should be) theirs.

The fourth criterion, *creativity,* has been applied by the Western world as the mark of the advancement of mankind. Humanity is brought closer to perfection through creativity. Therefore, creativity is a means of providing personal and national pride; and the activity in the industrial field that demonstrates creativity is scientific research and technological development, as illustrated by recent emphasis on invention and innovation within both advanced and developing countries.

These four criteria are closely linked but have not been seen as fundamental criteria of acceptability of the international economic system by the advanced countries. Rather, the U.S. government continues to urge the maximization of production for the world (efficiency) as *the* criterion of progress. OECD countries have, humanistically, been willing to share the returns of progress through aid. However, the developing countries are continuing to insist on trade, not aid or trade with aid, so as to participate directly in production and to have a voice in what is produced. The advanced countries have responded by reducing aid and not opening up the trade channels as fast as the developing countries wish. Therefore, developing countries wish a greater participation in the institutions of the international economic order through which rules are formed and implemented.

In the simile of the production pie, LDCs are saying that while they would like to see a larger worldwide pie, they are also interested in a larger piece for themselves—relatively, as well as absolutely. Further, they are not willing to accept a larger piece at the hands of the advanced countries; that is, they wish to participate as their share is cut. In addition, they are not at all certain that they wish to have the kind of pie that is cooked by the advanced countries; they would like one baked from their own fruits by their own recipes and techniques, to suit their own tastes and exercising their own creativity.

The fifth criterion of acceptability of new arrangements is *stability*—that is, greater certainty and order. Both governments and private institutions are increasingly adopting planning systems that require greater certainty in order to be successful, and many governments are considering national industrial policies to provide greater stability and certainty in income and employment. Such an order will undoubtedly lead to a loss of some flexibility and innovation, increasing the rigidity that results from bureaucracies. Certainty is sought even at the cost of some freedom. But it is important to ascertain the costs in the trade-off and minimize the loss of flexibility because rigidity stifles creativity.

Finally, every nation still seeks a degree of *autonomy* that will permit cultural diversity and political and economic self-reliance. The frequently cited increase of *inter*dependence has not been fully accepted, even though over several millenia it has been identified as existing or needed at various levels, from the philosophic to the mundane, and throughout many facets of the world economy and polity.

The existence of these six criteria of acceptability will make any negotiation on industrial restructuring rather complex. The criteria are complex in application; they conflict among themselves; they will be interpreted differently by various countries; there is no mechanism or institution where trade-offs can be resolved at present; and, probably the greatest obstacle of all, the six criteria stem from different academic disciplines, thereby preventing the formation of a theory of acceptability without first integrating long-separated bodies of thought. Thus, efficiency is based on economic theory; equity on social theory and jurisprudence; participation on political theory; creativity of psychology (intuition), science, and even theology; stability (equilibrium and certainty) on concepts from physics, economics, sociology, and political science; and autonomy of social philosophies, military theory, and wishful thinking ingrained by the siege mentality developed over centuries of strife. It is, therefore, impossible to turn to any one body of theory to provide guidance in finding a single ordering principle. The academic world is incapable of resolving the difficulties because of its narrow specialization and its lack of stimulation to those who might have operated at the interfaces of the disciplines and who could have provided an integration of ideas and values in a holistic fashion, which now seems prerequisite to worldwide (or even regional) economic integration.

Without a theoretical basis, and with multiple criteria requiring delicate trade-offs in multiple areas, it is likely that the order we seek will exist only in our minds and then only if we can mentally encompass a myriad of different modes, mechanisms, and arenas with varying degrees of dis-integration and integration among industrial sectors. Consequently, if greater industrial integration is to be achieved in the restructuring process, it is likely to arise, not globally, but regionally and sectorally, with different rules for activities undertaken in each region and different rules for the specific sectors being integrated under various communities of interest. But, we *can* achieve such an integrated restructuring, meeting many of the criteria of acceptability, if we are willing to seek new institutional arrangements, which are so urgently called for and so avidly avoided.

# 5 Potential Roles of TNCs

The roles that particular TNCs can or are likely to play in the process of international restructuring will differ according to their orientations. Some industrial sectors include several types of TNCs, whereas others contain predominantly one type, thereby limiting the options of policy makers. Concerns of governments differ over the three types, and the bargaining power of the TNCs with governments varies both according to the type and their duration in the host country. Therefore the extents to which they can satisfy the criteria of equity also differ.

## Types of TNCs

There are many ways in which one might characterize foreign direct investors: according to the sectors in which they operate, the degree of ownership or control by the foreigner, corporate organization, marketing areas, ability to appropriate returns to the enterprise, decision channels, size of assets, sales volumes, and so on. For the purpose of assessing moves toward or away from integration, activities of the companies may be distinguished according to the nature and closeness of the ties of affiliates to the parent company or other affiliates in terms of movement of goods, funds, and technology. Many other aspects of the operations of affiliates result from these particular ties to the parent. The three different types of international companies noted in chapter 4—resource-seekers, market-seekers, and efficiency-seekers—are really concepts as to how activities of TNCs are structured, for any given TNC may have all three orientations among its various affiliates, giving rise to different impacts in host countries.

### Resource-Seekers

The companies that are seeking natural or human resources are similar in their integrative effects to foreign investment in the later eighteenth or nineteenth centuries or the early twentieth century. Much of this investment had an enclave effect, not reaching very far into the host economy, and thereby

101

tying only a segment of the recipient economy to the investing country or to world markets. It is for this reason that many resource-producing countries have asserted national sovereignty over their resources and have sought downstream processing facilities. To the extent that this shift expands integration by economically involving more factors in the host country and lowering long-run costs, the result is efficient for the world economy—however disruptive in the short run. But it is virtually impossible to assess long-run costs, especially when producing countries are trying to alter the gains in their favor. All we can conclude is that the situation in natural resources lends itself to restructuring and that the present structure is sufficiently unstable to require new initiatives.

The same results can be seen today when a company relies on foreign sourcing by establishing an affiliate to produce components (or undertakes an assembly function) in Hong Kong, Malaysia, or South Korea; materials or components are received and worked up or assembled for shipment back to the home country. The effects of such integration are felt directly in the marginal shifts in the returns to capital and labor in the host and home countries, which will affect the comparative advantages of the two countries in other commodities to some degree. But since such sectoral integration is marginal in its costs and benefits to the investors, they will shift locations if the labor costs rise unfavorably. The resulting integration, therefore, is not as significant as one in which several factors underlie the integration and thereby provide means of making adjustments to economic changes without destroying the pattern of integration. The management of such a foreign branch plant is integrated with parent-company management—only at a low level—since it does not raise serious policy issues (except at the time of entry or exit).

Such branch-plant operations as the border plants in Mexico are advantageous to the local communities, and they provide the American companies with lower-cost inputs and components. However, there is little autonomy for the Mexican affiliate because it is very closely tied to the operation of the parent or other affiliates that it supplies. Its present and future are determined by decisions outside of the host country.

Consequently, although such investments restructure the location of industrial activity and add employment in local communities, their impact is seen in construction costs, employment, and the balance of payments for value added. However necessary this shift of sourcing may be for competitive reasons, the benefits to the host and home country are marginal and potentially temporary, depending on the technologies in the particular process and continuing wage differentials. Given the costs and benefits, these activities are not likely to be the subject of significant intergovernmental debate, although affected workers in the home country sometimes complain. Host governments like the contribution to wages and employment, and the size of such operations is not economically or politically distributing.

## Market-Seekers

Those companies investing abroad to serve the host-country market from production *within* that economy have a minimal integrating impact. At the extreme, no direct ties may exist between the host- and home-country markets; local operations can be supported by a flow of capital, management, and technology but without a corresponding return of goods. The production abroad is frequently import-substituting, thereby reducing international specialization. However, some new trade is generated through imports by the affiliate of capital goods and components or materials. Other new trade will undoubtedly arise in other sectors also as a result of economic growth, changing both imports and exports and forming a new integrative pattern, but the link with TNC activities will not be clear. Also, it will be difficult to know the distribution of benefits resulting from the new trade.

The *entry* of this form of TNC is dis-integrating, in the first phase, substituting as it usually does for imports. It remains dis-integrating if local production can survive only with protection or if it can export only with subsidies. But it forms a *new* pattern of integration if all that was needed was an initial push in order to become competitive, internationally, based on underlying (but undeveloped) comparative advantages in the host country. It then leads to a new structure of allocative efficiency, even if it does not export. The generation of new economic activity and shift in economic structure alters comparative advantages and would eventually raise the level of integration by increasing the overall volume of trade and other integrating investment flows—if government policy permitted.

If market-seeking investment is merely import-substituting, adds little to world production, and is not export-generating, the result will be to reduce the level of international integration, thus duplicating operations that exist in several countries. This result is costly in terms of efficiency criteria even if it satisfies that of participation. But its total (net) impacts cannot be known without tracing the indirect effects, and these will depend on other governmental policies and local investor responses, which cannot be attributed directly to the foreign investment.

This type of activity is illustrated by the automobile companies in many NICs (such as Brazil, Mexico, and Argentina) especially during the 1960s and 1970s. Since these foreign operations were separate (not necessarily different) from the activities of the parent or of other affiliates, the parent responsibility was usually not at the top levels of management but was generally given to a separate international division or company responsible for all foreign affiliates. The product line of the affiliate was *similar* to but different from that of the parent. Adaptations were made for the host-country market that made it unlikely to sell easily outside of the host country. The varied regulations that prevented imports into the country from the parent company or that required high local-content also raised costs, thereby reducing export opportunities. The local market was the principal (if not only) market that the affiliate could serve. (This picture is, of course, now slowly changing for the auto industry through NIC governments subsidizing exports.)

Where national markets are distinct, difficult to trade across, or highly protected, this TNC form has been found most suitable. Its concentration on the national market of the host country means that the affiliates are not significantly integrated with the rest of the company's operations. The growth of each affiliate is restricted to the growth of the national market. The level of technology applicable is also restricted by the product line that is appropriate for the host country, which in turn is partly determined by the size and sophistication of the market.

From the standpoint of international economic integration (allocative efficiency), therefore, it is difficult to balance the impacts of this type of investment. Restructuring by such shifts in location of activity will be judged by criteria of economic *in*dependence, stimulus to indigenous science and technology, the relative contribution to economic growth (employment and balance of payments), the accompanying effects on social welfare, and perceived equity in the distribution of benefits. Similarly, stimulation of such investment by the U.S. government through promotional tactics, cannot be based on a vision of greater integration of the world economy but merely on the contribution of the investment to U.S. economic (and political) goals within the host country.

*Efficiency-Seekers*

Foreign investment to create the most efficient network of worldwide production to serve multiple (standardized) markets has a much greater integrating impact—not only on trade but also on capital markets, consumer habits, and even management styles. These TNCs have been the *new* restructuring institution, generating new patterns of ownership, control, concentration, and economic power. Their ability to transfer funds, goods, and technology, and to shift production locations if necessary, ties the economies in which they operate in ways that influence not only trade and the balance of payments but also the level and location of investment and employment. These effects are close to the core of international economic policy and governmental responsibility.

The efficiency-seekers are new on the world scene (coming to the fore in the past twenty years) and are most appropriately called multinational enterprises (ME). Oriented toward serving a world market from least-cost sources anywhere in the world, the affiliates are integrated to some extent not only with the parent but also with each other. They specialize in the production of components or distinct product lines, trading the semifinished or finished products among the affiliates, with final assembly or sales and service close to the market. More than just markets and production are integrated; the parent headquarters adopts a centralized policy to make certain that the affiliates are in fact woven tightly together. This centralized policy includes financing, pricing, technologies, R&D, sourcing of components and raw materials, sales and distribution, product design, production layout, site selection, and even personnel policies—though each to varying degrees.

No TNCs have integrated all of these functions, but many have moved far toward this type of organization and centralization, and IBM comes close to it in several ways. Other TNCs also contain regional groups that are organized like a multinational enterprise: For example, Ford-Europe, Inc. has integrated the European affiliates, causing each of the national companies to specialize and produce parts for the others, with assembly occurring within several national companies. Philips (Holland) has also integrated much of its worldwide operations, standardizing and simplifying its product lines and reducing costs substantially. (This type of integration has not been possible within the Latin American region; there, Philips and others have operated more like market-seekers.) Probably some 400 companies have partial ME-type operations and more would be established if governments (especially LDCs) removed barriers to movement of goods, funds, and technicians. These companies are found in most of the major industrial sectors, though in a few—such as basic steel, cement, shipbuilding, and textile mill products—the ME-form does not appear.

What makes this form feasible is the reduction of barriers to the movement of goods, funds, and technicians across national boundaries, permitting it to reduce costs significantly through larger production runs and economies of scale to serve a wider market. Economies occur not only in production but also in marketing and transportation, in the use of scarce management skills, support of R&D, and in a better allocation of financial resources. The growth of the affiliate companies of a multinational enterprise is, therefore, tied to the total growth of the company, which depends on its ability to create demand or gain market shares in sales of a standardized product, the market for which is more related to international economic growth than to that of a single national market.

Some ME affiliates abroad primarily serve national markets, but they are significantly tied to the world market and therefore export and import a substantial volume of products. Some governments, such as Spain, Mexico, and Brazil, have found it feasible to insist that a substantial portion of local production be exported as a trade-off for permitting some desired exceptions to national guidelines (such as price or import controls or ownership of the affiliate).

* * *

Few TNCS are purely or completely only *one* of these types. Most TNCs operate some divisions as market-seekers, some function as raw-material- or labor-seekers, and some product groups or regional groups as efficiency-seekers; the choice depends on the market conditions, government policies, or technologies. TNC organization, management styles, and orientations both determine and reflect these market orientations. Government policies that seek to alter TNC activities or orientations will do so at some cost in efficiency to the TNC and the country itself. But national benefits are also obtainable in terms of other criteria of acceptability (as discussed later).

## Concerns over TNCs

The concerns of host (and home) governments over the activities of TNCs have been widely expressed but seldom addressed to their effects on international integration. The three types are frequently and inappropriately painted with the same brush—a tactic that results from a lack of understanding of the distinctions and, in the United States at least, from a bias against discrimination among different companies or sectors in its foreign economic policies. Without regard to the impacts of the different types, both the LAFTA and ANDEAN countries early stated that they would not seek economic integration if it occurred at the hands (or to the benefit) of the TNCs. Thus, there was a strong bias against *using* the TNCs to achieve the desired integration regionally.

As a result of worldwide recession in the early 1980s, all governments have altered their positions as to TNCs, thus becoming more receptive. But a variety of concerns have been expressed and remain under the surface. They will undoubtedly affect any negotiation on use of TNCs.

The primary concern that arose from the spread of the TNCs was that of *dependence,* both economic and political. This fear arose not only from the large size of the companies and their tendency to dominate activities in whatever sector they operate, but also from the fact that the companies tend to be headquartered in the old colonial powers, within which the United States and Japan are included, despite the absence of significant colonies in their history. Since the headquarters' companies made a large number of decisions concerning the activities of their affiliates abroad, the host countries felt that their own interests would not be taken sufficiently into account in the integration process. Integration is generally seen as dependence, rather than interdependence. Consequently, TNC dominance was seen as likely to remain even after industrial restructuring.

Perception of dominance through TNC decision-making was reinforced by the fact that many of the TNCs operate in key economic sectors, and restructuring to integrate these sectors is unacceptable to governments if achieved under strategies formed by the TNCs. Technological dominance by TNCs arises from control over the origins and flows of technology, and their market presence and control implies that integration would only open wider markets to their dominance.

The fear of economic dependence has been increased by a concern over potential *interference* by the TNC's home government. Thus, U.S. antitrust law, tax law, and controls over capital and technology flows have been extended into activities of U.S. affiliates abroad, whether or not such extension violated or controverted the laws of the host countries. Such extraterritorial extensions of U.S. law still pose an obstacle to cooperative intergovernmental policies among advanced countries and between them and developing countries. This obstacle can be reduced only by cooperative, participatory decisions among advanced and developing country governments.

For countries that have not developed in the Western traditions, there has been and remains for some a fear of *cultural* change through the spread of Western life-styles, values, goods, and familiar relationships through any direct investment not controlled by locals. Managerial styles that emphasize rapid hiring and firing of individuals so as to increase profits or decrease costs are not always acceptable. Also, values that emphasize gadgets, or a multiplicity of goods that are only marginally differentiated, are sometimes seen to be a waste of resources, especially when the masses lack basic goods and services. The idea that income and the market should determine what goods are produced is also not universally accepted by host countries. The desire to retain cultural differences is tied to the concept of self-identity: *vide,* the billboards in Peru encouraging citizens to "Be proud to be Peruvian"; the bumper stickers in Brazil asserting "Brazil: love it or leave it"; and the requirements in Belgium, Quebec, and some countries of the Mideast that local languages be used with nationals hired by foreign companies. Since the TNCs are the transmitters of a Western culture, which is both welcomed and rejected, the companies are subjected to a love-hate syndrome.

Still another concern arose over a perceived inequitable distribution of the benefits of economic growth at the hands of the TNCs. Questions were raised about the percentage return to capital invested by the foreigner, the direction and volume of trade, the cost of imports from the parent company to the affiliate, the charges for technology and headquarters expenses, the types of technology transferred and employment levels and skills needed locally, and the location of R&D activities. The TNC was seen as looking after its own financial interests first, leaving in the host country only that which is necessary to continue operations. Whether or not this was the fact, it was the *perception;* this view, in turn, created a demand for changes in TNC ownership and behavior, to make them more nationally (rather than internationally) oriented, and therefore blocking further integration.

The accumulation of these impacts on the host country gave rise to a feeling in host countries that the TNCs have considerable *power*—political, economic, and social—causing unwanted local changes. Not all of the types of TNCs have the same kinds of impact or the same power, even though they may be perceived to have similar power. The standard host-government policy has been to require joint ventures or government participation, gaining local control and a larger piece of the pie despite a potential reduction in the size of the pie as a result of dis-integration.

**Legitimacy and Power of TNCs**

The reaction of host governments to using TNCs to restructure industry regionally or internationally is directly related to their perceptions of the power of TNCs and the legitimacy of that power. Power is a function of options (choices), and legitimacy is a function of the acceptability of those choices to the parties affected.

What is sought among all countries is a means of containing or reducing (and thereby legitimizing or making acceptable) the power that the foreigner wields in the host country. The justification of power—that it comes from the consent of the governed—reinforces the demand that TNCs conduct themselves in a manner acceptable to those affected. This acceptability is the only basis for the legitimacy of the TNCs; the OECD guidelines for behavior for TNCs and the proposed UN codes of conduct are (ineffective and irrelevant) attempts at spelling out what is acceptable action. Moves to international restructuring will require intergovernmental guidelines to make the results acceptable but of a different sort (as discussed in part III). The willingness of governments to form more cooperative arrangements will be a function of the perceived power of the TNCs to alter the guidelines during the process of their negotiation or implementation.

*Extractive TNCs*

The power of the extractive companies has been substantially reduced as host governments have become stronger and recognized their own negotiating strength vis-à-vis the parent company. The strength of the parent company in extractive or branch-plant manufacturing operations lies in its control over the marketing of the product and supply of necessary technology. For development of natural resources, capital has often been available independently, even though quite large amounts are needed. Lately, the technology needed has become available outside of the extractive companies and from competitive sources in many countries. The weakness of the international extractive companies lies in the fact that they must go where the resources are; and the more restricted is access to such materials, the weaker the TNC's negotiating strength.

As a consequence of this situation, the extractive sector remains relatively weak in bargaining with governments, as is demonstrated in the increasing nationalization of these activities. Nationalizations result from the perceived benefits from local control (and ownership), since an entire operation can be taken over intact. Since such a loss is generally quite significant to the foreign investor, the threat of a takeover is a strong bargaining weapon in the hands of government.

This weakness of the TNC in the extractive sector is matched by its low level of legitimacy. Correct or not in terms of Western law or property rights, the foreigner is often seen as an illegitimate exploiter of the host-country's life-blood. In many countries, no individual or private company can *own* the minerals in the subsoil or the subsoil itself. Concessions given to such companies are, therefore, rights to develop nationally owned resources, which are to be held for the benefit of the people in the host country. Therefore the question of the distribution of the benefits is primary.

The resolution of this question has recently been sought under the proposition that, without local control, the host country would not *know* the distribution of the benefits, much less get a fair share; therefore, nationalizations occur. If all that happens under nationalization is a shift in ownership, the impact on international integration is slight, with trade moving much as before. However, the price of the minerals can, in cases such as OPEC, be raised so as to alter the distribution of benefits significantly, as the price of continued integration of the industry worldwide. In the case of petroleum, U.S. policy is, *assertedly,* to seek domestic and alternative sources of energy, which would result in international economic *dis*-integration and be to the long-run detriment of the OPEC countries. In this sector also, dis-integration and re-integration is occurring from the shift of downstream activities in petrochemicals to the oil-producing countries; whereas formerly Europe sold petrochemicals to Arab countries, the latter now seek to sell petrochemicals to Europe. But, given the ability of OPEC members to use the sale of crude oil as a means of opening markets to downstream products, one cannot conclude a priori whether or not the new structure of integration achieves an optimal restructuring (better allocative efficiency) for the countries involved. At present, consumer-countries are asserting that the situation is not satisfactory.


## Branch-Plants

Compared to the extractive company, the branch-plant component-producer, using low-cost labor, has greater negotiating strength vis-à-vis the host country, and its mobility is greater even after operations have begun. If pressures arise from the host government concerning its conduct or operations, it can simply move the equipment and technology related to it to another country (often merely increasing operations in a location where it already has a plant). The need to provide employment usually overcomes any concern by the host country. The fact that the investment is made because of the existence of low-cost labor puts a ceiling on pressures to redistribute the benefits toward host-country labor. And any attempt to nationalize or localize ownership of the facility if it requires technology from the parent would simply kill it. Governmental pressure against such plants is not likely to arise, especially when the investors have been invited to come in. Significant benefits accrue to the host country in employment, skills training, construction, foreign exchange, and so on. Also, the host government can insist on the use of local suppliers, technicians, and so forth to increase the ripple effects. Therefore, little question arises over the legitimacy of such operations in host countries.


## Market-Seekers

The market-seeker form of TNC raises few questions of legitimacy, also, partly because of its local-market orientation and partly because of its relatively weak power vis-a-vis host governments. Its power is greatest when it is negotiating entry into the host country and smallest after it has established facilities and committed its assets, although it regains some flexibility (options) after it has amortized its capital investment. Since the host government approves the entry of the TNC's affiliate *and* since its activities are almost wholly within the host economy, the power of the host government remains almost as great as that with local enterprises. (This relation is modified by the necessity to obtain technology from the parent and by the ability and willingness of the government of the parent company to interfere in its behalf in the event of a dispute with the host government.)

If the TNC-affiliate acts in unacceptable ways in the host country, the government is able to stop or redirect those activities to some extent. In the extreme, if the government nationalized the local affiliate of a market-seeker, it gains a self-contained operating unit, but the damage to the TNC tends to stop there so the injury is limited. But the government gains little and sends disturbing signals to other foreign investors. The company's bargaining power is probably stronger than that of an extractive company and it will negotiate at length since it fears that any such acts will turn into precedents elsewhere.

Despite the fact that fewer problems of benefit distribution arise for the market-seeker form, host-country groups and interests see a significant flow of benefits out of the country and wish them retained within; therefore, constraints on outflow and reinvestment of earnings are imposed. Much of the pressure against such foreign-owned companies also stems from the legitimacy of headquarters control, and the possibility of decisions that do not coincide with the national interests of the host country reinforce the concern over the distribution of the benefits and support moves to require partnerships with local citizens (banks, the public, or entrepreneurs, or even government agencies). The objective is to redistribute control and gains in favor of locals.

These constraints on ownership and control do not directly alter the extent or structure of international economic integration since the primary market is domestic. But if governments attempt also to require exports, conflicts arise with the parent, which is reluctant to share its overseas markets with joint-venture affiliates, since the costs of market development around the world will not have been borne by the local partner. (Only if each joint venture was in different products of a line, or different lines, would mutual cross-national marketing be acceptable.) The structure of ownership is one of the basic distinctions between the market-seeker and efficiency-seeker. It would be conceivable and appropriate to have joint ventures in the former, so long as none of the national affiliates were integrated with others or with the parent. It would be impossible to have joint ventures under the pure ME-form, since any interference by an outsider could upset the delicate balancing and specialization required to achieve worldwide least-cost. The desire of host governments to have local participation in ownership and control is satisfied at the cost of lower growth and little or no exports by the TNC affiliate.

An adequate understanding of the trade-offs involved would help governments in forming their objectives in industrial restructuring. There is no absolute advantage of one form over another; they each serve particular policy objectives and will do so in different ways. However, for a government to expect its national economy to be tied into worldwide export opportunities through market-seeking type companies is to expect the unreasonable, if not impossible. A restructuring that sought economic independence among countries would, therefore, give high priority to market-seeking investments, giving no impetus to international industrial integration. But the result would be a decline in worldwide efficiency if the national markets were not large enough to permit economies of scale and encourage competitive cost reductions.


## ME-Type

The integrating activities of the ME form provides it with power vis-a-vis governments and raises questions about its legitimacy. This worldwide orientation is seen as further evidence that MEs have no particular loyalty to any one of the host countries although the ME is likely to have such ties to the home country, which only exacerbates the concern in host countries.

The ME-type has greater power than the other two forms in the mere fact that its options are greater: choice of location of production, technologies, products, trade patterns, financial sources, personnel (who accept shifting and rotation more readily), sources of materials, inputs, and so on. The specialization it achieves in components or product lines means that it reaches economies of scale not available to other types of companies; it therefore has competitive advantages.

The movements of factors and goods across national borders affect many aspects of the national and international economies, giving rise to concern on the part of governments which have difficulty determining the impacts or the distribution of benefits and burdens. Consequently, the proposed OECD and UN codes of conduct starting with a request that TNCs provide basic operating information to governments; however, the form and extent of the data likely to be forthcoming is not likely to be useful.

Governments have varying degrees of power in negotiating with the ME-type. For example, the greater the specialization among affiliates, the greater the potential hostage value of any one of them; interruption in its operations could tie up the entire company. Still, the expropriation of such a specialized unit is not likely to benefit the host country significantly. Alternatively, governments can destroy the ME's structure through joint-venture requirements (as noted above), thereby reducing international integration.

It is the thesis of the succeeding chapters that the ME-type can make *special* contributions to the integration of the international economy (or regional groups) if that is a major purpose of international restructuring. But these capabilities have not been directed to the resolution of major foreign economic problems; so its power has been seen as illegitimate and its attributes have been nullified by LDC governments in efforts to gain control over the destiny of their eonomies. Only in making clear its contributions to major problems facing governments can the ME achieve the legitimacy required to permit it to continue operation in an integrating fashion, but through an approach that will achieve a more efficient world economy, a more equitable distribution of the benefits, and other criteria of acceptability.

## Guiding TNCs by Criteria of Acceptability

Most of the discussions on TNCs have been directed toward examining what they have been doing and seeking a means of preventing them from acting undesirably. Little effort has been made to determine how best to guide or use them to achieve the criteria of acceptability and create the kind of international industrial structure desired. In fact, the increasing constraints on TNC's activities have led some observers to consider that this type of direct investment will soon be disappearing and the protectionism rising in the world economy, fostered by the recession and floating exchange rates, has accelerated decisions by MEs to restructure their organizations and market orientations more nationally.

The effort on the part of many national governments to prevent the integration of activities among affiliates and centralized control by the parent, their removal of foreign ownership in the extractive sector, constraints on foreign-owned banking, the forced localization of services, and the pressure for joint ventures with local partners—all are seen as evidence that TNCs in LDCs will not be permitted to operate in an integrated fashion and that they will be pressed to run self-contained operations in national markets, with perhaps some exports to third markets.

In order to gain some of the benefits of integration, a new form of TNC arrangement would then likely emerge, under which nationally oriented companies would cooperate in separate functions, ad hoc projects, or long-term contracts as in research and development, technology transfers, concessions for extraction, and so on.

Much of the discussion of what should be done about TNCs is conducted without considering the nature of the industrial structure desired and the specific contributions each type of company can make to achieving it. Some *implicit* assumptions obviously exist as to the nature of that structure, and it is important to uncover these assumptions in order to test the desirability of guidelines for TNCs. An alternative is to design an appropriate restructuring and fit the TNCs within it. Since it is difficult to design an *entire* new structure, it is more likely that this approach would be implemented by determining key sectors in which the TNCs could make appropriate contributions and then to determine the ways to induce them to alter their organization and operations on an international basis. We should be more concerned to maintain and stimulate international production as a means to efficiency than to protect any form of corporate organization.

Both the organization and its mode of operation should yield to the criteria of acceptability.

Each of the different types of TNCs will respond differently to guidance from governments in pursuit of the six criteria of acceptability discussed previously. Each of them is able to make *some* contribution to these criteria, but in substantially different ways. And there are trade-offs between each of the various criteria and their specific implementation.

The ways in which various criteria can be implemented through activities of TNCs can be outlined as follows:

*Efficiency* can be achieved through

1. Least-cost combination of factors of production, locally or internationally.
2. Economies of scale in production serving local markets of adequate size or gained through international specialization.
3. Application of appropriate technologies to different markets.
4. Contributions of management skills where lacking.
5. Marketing skills to enhance customer information on knowledge of products.
6. Greater credit-worthiness, expanding investment opportunities.
7. Flexibility in product lines, responding to shifts in demand and factor supply.
8. Support of R&D in the most effective locations.

*Equity* can be achieved through

1. Contributions of capital funds to locations of capital shortages.
2. Flow of exports and imports, balancing market opportunities.
3. Flow of funds in the balance of payments, balancing drains on foreign exchange.
4. Transfers of technology, opening new opportunities for production.
5. Transfer of appropriate worker skills, to fill gaps.
6. Manufacture of products desired by mass consumers.
7. Distribution of tax revenue among countries to spread direct benefits to governments.
8. Hiring of local engineers and consultants.
9. Reinvestment of earnings.
10. Sponsoring of community developments.
11. Assistance in rural development.
12. Assistance to local companies in management and technical problems, and so on.

*Participation* can be achieved through

1. Introduction of locals into management and marketing areas of affiliates.
2. Acceptance of joint-venture partners (save for ME form).
3. Acceptance of local shareholders or debt financing, opening investment opportunities.
4. Determination of appropriate tax revenues by cooperative dialogues.
5. Cooperative determination of transfer prices.
6. Cooperation in local training programs.
7. TNC acceptance of host-country laws.
8. Dialogues on product standards and environmental controls.

*Creativity* can be stimulated by

1. Assistance to the host-country's science and technology community.
2. Introduction of indigenous R&D capabilities in affiliates.
3. Innovation of new products or processes in local markets.
4. Diffusion of a scientific and technical orientation within local industry.

*Stability* can be affected by

1. Expansion of local or worldwide markets.
2. Employment policies of foreign-owned affiliates.
3. Regional or international economic ties through TNCs, which spread fluctuations from one economy to another.
4. Use of earnings (reinvestment or pay-out).
5. Consistent or openly explained behavior.
6. Plant closings.
7. Location in depressed areas.
8. Public and government relations.

*Diversity* can be retained or altered by

1. The development of product lines specifically for indigenous demands.
2. Introduction of standardized, world-oriented products into local market.
3. Attention to cultural and religious differences.
4. Adaptation of management styles.
5. Social integration by foreign managers.
6. Use of local language.

Each of the forms of TNCs responds to governmental pressure by making different types of trade-offs. Given the power of governments vis-à-vis the extractive companies, as discussed earlier, the governments can achieve virtually any of these criteria that they wish if they are willing to pay for them.

At the extreme, governments can simply take over the *extractive* operations, borrowing funds if needed, buying technology as desired, and taking the risks of marketing. They can, therefore, set up any of the trade-offs that they wish among the various criteria noted above. If governments do not wish to take the concomitant risks, they will likely enter into negotiation with extractive TNCs, with the bargaining strength of the TNC being determined by the nature of the world markets within which it must sell and by the availability of alternative sources of raw materials. This strength varies considerably from petroleum through copper and aluminum to tin, rubber, and so on. A more stable, institutionalized structure is suggested in chapter 10.

Conversely, as indicated earlier, the *branch plant* form of TNC leaves most of the bargaining strength with the TNC as compared to the host government, since the TNC has a number of alternative locations, and it will be unwilling to make any trade-offs in favor of the above criteria if they are costly—simply because it is looking for the least-cost source of supply. Anything which adds to these costs is seen as a significant disadvantage, causing it to look elsewhere. The 1930s debate of social dumping is apropos because it stemmed from a comparative advantage in trade gained by use of (exceptionally) low-cost labor. It was argued that this condition warranted protection of home-country producers. The situation is now complicated by the fact that it is *our* TNCs that are benefiting from low labor costs abroad and potentially maintaining employment of other workers in the parent company. To accept such operations, the host government must place a high priority on employment alone and a second priority on exports to gain foreign exchange. Everything else tends to be traded off against these, which is obviously satisfactory to the TNC investor.

The *market-seeker TNC* undoubtedly makes contributions to *efficiency,* but they are related to the local market. Its economies of scale are limited to the size of a local market; the technology is appropriate to local market demands and social needs; managerial efficiency will be largely determined by local capabilities; and marketing efficiency is limited again by extent of the market and the competitive structure locally. But there are divergent views as to whether *equity* criteria also are significantly determined by the market orientation in that the flow of funds will be restricted by the size of the operation, which is again determined by the local market. There will be few exports but some imports of capital equipment and materials or components; the skills learned will relate to the technology imported; product lines will be determined by local market demands; and the tax revenue is simply that determined by the government and the size and profitability of the operations in the local market. For a TNC affiliate wholly oriented to the local market, there is less problem of an equitable sharing of benefits because there is little movement of factors or product among affiliates of the TNC or between the local affiliate and the parent. But the flow of earnings still raises problems.

Local *participation* in the TNC affiliate that is oriented to the local market can, of course, be quite high, increased by the possibility of joint ventures which bring local financing and local entrepreneurial and managerial talent into the activity; the government has the ability to set the tax revenue, and to determine any transfer pricing patterns for the affiliate; finally, local institutes can be drawn into training programs to increase their participation in technical and education preparation.

Any contributions to *creative* activity by this type of TNC are locally oriented and constrained by the product and market orientations of the affiliates. Thus support of the scientific community is likely to be oriented to the needs of the company; R&D activities will arise only to the extent that the local market expands to require them; product innovations will wait for local demand–pull; and dispersion of a scientific or technical orientation will depend on the growth of local industry related to the activities of the TNC affiliate. But more could be done to support community projects: education, training, and so on.

The contributions of the market-seeking affiliate to *stability* in the host country will stem from its ties principally to the local economy; therefore, it is unlikely to make a more significant impact of stabilizing or destabilizing the economy than local companies of comparable size in the same sector. Finally, *diversity* in the host society is maintained in the way in which the local culture and market desire, in that the company is responding to local demands. Of course, it can introduce foreign products and attempt to sell them, but the response still is determined by local customers. Most societies recognize that social orientations will change with industrialization and worsen with foreign investment. They still have the ability to set any limits to change that they desire.

In sum, the host country can buy virtually any contributions it wishes from this type of TNC, so long as it keeps the market nationally confined and protected from foreign competition. The trade-off is potentially against efficiency, with the cost determined by the size, extent, and sophistication of the local market.

The *efficiency-seeker,* or ME-type of TNC, has considerable capability to make trade-offs among the criteria of acceptability because of its worldwide integration, centralized decision-making, and oligopolistic market structure. In terms of *efficiency,* its contribution to effective combination of factors is potentially greater because of its ability to command factors from around the world; its economies of scale are potentially greater because of its serving multiple national markets; the technologies employed are of the most advanced and sophisticated in the world. It can draw from varied management and technical pools; its marketing capabilities are at the leading edge around the world. What each host country receives in terms of these efficiencies will depend on the particular activity located in the country and the extent of its ties with the rest of the ME's operations around the world. Each host country has the ability to bargain for particular activities, although they are, of course, limited by the competition for the same activities from other countries and by the efficiency objectives to the ME itself.

Because of the ME's ability to integrate operations around the world, it also has a substantial capability of making trade-offs among the elements leading to more *equitable* distribution of benefits. It can alter the flow of funds between the parent and affiliates and among the affiliates so as to increase the supply and minimize the costs of capital. It can allocate the location of production of components' final products and assembly in different patterns. It can design the flow of exports and imports so as to fill gaps in the sources of supply and minimize the burden on national balances of payments; it can draw from complex and diverse sources of technology to offer the level of technology desired by the host country (though it has not always done so in the past); it can raise the level of technical skills and labor training in the country to that in more advanced countries; the product lines can be more diverse and specialized than in the market-seeker form since the markets to be served are worldwide. Also, there is greater ability to negotiate tax revenue among the various countries involved—if this were found desirable and equitable.

The type of *participation* that is feasible with the ME is different from that of other forms of TNC in that, although joint ventures tend to be precluded, management opportunities are expanded for local managers, who may be chosen for positions elsewhere in the company. Local financing is made more secure by the fact that the operations are tied into the worldwide activities of the TNC. But the host country is substantially restricted in its ability to determine transfer pricing in that direct efforts of interference will have an effect on tax revenue and on export sales by the affiliate.

The potential contribution of the ME to *creativity* in the host country is greater than other forms because the ME is interested in scientific contributions from anywhere in the world and will frequently support scientific communities in a number of countries. Its R&D activities will be located wherever they can make a contribution to its long-run objectives of invention and innovation. It will innovate inventions wherever the products or processes are relevant or applicable to the market or manufacturing activities of an affiliate, and it gains by dispersing its scientific and technical orientation whenever it can into local communities.

The effect of the ME form on host country *stability* is both positive and negative. It is stabilizing in the sense that the operations of the affiliate are tied into a larger entity, which can smooth fluctuations. However, world-wide fluctuation may get transmitted back into the affiliate when national conditions are also unstable.

As to *diversity,* the ME is likely to bring into the host country products that are also desired by other markets and even to produce some that are not demanded in the local market if a particular affiliate is a singularly appropriate location for production of a given component. It is unlikely that ME affiliates will produce *only* for export; therefore, worldwide product lines will tend to be brought into the host country. Obviously, the host country can prevent this simply by prohibiting the ME affiliate from entry. Once again, it must determine the appropriate trade-offs in terms of its employment, income growth, product mix, and industrial strategies.

* * *

Although the different forms of TNC can make a variety of contributions toward the achievement of the criteria of acceptability in a restructuring of industry internationally, they will not automatically do so in the ways in which each host country desires. Therefore, negotiations are required not only at times of entry but also throughout the period of operation and in the event of termination of investment. During such negotiations it is important that governments recognize the limitations of the different forms of TNCs and that the TNCs themselves recognize the priorities of the host countries in achieving various criteria and goals. Both must recognize the necessity to make trade offs in the pursuit of their mutual or conflicting objectives. Under such an approach, TNCs can be guided to help achieve desirable restructuring, but governments must first agree on the nature of the new industrial structure and on the criteria of acceptability if it is to achieve greater industrial integration. Greater dis-integration requires no agreement at all.

## Selected Readings for Part II

Baranson, J. *The Japanese Challenge to U.S. Industry.* Lexington, Mass.: D.C. Heath, Lexington Books, 1981.

Behrman, J.N. *National Interests and the Multinational Enterprise.* Englewood Cliffs, N.J.: Prentice-Hall, 1970.

Behrman, J.N. and Fischer, W. *Overseas R&D Activities of Transnational Companies.* Cambridge, Mass.: Oelgeschlager, Gunn, and Hain, 1980.

Bezold, Clement. *The Future of Pharmaceuticals.* New York: John Wiley & Sons, 1981.

Bhaskar, K. *The Future of the World Motor Industry.* New York: Nichols Publishing, 1980.

Blake, D. and Watters, R.S. *The Politics of Global Economic Relations.* Englewood Cliffs, N.J.: Prentice-Hall, 1983.

Caves, R.E. *Multinational Enterprise and Economic Analysis.* London: Cambridge University Press, 1982.

Dunning, J.Y. *Economic Analysis and the Multinational Enterprise.* London: Geo. Allen & Unwin, 1974.

Frank, I. *Foreign Enterprise in Developing Countries.* Baltimore: Johns Hopkings Press, 1980.

Franko, L. *The European Multinationals.* Stamford, Conn.: Greylock, 1976.

James, Barrie G. *The Future of the Multinational Pharmaceutical Industry to 1990.* New York: John Wiley & Sons, 1977.

Kojima, K. *Japanese Direct Foreign Investment.* Rutland, Vt.: Chas. Tuttle, 1978.

Kumar, K. and McLeod, M.G. *Multinationals from Developing Countries.* Lexington, Mass.: D.C. Heath, Lexington Books, 1981.

Leroy, G. *Multinational Product Strategy.* New York: Praeger, 1976.

Solomon, L.D. *Multinational Corporations and the Emerging World Order.* Port Washington, N.Y.: Kennikat Press, 1978.

Stoever, William A. *Renegotiations in International Business Transactions.* Lexington, Mass.: D.C. Heath, Lexington Books, 1981.

Swedenborg, B. *The Multinational Operations of Swedish Finances.* Stockholm: Alqvist & Wiksell International, 1979.

Tilton, John E. *International Diffusion of Technology: The Case of Semi-Conductors.* Washington, D.C.: The Brookings Institution, 1971.

Tugendhat, C. *The Multinationals.* New York: Random House, 1972.

Vernon, R. *Sovereignty at Bay.* New York: Basic Books, 1971.

Vernon, R. *Storm over the Multinationals.* Cambridge, Mass.: Harvard University Press, 1977.

# Part III
# Industrial Restructuring and Integration

The industrial policies adopted by both the advanced and developing countries as well as the decisions of transnationals are, in fact, restructuring the industrial world. These new structures are not necessarily to the liking of the countries involved (not governments, business, or labor). Therefore, there is a constant effort, principally from a national viewpoint, to redress the situation. Only a few efforts have been made to structure international cooperation apart from agreeement on some very broad rules, whose application is not satisfactory to governments. Even the U.S. government has intervened when the rules did not result in situations that it considered sufficiently equitable.

If we are to move out of the present confused situation into one of the greater order and international balance, we will have to adopt new mechanisms and new orientations. The succeeding chapters suggest some new approaches among the advanced countries, between East and West, between the advanced and the developing countries, and among the developing countries themselves. Some sectors, such as the petroleum extraction and processing, will require even more extensive modification and cooperation.

# 6 OECD Industrial Integration

The history of the countries now forming the OECD group has been one of both international economic integration and dis-integration over the past two hundred years. The primary thrust has been toward increasing integration, but backsliding and detours have occurred repeatedly, redefining the nature and scope of acceptable integration. The ME-form of TNCs has helped to integrate the OECD region (particularly the European Community) and should be used to accelerate integration while reducing some of the tensions currently arising out of restructuring under national industrial policies.

## OECD Industrial Integration through Trade and Investment

Prior to World War II, economic integration among the OECD countries occurred almost wholly as a result of trade among them. (U.S.–Canadian investment was an exception.) But over the past thirty years, integration has increasingly and most significantly resulted from the international movement of factors of production through direct investment; even much of trade has arisen for these movements. Classical trade theory postulated that the movement of products would be an adequate substitute for the movement of factors; it assumed that the factors of production were substantially immobile across national boundaries. As a consequence, international economic integration (industrial, agricultural, and extractive) would occur through specialized production based on comparative advantages within each of the trading countries. The nature and extent of specialization determined the degree of integration of the economies, and specialization would continue to the point of maximum efficiency for the system so long as markets were left free.

Of course, this system applied only to the major countries—the colonial powers—since the trade of the colonies or mandated territories was controlled by the metropolitan countries. The major trading countries of the nineteenth century were not necessarily the largest in terms of basic

123

resources, land areas, or population. The United States, Soviet Union, and People's Republic of China were not proportionately large traders because their internal markets were so large; India was still a part of the British Commonwealth. International economic integration was propelled by the trading activities of countries such as the Netherlands, Portugal, Britain, France, and West Germany. The United States entered the picture strongly after World War I and has essentially supported the classical prescription for international integration from the 1920s, with aberrations, as indicated in chapter 3.

It was recognized that the pattern and extent of specialization would change as comparative advantages changed, and that comparative advantages were themselves altered by changes in exchange rates, shifts in demand both within and among countries, discoveries of new resources, development of new labor skills and technology, and expansion of the size of the market through the process of economic development. Thus the size and composition of the outputs resulting from international economic integration would be constantly changing, as would the distribution of the benefits. Whatever distribution arose was *presumed* to be acceptable to the notions involved.

Private direct foreign investment occurred in response to changes in market size (demand) and the relative production advantages (factor endowments such as resources, labor, and capital) around the world; but it also frequently followed the national flag rather than economic signals. Such investment both responded to and altered comparative advantages by changing the factor mix—capital, labor (skills), management, and technological inputs—of both the capital-exporting and capital-importing countries. One consequence has been a change in the nature of specialization: from a pattern of different countries concentrating on different *sectors* of production to one of specialization in subsets of sectors (product lines) and even components. Trade is, thereby, composed of multiple exchanges within the *same* industrial sectors, and even within the same TNC—intra-company trade. Production structures show all advanced countries active in almost all industrial sectors with notable exceptions, such as the absence of automobile production in Switzerland. Even aircraft are exported only after numerous exchanges of subassemblies and components among suppliers in purchasing countries and the major producers.

National governments have not been willing to leave the nature and extent of international economic integration completely to the determination of the free market. Free-market integration implied a reliance on foreign sources of supply and demand for national prosperity, which was seldom deemed wholly acceptable by any country, especially when it felt its sovereignty threatened through economic or military power or its economic gains inequitable. Interferences by national (advanced-country) governments were, therefore, never wholly removed even during the so-called free-trade period in the late nineteenth century.

These interferences were employed for the purposes of preventing undesired dependence (due to specialization) and of gaining more of the benefits from trade. Classical trade theory provided no explanation of *how* the benefits of expanded world trade were to be divided. It merely asserted that the entire world product would be larger under free trade and that all nations could be better off. It did not assert that all would in fact be better off, although this was implied. Benefits were supposed to accrue in the same proportion as national production to total (trading) world production. Even if all were better off than previously, the *gap* between the weaker and the stronger or the richer and the poorer was not necessarily closed by adherence to the free-trade doctrine.

Consequently, no government was persuaded to risk full reliance on the classical thesis. Over the past two centuries, protectionism was strongly employed by France and Germany and only less so by Britain and the United States. It was not until the Reciprocal Trade Agreements of the mid-1930s that the United States began to pursue a liberal trade policy under bilateral agreements to reduce duties. After World War II, it was able to persuade major trading countries to liberalize their trade policies, by being willing to open its (much larger and more significant) market and offering foreign aid. However, tariffs have never been eliminated; quantitative restrictions remain, and other nontariff barriers to trade have increased; subsidies have been repeatedly applied; orderly marketing arrangements have been adopted; agricultural policies have remained a major exception in OECD trade practices; and cartel arrangements have been permitted by some OECD governments. *All* of these have been adopted for the purpose of attempting to dictate the nature and to limit the extent of international economic integration by influencing the location of production and pattern of trade. Consequently, comparative advantage and market-dictated specialization will not be permitted to determine the extent of reliance of one country on the economies of others.

To help restructure industrial activity after World War II and, it was hoped, accelerate worldwide economic development, the United States (more or less strongly) promoted direct private foreign investment from 1945 to the present—first to Europe, then to LDCs, and more recently to help specific areas such as the Caribbean. Potential recipient countries provided incentives to attract such investors, and several countries (including Canada) applied regulations that prevented the sale of particular goods in their markets unless a minimum portion was made locally (local-content requirements), thereby effectively forcing direct investment.

The result of U.S. private direct investment (predominantly flowing to Canada and Europe) has been to alter the nature and degree of industrial integration among these advanced countries. Industrial integration within the European Community occurred in the 1960s largely at the hands of U.S. TNCs, who were attracted by the possibility of manufacturing and selling within the potentially large and open Common Market. The decisions by these companies as to where to locate their manufacturing plants set the pattern for industrial integration, and those countries within Europe that did not like a particular pattern attempted to alter it through incentives and subsidies. Belgium and the Netherlands were the most eager for such investment; France was the least receptive in the 1960s. France was willing to have European integration—through trade, but not through foreign investments, and certainly not at the hands of U.S. companies. But the existence of the Common Market in Europe effectively prevented France from controlling the influx of U.S. companies, which in turn determined the location of manufacturing activity (altered only by the incentives and guidance of host countries).

While the United Kingdom was outside of the Common Market, the U.S. TNCs saw an investment there as an opportunity to reach the entire British Commonwealth and later (if Britain joined the European Community, as it did) as a favorable base for operations within an expanded European market. The delayed entry by the United Kingdom meant that many companies established facilities both in the United Kingdom and on the continent, which they would have preferred not to do had they been permitted to operate throughout Europe as a single market. The structure of European integration, therefore, has been altered by the fact of the community's delayed expansion (with Spain, Greece, Turkey, and Portugal still seeking full membership) as compared to what it would have been had the companies had an earlier choice of location in a ten- or twelve-country market.

To the extent that U.S. direct investment in Europe resulted from the inability to export from the U.S. into those markets because of trade barriers rather than market or location factors, the existence of the investment has altered the structure of integration between the United States and Europe as compared to what it would have been under freer trade. Also, investment incentives have altered production locations behind the trade barriers.

The removal of barriers or incentives in the future will not cause the structure of integration to revert to what it would otherwise have been. Consequently, we can assume that the European governments wished to relocate industrial activity in their own countries (through protection and inducements to direct investment) rather than rely on U.S. industry for imports. Thus they formed a type of industrial strategy without an expressed policy on industrial patterns. The choice made, in effect, was to gain local production in certain lines, rather than to produce other products for export to the United States in exchange. Preference for production in specific sectors constitutes a de facto industrial policy, even if it is not called by that name. Tariffs produced a similar result previously, but since they are used less now because of GATT negotiations, other techniques are employed to the same end. (Though the end of obtaining national capabilities in certain sectors is the same, the results are different because of the different means used. Thus, protection raises prices, but mere investment incentives leave the investor open to competition and thereby should be cost-reducing, or at least not price-raising.)

TNCs have also produced a type of industrial integration between the United States and Canada that would not have occurred under freer trade. Canadian tariffs prevented a substantial amount of exports from the United States, inducing companies to invest there for local production and sale. Canada also provided some incentives for plant location. When the balance of trade in automobiles and automotive parts was significantly against Canada, the U.S.–Canadian auto agreement resulted as discussed in chapter 3. Governments thereby altered the nature and extent of industrial integration between the two countries through the operations of TNCs.

The degree and nature of industrial integration between the United States and Japan are dictated principally by governmental trade and investment policies, which in Japan reflect carefully considered industrial policies (as discussed in chapter 2). Japan's traditional industrial base was seen as insufficient to provide the high-level prosperity that it sought; therefore, it altered its basic comparative advantages by adding foreign technology to ample manpower which could acquire new skills readily, and supported these by substantial local capital. The Japanese were also unwilling to permit integration to occur at the hands of the TNCs. But unlike the French, they were able to adopt independent policies unaffected by close and open trading ties with other countries.

New policies on industry are emerging among the OECD countries in response to pressures of international competition and recession. The question of location of industrial activity (or the international division of labor) will be resolved one way if by free-market criteria, another way if by the movement of direct investment under decisions by TNCs, and in still other ways if by governmental decisions—taken unilaterally under industrial policies, as discussed earlier, or cooperatively through the TNCs, as proposed here.

## An OECD Industrial Policy?

The OECD countries have been influencing the structure and location of industry nationally and among their members through their trade and investment policies, but they have not yet adopted concerted industrial policies. They will continue to influence industrial location by direct and indirect means, but they are eventually likely to come to the realization that industrial policies should be formed positively and under agreed (regional) strategies, rather than negatively and indirectly as a by-product of national policies. This recognition is likely to arise from pressures in the shifting orientations in international economic policies: the difficulties of moving any further toward liberalized trade through the GATT; the inadequacy of the IMF in stabilizing exchange rates; international debt problems; and the difficulties in handling specific industrial sectors under ad hoc bilateral or multilateral orderly marketing arrangements (OMAs) constitute an international industrial policy even though not adopted with a full consideration of the objectives and the best mechanisms for industrial restructuring; they tend to be protectionist rather than development-oriented.

If there is any justification for the use of rationality in economic policy, it is to seek desired goals by effective means. An OECD industrial policy would seek to channel industrial activities into those sectors that would produce the desired results for mutual goals of wealth and power, while at the same time seeking to minimize economic and social costs in an equitable fashion within the region.

An OECD industrial policy would be constructed out of the following activities:

1. selection of specific national industries to foster or help decline;
2. decisions as to the appropriate location of various industries (within or among countries) and whether to move jobs to people or vice versa;
3. provision of appropriate infrastructures for their development;
4. determination of production capacities for national industries by sector;
5. facilitation of R&D activities;
6. adoption of promotional techniques (including financial support and the selection of key companies to operate at the leading edges of change) and other methods of governmental guidance of the operations of individual companies or industry sectors;
7. determination of appropriate degrees of concentration and rationalization of an industry sector;
8. determination of the principal market orientation of each industry sector (national, regional, or international);
9. amelioration of impacts on employment from locational shifts; and
10. agreement on acceptable modes of discrimination against non-OECD entrants into the specific industrial sectors.

Many of these are employed presently in some fashion by OECD countries. Since a regional industrial policy involves a distribution of industrial activity among member countries, it would need to be set within a still wider policy concerning the *distribution of benefits* of industrial development. OECD countries have not yet agreed upon the criteria for acceptable distribution; in fact, they have not even tried to develop them. Rather, the issue is approached only under ad hoc pressures (as with steel) and spur-of-the-moment solutions are found that reflect the current negotiating strengths and skills of various parties. The agreement comes unstuck when conditions or strengths change because there are no agreement on the underlying ordering principle for OECD economies.

The benefits to be distributed include income and employment; access to resources, technology, and markets; opportunity to participate in decision-making and invention; and governmental revenue. Only access to markets has been given attention within international rule-making; but OECD members have often broken these rules in order to gain a more favorable position with reference to one or more of the other benefits, especially if the *costs* of rule-breaking are borne by others. Restraints on entry and imports, relocation subsidies, low-cost loans, export subsidies, preferences in governmental purchases, tax rebates for negotiations, and so on, are justified on ad hoc bases rather than by a considered policy toward industrial development for each country, much less for all OECD members collectively.

Aside from coal and steel, the closest that European countries have gotten to an industrial policy is in the sectors of nuclear energy, nuclear research, aircraft, and electronics. The Colonna Report of the late 1960s proposed the adoption of European Community industrial policies in aerospace, aircraft, and electronics. This has not yet been achieved, but there are still discussions on these issues.

The application of OECD industrial strategies could be as finely drawn as a single product line (such as the elimination of production of baseball equipment or sewing machines) or as extensive as guidance for the entire electronics industry. The adoption of sectoral OECD policies would alter investment opportunities around the world and change the ability of TNCs to penetrate markets, obtain financing, and develop competitive strength, thus altering the distribution of benefits and burdens and shifting the location of R&D programs and capabilities. The international geographic shifts that have occurred in several industrial sectors (such as electronics, home appliances, sewing machines, cameras, shoes, textiles and automobiles) have necessitated unwanted adaptations and adjustment within advanced countries. OECD members have sought to avoid these changes because they considered them an unacceptable burden or because they considered retention of these capabilities important, but they have done so on a national basis only. The history of the development of OECD countries demonstrates that the redistribution of industrial activity even *within* countries has been difficult to accommodate: the movement of industry from New

England to the South in the United States, from England to Scotland in the United Kingdom, from the North to the South in Italy, from Paris to the periphery of France, and from the center to the extremities in Japan. In each case, incentives have had to be offered to encourage these internal moves, and relief has been extended to some of the damaged areas. The willingness to foster *internal* shifts within a country illustrates the necessity to have a community of interest among those involved and an ability to move factors of production (especially labor) so as to protect against a loss of personal income of citizens.

Governments are, by their policies on trade and foreign investment, already shaping the character and extent of industrial integration among the OECD countries in the absence of a formal policy aimed at creating a more desirable pattern of industrialization and distribution of benefits. Rather, the determinations are made under a variety of pressures and concerns voiced by special interests or by uncoordinated governmental agencies, using many of the techniques identified with industrial policies but without the ordering or coordination of such strategies. It would seem highly fortuitous if such an uncoordinated process achieved the economic and social goals desired by each of the member countries or among them, and at a reasonable cost in resource terms. The issues confronting the OECD countries involving resource conservation, duplication of industrial capacity, and overlapping plans for industrial expansion will lead to costly responses on the part of member countries unless coordinated sectoral industrial policies are adopted on at least a *regional* scale. But this is a cost we may have to pay for not having yet learned how to achieve the prerequisite community of interest. Yet it is time that we extended the concept (and practice) wider than the nation-state.

The next moves should be toward regional industrial policies, although European regional agricultural policies have not set an attractive example. OECD agricultural policies have not been adopted for lack of criteria of sharing of costs and benefits and the absence of the underlying community of interest. Regional agricultural policies have not been singularly successful in generating efficient production, but that was not and is not their purpose. Their objective has been to *distribute* the benefits of agricultural employment within rural areas and among member countries, even at considerable additional cost, with these costs shared in an agreed way. Although these costs are high, they must be offset against alternative costs of the movement of workers, urbanization, infrastructure shifts, social dislocation, welfare and unemployment benefits, worker training, and so on, as required if more people left the farm. (Of course, these trade-offs should be balanced off, but they are difficult to measure; and even if they were neatly calculated and tilted in favor of no supports, some people might prefer to stay in rural areas and are enabled to do so by the political influence to obtain the subsidies.) Development policies need to consider the alternative of moving jobs to people versus people to jobs and the attendant lifestyles involved and impacts on the quality of life. This can be done only with effective participation of those affected.

Policies enhancing labor mobility, the level of jobs offered, and the skills to be utilized have been adopted by several of the OECD members, all of which would be an integral part of OECD industrial policies. Foreign investors are encouraged to employ labor of various types, and training and retraining facilities are often provided by the host governments. Similarly, attempts have been made to regularize employment so that workers are not terminated without opportunities existing for prompt reemployment and without the necessity to move geographically in order to find new jobs. Rather, governments seek to move industry to where labor is. An international impact of West Germany's and Switzerland's efforts to move workers to jobs has been the disturbances caused by temporary immigration of Spanish, Turkish, Italian, and Yugoslav workers. These moves have upset local communities in Europe and caused further difficulties when workers became unemployed and tried to remain or had to return to their own countries. National industrial policies would tend to attract foreign workers temporarily into the economy, but cooperative regional industrial policies would tend to move jobs across borders to the workers.

Similarly, governments have attempted to prevent termination of company operations until adequate efforts have been made to maintain some industrial activity in the same community. The concerns of government are joined with those of labors unions over both the termination of operations and even shifts in the product lines or technologies employed. All of these concerns are aimed at maintaining employment levels so as not to put the burden of adjustment on the workers. These practices are sometimes sector-specific in that labor is concerned to retain the jobs they have rather than shift to some other employment. Such constraints affect industrial location regionally.

Moves toward codetermination and industrial democracy which have arisen within European countries are also in the direction of *national* industrial policies, for labor will look after its own interests first, seeking to protect specific jobs in particular industries. This is likely to result in new rigidities in terms of product changes, technological shifts, and the mobility of labor as well as long-delayed decisions on location of new operations. It is not at all clear that the interest of a given Works Council in an affiliate would fit with goals of the TNC-parent *or* with the interests of OECD governments in a more nationalized sector. For example, if OECD governments concluded that a given industry ought to be permitted to be deployed into another country, labor would likely oppose because of the substantial burden on the workers in that specific industry. Among the techniques that would support such shifts would be retraining of workers, relocation of industry, and industrial expansion.

To date, within the OECD, no effort has been made to achieve agreement on industrial strategies, although some ad hoc agreements were reached within the European Community. Although there is an Industry Division within the OECD secretariat, no effort has been made to develop the kinds of guidelines that would constitute an industrial policy for the member countries. The OECD countries remain in a (pragmatic?) halfway house between national industrial policies and regional free-market approaches modified by ad hoc intervention.

This mixture of policies avoids the complexities of industrial policies and the agonies of trying to form coordinated positions, with traumas faced only *in extremis* when a given sector becomes greatly unbalanced. Also, the rejection of free-market determinations avoids the inequities arising from unconstrained competition at national and international levels. Governments are not willing to permit the free market to determine how industrialization progresses, nor are they been willing to let TNCs make all decisions relative to the location of plants, rates of expansion, employment practices, and trade patterns. Consequently, again, governmental decisions will be necessary, and they will be essentially protectionist if not moved onto a regional scale at least.

**Pressures for Coordinated Industrial Policies**

No moves toward the creation of coordinated OECD sectoral strategies are likely until governments face substantial pressures because the problems of industrial restructuring are excruciating. Nor are governments currently organized so as to be able to make the necessary trade-offs effectively. Without strong pressures, governments will continue to meet specific problems in an ad hoc fashion, thereby gradually creating a set of on-and-off national industrial policies without careful consideration of regional effects. (One might even suggest the existence of a decision-law that explains this bureaucratic behavior of problem avoidance—viz., no government official will seek to decide a problem for which each of the perceived outcomes offer less benefit than the [personal or departmental] cost of seeking a solution. *Not* taking decisions is more easily explained than errors, so the costs of decision-making are always deemed high. Further, any compromises appear to reduce the social benefit to some, so that they are not deemed worth the personal cost of grasping the more complex and long-term problems. Therefore, strong pressures are needed for action. Or, as stated long ago: "The worst evil is a tolerable evil.")

In the present world situation, several pressures are mounting that will likely induce consideration of regional industrial policies.

The competition from TNCs that is eliminating desired *national* companies—as with the oil industry in West Germany, the computer sector in France and Britain, automobiles in Britain, and, potentially, autos and steel in the United States—is one such pressure. The elimination of the last national participant in a given industrial sector leaves the host government feeling wholly dependent on foreign decision-making and at the mercy of foreigners as to the distribution of benefits resulting from activity in that sector. This result is likely to be unacceptable in key sectors. Even high concentration of foreign ownership and control in a key sector may be deemed unacceptable, as has been asserted to be the case in the electronics industry in Europe (Britain, France, and West Germany). To prevent this concentration, or the extreme of complete elimination of all local participants, requires the attention of the host government so as either to prohibit TNC initiatives or to gain some control over the final situation. To prevent sectoral wars, agreement will be necessary.

Concern over the maintenance of *competitiveness* in international trade of critical sectors has increased government willingness to support key industries or companies. But efforts by several national governments to expand capacity and strengthen the same sectors will end in frustration, costly duplication of facilities, and unprofitable sales (i.e., as misallocation of resources) unless coordinated across national boundaries.

Several industry sectors seem to be prime candidates for coordinated strategies for maintaining competitive strength. The high-technology group of aircraft, aerospace, electronics, chemicals, and petrochemicals have become priority sectors to provide high-wage jobs and export opportunities. But the lower-technology, mass-consumption industries such as textiles, shoes, and food are also priority because of large-scale employment and service to basic needs. Another group comprises industries that are readily mobile across national boundaries and, therefore, are easily subjected to inducements or constraints by host governments to locate in their national markets; these include autos, metalworking, some chemicals, and pharmaceuticals.

The communications sector is already under substantial regulation and includes an international company covering the communications satellite network. Government interest in communications and its extension throughout the world economy will undoubtedly lead to a regional, if not international, industrial policy for this sector in the not too distant future. Similarly, the necessity to develop alternative sources of energy and to husband those that exist is highly likely to lead to an international industrial policy for that sector, despite the difficulties seen in the operations of the International Energy Agency. The sizable input of energy in some manufacturing sectors is likely to be a wedge through which coordinated industrial strategies are applied in other sectors.

A third pressure is the desire on the part of governments to *disperse industrial activity* within regions of the country and even across national boundaries. The recognition that it is easier to move industrial activity to workers than workers to industry has caused a shift in attitudes toward labor migration and governmental guidance of industrial location. Rather than import the workers, as West Germany did, the French government decided to encourage industry to move toward the lower-wage regions in Europe and even to LDCs. Policies aimed at relieving depressed sectors of the economy (resulting from dying extractive industries or shifts of demand or new technology within industrial sectors) will reinforce the perceived need for coordinated industrial policies.

The capability of some TNCs to *alter trade patterns* either favorably or adversely for any given country is another pressure on governmental recognition that they may have to defend some sectors against foreign decision-making or move to more coordinated approaches. Governments are already urging TNCs to alter their trade patterns to improve host-country balances of payments and some have negotiated agreements for predetermined export volumes (for example, Canada, France, and Spain). The U.S. government has urged Japanese auto companies to invest in the United States so as to reduce U.S. imports and maintain U.S. employment and, hopefully, to reduce competitive pressures on U.S. auto companies since all would presumably have similar cost structures. These initiatives have already formed the basis for bilateral (then regional?) sectoral policies.

Technological changes and technology transfers cause shifts of entire product lines and geographic shifts of industrial activity, followed by shifts in manpower skills and employment. These constitute another pressure on both governments and labor unions to become concerned over company decisions as to regional location of industrial activity. Labor groups have sought to slow down or eliminate some of the foreign investment shifts (for example, the foreign investments by Philips of Holland and Volkswagen of West Germany, during the latter 1970s), thus constituting a step toward regional industrial policies in the sense that specific locations of operations of specific industries were involved.

Finally, the desire for local R&D capabilities, so as to reduce the brain drain and to create opportunities for scientists and engineers within their own country, has caused most governments to focus on an industrial structure that would support, complement, or require R&D facilities. To use R&D resources effectively will eventually require coordination among OECD countries in location of activities and even science policy.

Obviously, none of these pressures is by itself overwhelming; however, collectively, they are pressing in the direction of coordinated industrial policies. But the existence of (rigidified?) national policies will make it more difficult to agree on next steps. Without a concerted or cooperative policy, industrial patterns will be influenced by ad hoc and on-off efforts at the national level, with unanticipated results and probably inefficient resource allocation, not only in a market sense but also (more importantly) in the terms of achieving broader social and economic goals regionally or internationally. Regional industrial policies appear mandated, but they will not be developed until the means of implementation are at hand and the potential gains are visible.

## Contributions of TNCs

One of the obstacles in developing regional industrial policies for the European community or among the OECD countries is the lack of agreed (acceptable) means of implementing decisions as to the distribution of benefits and burdens. A second is the lack of agreed criteria of acceptability, as noted in chapter 4. It is not yet recognized that the TNCs themselves provide such a mechanism since they can be guided into the fulfillment of criteria for sharing costs and benefits. Some of the TNCs are already being used in this fashion in specific industrial sectors (aircraft, autos, and electrical machinery), but these arrangements are seen as exceptions rather than as forming new rules. Through such a mechanism, to help make the myriad trade-offs necessary to accommodate multiple national interests, the rigidities and conflicts of industrial policies can be mitigated.

We are currently in the advantageous situation of being able to start from the other end of the continuum by designing regional industrial policies first, dovetailing OECD member's interests in key sectors, and fitting emerging *national* industrial strategies within the regional goals. Such a move does not have to be made across all industry sectors, and certainly not simultaneously; some sectors are not significantly involved in trade or direct investment (e.g., residential construction). But the inclusion of several sectors would permit trade-offs *among,* rather than only *within* them, making accommodations easier.

However, governments have shown themselves reluctant to trade off participation in one key sector for a role in another; they each seem to insist on a significant role in *each* key sector. They are not yet willing to accept an interdependence that excludes participation in any one key sector. Such exclusion is, of course, accepted among provinces within a nation and by economically small countries, but not by major nations. And, so far, they have been willing to pay the costs of such duplications, except in extreme cases. Not to recognize desirable levels of interdependence among advanced countries but instead to insist on high priorities for *national* industry increases resource costs at a time when efforts should be made to husband all resources to achieve allocative efficiency.

If the OECD countries were able to determine a means of sharing industrial development and markets, a number of other contentious issues would be more readily handled. Many of the arguments over balance-of-payments deficits would be significantly reduced, and protection of the interests of labor would be eased (as would be moves toward tax harmonization and the integration of capital markets). Presently, policies directed specifically, and separately, at balances of payments, exchange rates, taxation, trade, dispersion of industry to depressed areas in a country, labor, and competition frequently have as a major purpose or effect the structuring of or maintaining a desirable pattern of industrial activity. An overt industrial policy would be directed primarily to the desired structure, with these other aspects decided within and falling out of the industrial strategies. The focus of national conflicts and interests would be shifted to the fundamental (but unrecognized) questions of who produces what and where? And who receives what and why?

No government will reduce its attention to specific ad hoc issues nor give up the techniques of intervention unless there is a different policy orientation that addresses the fundamental problem of the location of industrial activity (the international division of labor) and the consequent distribution of benefits. Not all industrial sectors are subject to these pressures; many will still be guided quite acceptably principally by market forces. There is no need, therefore, to try to *substitute* for the market where it is appropriate. But where governments have already largely mitigated its influence, a new policy orientation should be adopted by the OECD members, who do most of the world trade and investment among themselves. Otherwise, each country will develop its own industrial strategy and negotiate the best deal it can with relevant TNCs to promote *national* industrial development, leading to duplication of industrial capacities and, thereby, increasing pressures on markets (consumer, capital, and capital goods) that will lead to still greater protectionism. There is little recognition in policy that such duplication is costly and self-defeating and that all could participate more efficiently through coordinated policies. This coordination can be effected through the ME-form of TNC by guiding its multinational investment patterns, employment practices, trade, competitive practices, and dissemination of technologies.

Given present orientations, however, which are reflected in diverse policies on trade and industrial development and restrictions on foreign investment, governments have often reacted against the integrating effects of the ME-form of TNC. The thrust of most governmental regulations on foreign investment and trade has been to reduce the opportunities of MEs to integrate operations across national boundaries. Yet it is just this capability that fits with objectives of regional economic integration, which should lead to greater ability to achieve common goals. Further, the ME-form is most suitable in the high-technology industries in which all OECD countries are seeking expansion and greater international competitive strength. Not to recognize that the ME is most effective in achieving goals of industrial integration is to overlook one of the major mechanisms for meeting the several criteria of acceptability noted in chapter 4.

The ability of these companies to balance off interests of various parties in terms of the distribution of benefits has been well recognized in some sectors where a government (as purchaser, negotiator, or controller) has insisted that parts of the final product be produced locally and that repair and service facilities be set up. Where the potential supplier is an ME, with local facilities already established in the purchasing country, such requests can often be fulfilled without significant, if any, cost increases. When the local supplier is an independent national company, the cost of shifting the locus of production is greater but frequently acceptable to the government (and to the foreign supplier) in order to achieve the desired income, employment, and balance-of-payments effects. When the demands for local production require investment in new plant or establishment of a new firm (by a local or foreign company), resource costs rise considerably, but governments are also willing to bear such costs at times. Concerns of governments over TNCs were reduced when the existence of the ME-form in several countries permitted reduction of the costs of achieving locational goals while maintaining desirable levels of inter-TNC competition.

Even when governments require that, in a given project, the impacts on the balance of payments be equitable or that the impacts on trade be balanced off fairly precisely, the complex operational structure of the MEs permits many of them to achieve a rough balance of imports and exports among countries where they have producing facilities. Further, the desire of several OECD countries to have national R&D centers in specific sectors can be met by TNCs: Market-seekers put R&D labs close to markets if they are sufficiently differentiated, and the ME-form operates under a centralized and integrated strategy that farms out various R&D projects to affiliates, retaining a type of specialization that prevents duplication and yet makes available to each affiliate the results of company-wide discoveries and innovations.

The MEs themselves could take an initiative to demonstrate their usefulness in pursuing the objectives of regional or international integration. They could set forth programs of investment, product development, employment regularization, R&D relocation, technology transfers, patterns of trade, and so on that would demonstrate to host governments the company's understanding of their concern for the distribution of benefits and burdens. In some instances, all that the governments would seek is to be informed of the decisions of companies sufficiently in advance to make adjustments in public policies so as not to force the burdens of adjustment on depressed or weak sectors of the economy. Where there are clear trade-offs between efficiency in production (permitting more competitive prices) and an equitable distribution of benefits or burdens, the company's awareness of these impacts and its communication of them to governments would provide the policymakers with better information as to the effects of particular policies. It is not at all clear that governments would seek constantly or even repeatedly to force changes in business decisions so as to achieve greater equity if the constraints tended to rigidify operations, reduce innovation, or significantly reduce efficiency.

But a continued lack of appreciation on the part of the companies of the problems facing governments and an unwillingness to adapt to them are highly likely to produce unyielding governmental guidelines and restrictions that *will* reduce efficiency (and in unanticipated ways) to the detriment of both company and government objectives. Given the complexities of the trade-offs that TNCs make in their everyday operations, balancing multi-governmental interests (as illustrated *in extremis* by the rationing of petroleum by the oil companies during the Arab embargo), governments are likely to avoid taking responsibility for many of them. However, governments are concerned to know how these decisions are being made, and under what criteria, in order to alter them if they consider necessary. Therefore, communication of TNC policies and practices will become more necessary and required by governments. Without this cooperation, governments are likely to inject themselves more directly into business decisions, even to the point of placing a public official on boards of directors in order to know *ex ante* what decisions are being taken.

Whether or not governments can be brought to a cooperative mode depends strongly on their own vision of the new international industrial structure. If they see it as a grouping of nationally oriented industries in which each government is seeking to redistribute the benefits to itself, then the pressures to dismember the MEs and force them into partnerships with local private or governmental parties will continue, leaving the nationally oriented market-seeker as the predominant form of TNC, with little integration of industrial activities resulting. If, on the other hand, governments want to see the world move toward greater integration, with concern for the acceptable distribution of benefits and with consequent greater efficiency, they should examine the ME-form to see how it may be used in implementing their objectives.

The experience of the COMECON arrangements (see chapter 7) and of the NATO coproduction agreements indicates that once the decisions as to the distribution of production and basic benefits in the location of technologies and patterns of trade are determined, the concerns over precise company behavior or tax revenues or duties, competitive behavior, employment levels, and so on fall into third or fourth-class priorities. In fact, in many of the arrangements, these aspects were simply forgotten as unimportant or as falling acceptably out of the basic decisions on who did what.

The shift to a focus on sectoral policies, rather than on trade policies or even codes of conduct for foreign investors, would bring a similar reordering of priorities. Since the underlying concern of governments even in trade policies has been with the location of industrial activity, a shift in policy emphasis to industrial location would put the problems of trade in a new perspective, setting them within the larger framework of regional industrial policies.

The continuation of policies that seek to alter marginally decisions already made by companies, in an effort to shift their decision or the distribution of national benefits and burdens, will not likely remain satisfactory to governments. If companies can themselves see the trends, they will take an initiative to work in tandem with governments to produce a more efficient and equitable structure of industrial activity among the OECD countries. But, in the Anglo-Saxon part of the OECD, there remains a strong disaffection with close ties between business and government, stemming partly on the side of business from a fear of increasing rigidity in the industrial system as a result of intervention by the government, which has been seen also as under the strong influence of labor interests. Other countries are strengthening business-government ties, and the Anglo-Saxons should at least examine whether they cannot find a similar accommodation nationally without incurring the costs of rigidities and lower rates of innovation so as to form the basis for wider cooperation within the OECD.

## A Beginning: Sectoral Strategies for Autos and Aircraft

Assuming that the OECD countries accept greater interdependence and seek to reduce costly duplication in industrial development, prime candidates for cooperative sectoral efforts would be autos and commercial aircraft. The arrangements might work out something as follows:

1. In each of these sectors there is likely to be only a half dozen or so major companies producing a full range of products within the OECD countries. The size and structure of the markets place a premium on economies of scale and specialization, requiring high productivity and effective management. Consequently, only a few major companies are likely to survive, unless strong government interference is applied. But this reduction in number can make regional sectoral industrial policies easier to form and implement.

2. Each of the major surviving companies could be induced to maintain subsidiaries in each of the OECD member countries by techniques already employed or by new agreement, as in the U.S.–Canadian auto arrangement. Several of the subsidiaries would contain assembly operations, and each would specialize in particular phases of production, as is currently being done by major auto manufacturers in several of the OECD countries.

3. In aircraft, each of the several companies would produce different items in any given country, although this might require new investment since the aircraft companies have few affiliates abroad, or a network of local subcontractors could be maintained, as done now. If the country were large enough, it would have a sufficient number of subsidiaries producing different parts of aircraft so that in a national emergency full-scale production of aircraft could take place. Of course, production of a national aircraft would require new designs, but the production equipment would be in place and the shifts could be accomplished in any emergency. (In peacetime, a national aircraft is not viable for any but large countries [the United States, in reality] because the national markets in OECD are too small. Consequently, European countries have turned to regional cooperation in some commercial aircraft. But as yet there is no sectoral policy for the European Community as a whole in commercial aircraft; and military aircraft are still principally a national responsibility.)

4. In autos, each of the national subsidiaries would have assembly operations and would specialize in a given product line (such as heavy trucks) or specific components production. All countries would have some local suppliers of components that would be produced by independent companies serving several major auto companies. Under governmental guidance, each company could be induced to produce items different from other companies in any given country, providing a wide range of employment experience and technologies in order to permit local production of a complete vehicle if needed in an emergency.

5. All sales by either auto or aircraft companies would then involve production in several countries, forcing a sharing of production, employment income, and technologies, as well as an expansion of trade based on specialization.

6. Open competition—bidding on government contracts or market competition—would exist among the companies. Each bid would be fulfilled by production out of several countries. Where government contracts were concerned, as with military purchases of either autos or aircraft, special sharing requirements could be met fairly readily by any one of the companies through its operating units in several countries.

7. Managerial and production efficiency would be rewarded through companies being able to produce appropriate but low bids to government purchasers or appropriate products at low prices to the consumer, as is now being forced in the auto industry through the search for the least-cost production of the most efficient low-price cars. This search has resulted in virtually an identical car design and performance by a number of companies, as evidenced by the similarities among Volkswagen's *Rabbit,* Renault's *Le Car,* Ford's *Fiesta,* GM's *Chevette,* Toyota's *Corolla,* Nissan's *Datsun,* Honda's *Corrolla,* Fiat's *124,* Chrysler's *Omni,* and American Motors' *Gremlin.* The world car is next, with standardized performance aspects such as front-wheel drive and safety features. But the results of this competition are of increasing concern to governments, some of the companies, and labor. The pressures on Chrysler and on British Leyland led to large governmental support. To ease that pressure, the U.S. government has urged Toyota and Nissan to follow Volkswagen into production in the United States, as Honda has recently done. Such a response would be a step along the road to a regional, sectoral industrial policy, and Europe is likely to follow as Japanese companies penetrate the European market further.

8. In aircraft, all operations in production of certain models could be under a single company yet located in subsidiaries in various countries so that production could be shared out and still controlled under a single managerial authority. This would eliminate present governmental techniques of forcing the use of a local supplier (at the cost of inefficiencies and higher aircraft prices) or of multiple efforts to produce a single (150-seat) model for which the market offers a volume of sales sufficient only to support one producer with desired economies of scale.

9. In both industries, cross-border specialization is already occurring—at the hands of TNCs in autos and under government pressure in aircraft but without the efficiency of a single TNC organization and production ties. In both sectors, governments are showing a concern for the maintenance of local production facilities and a fear of potential shifts in the location of production, causing problems of unemployment and raising conflicts with labor. But they have not taken the next steps to achieve their goals, which involve encouragement of appropriate cross-border mergers (or establishment of new affiliates) so as to create companies that had facilities in each of the countries with open competition among them in all of the countries.

10. For the smaller countries, an alternative to having several foreign affiliates is to have one or more companies (local or foreign) producing a specialized component (undercarriages in aircraft and transmissions in

autos, for example) for *all* or several of the major companies so that the country was always included as a potential supplier in bids by major manufacturers or in current operations. Obviously, other independent suppliers could compete, but there would have to be an agreement that the majors themselves would not establish full capacities in these components and would rely on some outside suppliers within the OECD.

To form such an industrial structure would require an acceptance by governments of the elimination of a single, self-contained national industry in favor of a regionally oriented, specialized industrial structure. The latter would gain the desired economies of scale and provide greater diversity to the consumer, while at the same time permitting national sharing in the benefits of production and foreign trade. The result would be a type of organized free trade, having as its objective the provision of answers to problems of distribution, which classical free trade did not resolve acceptably.

Similar industrial strategies for chemicals, electronics, pharmaceuticals, and textiles would be more difficult in that a larger number of companies were involved and easier because of the greater flexibility at the margins offered by more numerous products and producers. The facts that each major company is already located in several OECD countries and that each produces numerous product lines make the assurance of the maintenance of some participation by each country in each sector easier. If there are key product lines (as the mainframe computers in the electronics sector), each government could have, by agreement, an affiliate of one TNC located there that would make or assemble these items locally. Once again, maintenance of a national supplier (even if foreign-owned) is the crux of the matter.

To the objection that these agreements force a concentration of industry, it can be replied that the result could be made *more* competitive than existing situations in which national champions are heavily subsidized but prevented from achieving international (or regional) specialization and where competition is likely to be eliminated by the present quotas and government procurement practices. The industrial strategies need not dictate to any given company how it sets up its OECD-operations but would induce each to build some facilities in appropriate dispersion so as to provide each country acceptable benefits. Guidelines rather than rules would be provided, but the specific application of the guidelines could be left to each of the companies.

If any government insisted on *certain* activities taking place in their country, more detailed agreements would be necessary to set such a pattern, and some additional costs would have to be borne by the requesting government. But given the opportunity to attract operations from several TNCs, the request would probably be fulfilled. Where it was not economically feasible for *any* of the companies to locate activities in a given country, consideration would then be given by the OECD countries as a group to alternative means of providing equity. It could be resolved by offsets in provision of production in other industry sectors—rather than the one under consideration—or by group subsidies to the relevant TNC. Such trade-offs lead quickly to the recognition that the industrial strategies would be still more efficient if they were developed for several sectors simultaneously so that each sector does not have to be divided completely among all of the member countries. Some specialization could then occur *among* sectors—as is necessary for small countries anyway—and not solely *within each sector.* Thus some countries would not be in some sectors at all, but more heavily in others. Once again, this approximates organized free trade, making sure that all are participating in an acceptable manner. Otherwise, participation is a matter of fortuitous resource endowment, economic strength, and political negotiating ability rather than equity.

## Obstacles to OECD Cooperation

The previous section implies that all that is required is for a few attitudes to fall in line for the OECD members to generate a set of regional industrial strategies. There are, of course, many obstacles in the path. They range from philosophical differences, to narrow national interests, to pressures from outside of the OECD region, and to the absence of a strong community of interest as yet.

One of the most difficult obstacles to overcome is the widespread conviction within some of the OECD members that the only acceptable way to control the economy is through aggregate and indirect policies (mainly monetary and fiscal), since this provides the maximum freedom for individual decisions and prevents discrimination among participants in the market. The difficulties of further OECD cooperation are shown in the lack of coordination even in this set of policies. It has been exceedingly difficult to get OECD members to coordinate interest rate policies, monetary aggregates, and tax and expenditure policies to prevent pressures toward recession of inflation from being passed from one economy to another. One of the reasons for the lack of coordination is the absence of a dominant economy that could accept the leadership in bearing the burdens of adjustment simply because of its size and flexibility. The fact that no economy can play this role in monetary and fiscal policies indicates that there may well be a similar gap in assumption of burdens for adjustments within any industrial sector.

A second obstacle is related to the first in that the structure and complexity of industrial patterns among the OECD countries makes an *overall* agreement on industrial policies difficult—not only because of their scope but also because of the difficulty of perceiving the results of multiple sectoral strategies and where any burdens of adjustments would fall. However, it is likely that within the OECD region, the burdens of adjustments would be *marginal,* especially if they were accommodated through growth within each sector. Since virtually each major sector exists already within OECD members, adjustments to changes could be made at the margin rather than through the demise of an entire sector in a country. Further, only key or priority sectors are likely to be involved among the OECD countries: automobiles, steel, electronics, chemicals, aircraft, electrical machinery, pharmaceuticals, communications equipment, rubber, nuclear power, and military materiel. This leaves a large number of sectors for which specific industrial strategies would not be needed. This does not minimize the difficulties; it merely means that macro and micro *planning* are not necessary for the entire economy in order to achieve the objectives of industrial policies within this region.

A third obstacle to industrial policies is the likelihood that rigidities would be built into sectors for which there were cooperative arrangements. This likelihood stems from the expansion of government regulation and red tape, leading to delays and costs imposed on companies to meet changing government demands. It also stems from labor's interest in the maintenance of jobs in particular locations and therefore in the unwillingness to permit shifts in industrial activity, even at the margin, and even when they are the result of growth. Finally, there is some likelihood that such agreement would lead to a reduction in innovation because of the perceived reduction in uncertainty and competition on the part of major companies.

Each of these obstacles is real but not overwhelming—that is, there are offsetting approaches. For example, an industrial strategy that induces major companies to locate in different countries within the OECD could still leave them to compete among themselves as at present. In fact, governments might well be induced to reduce barriers to competition (in government procurement or across-national boundaries) given the fact they were guaranteed that an acceptable portion of the industrial activity in the sector would remain within their country.

As to labor, there is some evidence that experience with codetermination has led labor to a greater understanding of the constraints on managements and the necessity to maintain flexibility in the growth patterns of the company and industry. The slackening of innovation appears not to be specific to situations in which there are intergovernmental agreements, because many of the advanced countries are now questioning why innovation has tapered off within the last five to ten years. One of the reasons adduced by some industry observers is the increased *uncertainty* through policies of stagflation, making it difficult to estimate future profitabilities of capital

investment. The greater certainty provided by agreement as to governmental approaches to TNCs is likely to stimulate increased private investment.

Obstacles of quite a different sort will arise in the necessity of the
OECD countries to make adjustments in their industrial patterns with reference to both East-West relations and North-South relations (as discussed in
chapters 7 and 8). These adjustments cannot wait until the OECD patterns
have been established, and therefore any OECD negotiations would have to
take into account adjustments required with reference to other regions.
However, none of the other regions are as important to the OECD members
as the industrial patterns within that region itself. By far the largest portion
of international trade and international production occurs among the
OECD countries, and the sectors that are key within this region are not
those that are in strong contention between the East and the West or the
North and the South. The fact that somewhat different sectors or product
lines will be involved in many of the negotiations with other regions reduces
somewhat the overlap in the formation of industrial policies.

Two quite fundamental and related obstacles remain: One is the
absence of agreed *criteria* of *acceptability* of any industrial strategy, and the
other is an absence of a *community* of *interests* sufficient to cause the
acceptance of bargains that may be perceived to be somewhat inequitable.
People and governments tend to know what is not equitable, but it is much
more difficult to delineate what is equitable. If a given bargain appears later
to be inequitable, there must be a sufficient community of interests either to
adjust it (as Britain had demanded of the European Community in terms of
the common agricultural policy) or to accept an unequal bargain in the anticipation that later arrangements will balance off the inequities; that is, a
continuing process is in place from which equity is anticipated.

Related to the absence of criteria of acceptability is the fact that many
of the trade-offs involved are non-commensurate, even if they are measur-
able, which many of them are not. For example, the grant of production for
a given country in one industrial sector might be balanced out by the acquisition of R&D capabilities in another country in another sector. It is difficult to determine the balance among such activities. Therefore, negotiations
are likely to be reduced in scope so that agreements balance off contributions within a single sector, trading $A_1$ for $A_2$ rather than contributions
among different sectors, as A for M, or $A_1$ for $M_4$. This restriction would
reduce the scope of specialization and therefore allocative efficiency among
the OECD members. However, with experience, more complex arrangements are likely to be achievable.

Success depends entirely on the development of a community of interests that places the process of decision-making above any specific bargain.
We come back, therefore, to a central proposition of all international coop-

erative efforts: The means exist, and governments can have almost anything they are able and willing to pay for in terms of industrial development. There remains simply a lack of *will,* which is tied to the absence of a conviction of mutual responsibility for the development and evolution of the community of man.

# 7 East–West Industrial Cooperation

The primary problem in accelerating East–West industrial cooperation is a divergence of rules concerning the ways in which business is to be conducted and business entities are to be formed. The West is much more open and offers more leeway to private decisions than do countries of Eastern Europe and the USSR. With few exceptions, Western companies cannot produce in the Eastern countries save in some form of partnership owned and controlled by the host government. Similar rules do not hold for Eastern business entities seeking to operate in Western countries; generally they are accorded rights similar to any foreigner. (Exceptions do exist in tariff differentials, but this is generally not so in investment opportunities or business negotiations.)

This difference in the rules of the game was one of the reasons for the demise of the Charter of the International Trade Organization (1949), which was primarily directed at tariff reductions but which set forth rules for trade between the capitalist and socialist countries and also on worldwide foreign direct investment. It was clear to analysts at the time that it would not be possible to determine the distribution of benefits from a reduction of barriers to trade if the socialist countries continued to play by their rules while the West opened its markets. The socialist countries have, in the main, continued to insist on their rules, and consequently the extent of industrial integration through trade or investment is greatly circumscribed.

Without a set of mutually agreed rules governing the nature and extent of economic cooperation, there is a strong tendency for each nation to seek a better bargaining position so as eventually to set the rules of behavior in its favor, thereby increasing its gains. The absence of criteria for distribution of gains among the European socialist countries—the COMECON, or the Council of Mutual Economic Assistance (CMEA)—has slowed progress toward economic integration even among its members. Although a substantial degree of specialization exists among them, the Eastern European countries have remained unsatisfied with their gains compared to the USSR's. Consequently, a debate has continued within the COMECON over the nature and extent of regional industrial integration and, further, the more West-leaning Eastern European countries over the role which Western TNCs might play in their industrial development.

In terms of East–West cooperation, the continuing disagreement on the rules of the game gives rise to repeated complaints by all parties over their treatment. For example, the Soviet Union and several of the Eastern European countries complain about the technology and trade controls imposed by the United States and the OECD countries under the COCOM arrangements. They also complain about tariff discrimination applied by the United States against imports from the USSR and some of the Eastern European countries. In turn, the Eastern countries do not readily open their economies to U.S. trade or investment, and it is quite clear from the procedures that they have applied that the achievement of East–West industrial integration at the hands of TNCs is not acceptable to them. Several Eastern analysts have argued that too large a part of the benefits of regional markets goes to TNCs in expanded (oligopolistic) profits; this distribution of benefits is seen as unacceptable by the Eastern European countries so they do not allow entry of TNCs into their economies except under quite limiting conditions. Further, foreign ownership and control of enterprises remains unacceptable.

These constraints and regulations demonstrate that *inter*dependence will be circumscribed as necessary to maintain close ties within the COMECON and to reallocate the relative gains between the host country and the TNCs. Even so, over the past several years, some of the Eastern European countries have shown considerable interest in widening the scope and nature of economic cooperation between the East and the West, and the Soviet Union has itself taken some initiatives ad interim.

Under one hypothesis, it is desirable to broaden East–West economic çooperation so as to reduce the threat of war: Commerce leads to peace. Another hypothesis is that the USSR is a natural enemy of the West and, therefore, any trade or economic benefit to it will harm the West: A stronger USSR hastens war. If we adopt the first hypothesis, TNCs could be used to achieve any of three types of industrial integration: a greater specialization among the COMECON countries themselves; a closer degree of integration between the Eastern European and Western European countries; or integration of the Eastern European countries with the Third World. The integration could occur through market specialization, transfers of technology, cooperation in research and development, coproduction, and redirection of trade.

To determine how best to use the TNCs, we need first to look at the objectives that closer industrial cooperation would achieve, the present rules and extent of cooperative arrangements, the limits of success of the present arrangements, and the alternatives available for new policy approaches. An assessment of each of these aspects of the problem is complicated by the fact that the interests of the United States are not identical with those of its Western European allies, nor are the interests of each of the

Eastern European countries in expanded East-West contacts the same as the USSR's. Development of cooperative arrangements will vary according to which parties are negotiating. Consequently, the development of a single set of rules applied to East-West industrial relations is unlikely; sectoral or even company integration remains more realistic.

**Purposes of East-West Industrial Cooperation**

The Economic Commission for Europe (ECE) described East-West industrial cooperation as follows:

> Industrial cooperation in an East-West context denotes the economic relationships and activities arising from (a) contracts extending over a number of years between partners belonging to different economic systems which go beyond the straightforward sale or purchase of goods and services to include a set of complementary or reciprocally matching operations (in production, in the development and transfer of technology, in marketing, etc.); and from (b) contracts between such partners which have been identified as industrial co-operation contracts by Governments in bilateral or multilateral agreements.[1]

This definition carries industrial cooperation beyond trade policies to include different means for allocating production: licensing, turn-key plants, coproduction, subcontracting, joint ventures, and joint construction or tendering.

The interests of Eastern European countries in such cooperation arise from their desire to gain access to western technology and know-how, to a supply of more sophisticated goods, especially capital equipment, and to capital for accelerated development, in order to rationalize investment structures, diversify industrial production, improve efficiency, and utilize existing capacity better. In addition, these governments seek means of substituting local production for imports and of generating exports into Western and LDC markets. They seek foreign exchange to meet their increasing import needs and, in order to gain it, are willing to undertake some degree of integration into the world economy; this is true of at least some of the Eastern European countries although the USSR is still recalcitrant. Finally, a major interest lies in acquiring managerial and marketing skills faster than was possible under independent licensing arrangements. Many of these licensing agreements have had to be renegotiated in order to permit transfer of later technologies and to add the necessary transfer of managerial and marketing skills. New forms of cooperation are being sought therefore to permit wider exchanges of technology without having to go through the renegotiation process and to open Western markets to Eastern European products.

Western governments have seen such cooperative arrangements as bridgeheads to wider economic cooperation, which might reduce the likelihood of political confrontation, as well as opportunities for business to serve markets wherever they existed. The U.S. government has long operated under the views of the nineteenth-century British Parliamentarians Cobden and Bright that a reduction of international tensions results from the expansion of commercial ties and that economic prosperity generates peace. Other OECD countries have been less sanguine, but they have sought closer ties for the direct economic gains. West Germany has regarded cooperation also as a tool in its *Ostpolitik* or opening to the East to maintain ties with East Germany. In the main, the form and extent of such cooperation have been left to the individual Western companies to negotiate. Although bilateral clearing arrangements and trade agreements exist between pairs of Eastern and Western European governments, they do not *require* specific commercial deals or arrangements; they merely express agreement on the part of Western governments to *permit* certain volumes and types of trade or exchanges. Their general arrangements are then followed by specific agreements that detail expected performance of each party.

TNCs are willing to enter into various types of contractual arrangements in the Eastern bloc in order to gain access to raw materials, to establish operations where cheaper labor exists, to gain a market share in Eastern European countries, to gain some revenue from transfers of technology and management skills, and possibly to penetrate markets in less-developed countries through production in Eastern Europe. Since occasionally these diverse purposes coincide with the requirements of the Socialist countries, a number of agreements have been consummated, although they are not of the number or size that Eastern European countries thought possible when they began to open the door to these contractual relationships.

In its 1973 assessment of East–West industrial cooperation, the Economic Commission for Europe (ECE) noted that four distinct problems had arisen in the successful development and implementation of cooperative arrangements: (1) information gathering and dissemination on specific opportunities; (2) financing of projects; (3) special treatment under trade and commercial regulations of goods made and traded under cooperation contracts, and (4) establishment of an adequate international normative framework for industrial cooperation contracts.[2] Conditions have not changed in the past decade.

Of particular concern to TNCs is the last problem—that of an institutional framework or industrial cooperation. To achieve a structure of cooperation that leads to industrial integration, more is needed than the marginal suggestions made by the ECE, which were limited to "an intergovernmental multilateral code or guidelines indicating the norms which should be applied and the objectives which should be sought through industrial cooperation agreements . . . ," facilitation of the socialist international partnerships through changes in national legal systems, agreement on the forms of contracts to be employed, mechanisms for international commercial arbitration, and arrangements for certification of quality and performance.[3] These suggestions show no priority for more extensive industrial integration; this probably therefore remains a Western, or even an Eastern European goal (Romania, Yugoslavia, Poland), but certainly not a focus of the Soviets.

Incremental and institutional adjustments to the contractual procedure seem inadequate in fostering industrial integration, and, in fact, they would be disintegrating, given the autarchic orientation of the Soviet Union. Determination of the ways of using the TNCs in Eastern Europe requires an assessment of the success (or failures) of cooperation under the present rules in achieving higher levels of integration and of the alternative approaches available to use their capabilities better.

## Cooperation under Present Rules

The present rules for cooperation in co-production arrangements and transfers of technology are based on contractual relationships. Both the Soviet Union and the Eastern European countries seek to determine, by contracts for specific projects, the type and degree of industrial integration between the East and the West and the distribution of benefits from each project. The contracts are not the same as joint ventures nor do they lead to the kind of integration that occurs under the ME-form of the TNCs. Rather than risk-taking being commensurate with ownership, risks are determined by contractual roles. Since these contracts are governed by national statutes of the Eastern countries, there is little room for maneuver on the part of the TNCs in terms of basic policies. Any company's negotiating ability must be focused on specific contractual provisions, with its ultimate weapon being that of rejecting an agreement. Given the fact that there are almost always other companies (U.S., European, Japanese, and some of the advanced LDCs) willing to negotiate an agreement, even this bargaining card is somewhat diminished.

Given the monopsonistic position of the Socialist agencies—reflected in their governmental control over entry and sales into their own markets—and given the fact that they have sovereign power, the ability of the TNCs to alter the basic nature of the arrangements is small.

However, this does not leave the companies without any negotiating power. On the contrary, they are able to offer entry into Western European markets, which is highly desired by the Eastern European countries, and the opportunities offered for alternative uses of capital and human resources mean that the Eastern European governments must make some accommodation to the desires of TNCs.

On the basic issue of the desired extent of East–West industrial integration, there seems still to be somewhat of a standoff. TNCs generally want to serve the host-country market and to find an entreé into the other members of the COMECON. Each of the Eastern European countries wants some degree of integration with the national markets of Western European countries. They are seeking neither to enhance integration *among* the members of the COMECON through such arrangements nor to encourage the integration of the COMECON and the Common Market. Rather, each of the Eastern European countries seems to wish to associate itself bilaterally with members of the European Community and the United States. Differences of degree exist among them, however. The USSR stands apart as being less interested in industrial integration than the rest: It plans more strictly, has its own large market, and gains much from ties in the COMECON, where it is usually in a deficit position in trade and uses surplus exports to reduce these debit positions. Hungary, Czechoslovakia, and East Germany are more closely tied to USSR industry than Poland, Romania, and Yugoslavia have been. Among these last, Poland has less industry and therefore less ability to mesh with Western activities, and its recent difficulties likely mean a reduction of Western ties, which in the 1970s were relatively significant. Romania and Yugoslavia have pulled themselves significantly out of COMECON constraints and have been more avid in seeking integration projects.

Presently, neither Western European governments nor the United States have formulated clear policies on East–West economic *integration* and are, therefore, not able to guide U.S. and European companies in their negotiations. Contrarily, they let the companies react to the initiatives or opportunities in the East and take no constraining position save on the flow of sophisticated technology, high-technology products, and the use of credits to finance socialist projects—all based on national-security interests.

This is not a positive policy of guiding the nature or extent of the contacts but simply one of limiting particular relationships, at the margin, and in some cases under an umbrella agreement. Since the initiative and final determination of the degrees of East–West integration are left to the Eastern countries, it would seem highly doubtful that the results redound significantly to the benefit of the West. But even if they are likely to, more careful analysis would be necessary to demonstrate that fact.

Under present policies, the USSR has pursued industrial non-integration, in which it has achieved a *controlled* application of Western technology within its economy, without letting that technology or the methods of transfer significantly affect the economic, social, or political life of the country. Commercial contacts are closely controlled, and imported technology is absorbed completely into the *Soviet* system, rather than opening the system to Western-style management or to wide business ties. Technology inflows cannot realistically be expected to pull the USSR toward the West in any significant form of industrial cooperation. The Western countries must decide whether this result is acceptable, for they are strengthening East–West separation.

A strong case can be made that Soviet intentions are not only to absorb Western technology into its system to strengthen it but also to use Western technology to achieve greater dominance over the Eastern European countries by moving its own industry into the higher-technology sectors, while keeping the others in lower-technology sectors. The USSR also appears to want the same type of dominance over other, supposedly nonaligned, nations. If this is Soviet policy, and if it is implemented successfully, the West will have contributed to its own declining influence.

The analysis leading to this result relates to the objectives of the Soviets in seeking cost-reducing technologies and access to Western markets. The Soviets recognize that they must find means of reducing costs of a variety of goods so as to satisfy their populace and to reduce the frustrations from continuing heavy military expenditures. In addition, if they are to pay for substantial imports of food and equipment, they must increase their exports, which can be done only through cost reductions or pressure on COMECON members; but the USSR remains a net debtor to the region. It is, therefore, seeking technologies and plants that will increase productivity quickly and significantly. Turn-key plants are a high priority, from which the Soviets will learn not only the construction of the plants but also the built-in technologies. They will also obtain training of their personnel, who can train other Soviet engineers and production workers; and subsequent plants will require no outside help. Their emphasis on technology imports results from the Soviet view that their industrial failures to date have been a result of poor technology rather than related to motivation or organization.

The Soviets are also seeking access to markets not only to pay for imports but also to achieve economies of scale through expanding production beyond that needed for the domestic market. Market access, then, becomes another technique in cost reduction. An inflow of management and technology, as well as equipment, is necessary in order to achieve productivity goals in the Socialist countries, so limited industrial cooperation is promoted, but behind a wall of protection. This protection extends not only to the flow of consumer and semifinished goods but also to the import of capital and equipment, to the selection of technologies, and to communications between foreign supplier and user firms in the USSR, although this last barrier is being reduced somewhat. Despite the need for a wide range of technologies, the determination of what technologies, goods, or capital should flow into the Soviet and Eastern European economies is not left to many market criteria or to negotiations between socialist firms and Western TNCs. Only a few Eastern European governments permit their companies to enter directly into international business negotiations (notably, Hungary).

Economic *competition* within the bloc has been restricted for the purpose of strengthening the USSR's economic base. Western technology then helps the USSR to challenge the West, both politically and militarily, in the nonaligned countries. To continue to play this game by *Soviet rules* is to strengthen their position relative to the West's.

Counterposed against this view of the USSR's increasing strength and capability are a series of doubts as to whether its efforts could succeed even if this were the Soviet objective. Are the Soviets so knowledgeable and flexible that they can, in fact, restructure their system to use technological changes efficiently and meet the varied and changing demands on world markets? The Soviet themselves apparently do not think that they are all that capable, because they (and the Eastern European countries) insist on *controlled* access into Western and LDC markets in a number of instances. Only in a few lines have they shown themselves capable of meeting Western products in European or LDC markets on a competitive (unsubsidized?) basis. Their economic planning system seems slow in adjusting to complex changes in technology and markets, which often leave them behind with obsolete plant and processes. Also, they tend to replicate Western technologies rather than use the know-how to make their own advances in commercial products. These inadequacies are reinforced by the state monopolies in trade, which tend to rely on bilateral trade arrangements to close out competition. It is conceivable, therefore, the Soviets have little knowledge of precisely what they need now commercially or will need in the future to achieve objectives of (economic and political) domination which they are presumed to have.

Deficiencies in the Soviet planning system indicate that they are not as able as Japan was to adopt and adapt Western technologies. If they can, they may be able to use Western technology to defeat the West; if they cannot, they will merely have paid for progressively obsolescent systems. At present, it seems that substantial changes would be required in the Soviet system to utilize effectively the technologies that they are seeking. Western cooperation could, of course, be a very strong catalyst for growth and innovation in the socialist countries, but it will be severely limited by socialist planning rigidities and decision-making, which still give priority to national-defense industries and capital-equipment sectors.

To assess more specifically what is happening in the present pattern of industrial cooperation, we may look at some of the contractual arrangements between the East and the West, noting the reliance on different business forms in the West.

*Turn-key Projects*

The Soviet Union has bought large turn-key projects as a fast route to industrial development, but Eastern European countries have relied mainly on other contractual arrangements. Such projects are available principally to Soviet Russia, which is itself large and wealthy compared to the Eastern European countries. These latter face a lack of foreign exchange and have small domestic markets. They are not able to expand these markets significantly by penetrating other East European markets or the Soviet Union in the more advanced technology sectors because the Soviet Union seeks to develop this capacity itself. If the East European countries tried to commit substantial resources to specific (high-technology) sectors to achieve higher levels of productivity and competitiveness, they would be required to specialize even more than they do now and, thereby, (in their view) become still more dependent on either the USSR for industrial products or markets or on the West, where the TNCs dominate. The TNCs not only have the technologies and product lines sought by the Eastern European countries, but they control substantial access to Western markets.

The push of the Soviets for dominance in high-technology sectors and their reliance on turn-key projects increases the role of the larger TNCs in East–West cooperation. The medium- and small-sized companies are not able to sustain the kinds of project risks that characterize such large-scale operations. Even some of the largest companies have formed consortia in order to undertake (or have backed away from) some of the sizeable projects offered by the Soviets.

The nature of these turn-key projects is such that they provide for very little integration of Eastern and Western Europe. They are principally for the domestic market in the Soviet Union plus export to COMECON countries, and there is little continuing relationship at either the technological or managerial levels with Western suppliers. They provide little opportunity, therefore, for the use of TNC capabilities in international integration. Rather, they are a technique of competitive duplication of Western industrial facilities.

*Co-production Projects*

Co-production involves a specialization by each partner in the East and the West in the production of certain parts of a final product (assembled later by one of the partners or both) or in the production of certain items of the product line which are then exchanged among the partners. Technology flows from the West to the East, and marketing is done by the Western partner for the joint products that are to be sold in the Western markets. Co-production arrangements have in a few instances become fairly complex, involving in one instance as many as four countries (Germany, Australia, Hungary, and Czechoslovakia). Co-production has also been used in R&D activities: in at least one case, a wide range of R&D results and documentation was exchanged between the two partners.

There are many successful examples, beginning with the Fiat agreement to set up a complete auto plant in the USSR. Not all such negotiations have been successful, however. In the late 1970s, General Motors (GM) negotiated with Poland to produce (20,000) truck vans jointly, with a substantial number of them to be marketed in Western Europe through GM outlets. Polish industry was to gain an increase in employment, a wider range of products at reduced costs and larger economies of scale through sales into the export market, as well as some foreign exchange. The advantage to GM would have been a supply in Western Europe of a model (under its own name) that it would otherwise not have had available in that market since its size fit a niche not produced by GM in Europe. For undisclosed reasons, the agreement was not finalized.

Such co-production arrangements do provide a degree of integration, but the greater gain would seem to go to the host country in the generation of new products out of imported technology, employing local labor. Where this is the case, the operation is similar to that of a market-seeker with the Western TNC owning a small minority share in the affiliate. Where the production of the affiliate is largely exported back into Western Europe or into markets in LDCs served by the TNC, the arrangement is similar to a manufactoring contract (or a branch plant in the definitions of chapter 4), which provides a type of integration, controlled almost wholly by the TNC.

*Joint Ventures*

So-called joint ventures in Eastern Europe are quite different from those among Western countries. They do, to different degrees, involve comanagement, coownership of capital, and some sharing of profit and risks. But the regulations under which they are formed in the three countries that have permitted them—Yugoslavia, Romania, and Hungary—make them virtually contractual agreements. These joint arrangements sometimes are restricted to marketing only, sometimes involve production, marketing, and R&D activities, and sometimes are a simple joint-tendering for a construction, infrastructure, or extractive project.

Still, they are a significant step toward integration between the East and the West and merit careful assessment as a means of increased cooperation. Yugoslavia has the most developed program, and though Romania and Hungary have shown a desire to move toward its more liberal approach, it is used here for analytical purposes.[4]

The analysis shows that the Yugoslavian joint venture faces seven major problems: (1) the difficulty of integrating any joint venture into the worldwide operations of the TNC, leaving it with a sales orientation to the local market or as component supplier to the TNC; (2) the degree of profitability; (3) a reluctance to transfer sophisticated or secret technology to such a joint venture; (4) the difficulty of termination; (5) an implicit export requirement; (6) differences in management systems; and (7) a desire on the part of the foreigner not to create a new competitor.

**Characteristics.** The requirement that arrangements with TNCs be joint-ventures, with majority ownership held by the socialist owners of the Yugoslav, Romanian, or Hungarian enterprise, means that formation of ME-type activities is basically foreclosed. Since foreign ownership in the extractive or import activities into Yugoslavia is prohibited, only two forms of association remain: the branch plant and the market-seeker. Both will readily permit joint-venture relationships, but their market orientations are quite different. The former is essentially for export back to the parent or its affiliates and the latter is for sales within the host-country market. Although both can encompass joint ventures, trade-offs in each are necessitated by the formation of the joint ventures. That is, less is gained by both the joint-venture partner and the host country compared with 100 percent ownership by the TNC. These losses must be set against the advantage to the host country of participation by local partners.

Similarly, the requirement that management be predominantly reserved for host-country nationals means that the exposure to foreign management techniques, which might permit cost reduction and greater exports, is significantly reduced. This is not to say that the foreign techniques are better, and certainly not *best,* but local management skills can be sharpened by exposure to those employed by others.

For capital-short countries, the insistence on joint ventures means that there is less foreign capital made available to the country. Where initial capital funds are available locally, the host country tilts frequently in favor of joint ventures rather than wholly owned foreign affiliates. But the fact that the two partners have to put up additional capital for expansion means that the further growth of the company is dependent on the capital available to the local partner (usually that earned in the venture) whereas the TNC usually has sufficient capital to expand at whatever rate it wishes. TNCs

TNCs face competing requirements for their capital, and they would prefer to place it where they have more than a minority position.

In the case of the branch plant, joint ventures are sometimes acceptable, even though it may be necessary to produce components or products in strict conformity with plans and procedures determined by the TNC. Obviously, the TNC is not going to buy components that do not meet its standards, and it will require production according to schedules meeting its needs. The local partner *can* profit from this arrangement, which is essentially a manufacturing contract in which the total output is purchased by one company. If the affiliate is majority-owned by a local majority partner, ancillary contracts concerning production and technology will permit control by the TNC. Since the sales of this entity are guaranteed and prices are agreed to beforehand, there are few surprises for the local partner.

The frequently expressed view that the joint venture is the obvious way in which foreign decision-making can be prevented and a sense of partnership created does not hold for the branch-plant form. Even if the branch plant were owned 100 percent by *local* capital and managed by locals, it would not remove the domination of the foreign company in the venture, although the local management and labor would learn techniques that could assist their growth in other ventures.

The joint venture can be much more of a cooperative enterprise under the market-seeker form of TNC; the foreign partner does not necessarily have to have control over the product, its quality, prices, markets, and so on. On the contrary, the local partner may have much more capability in some of these matters than the foreigner and can contribute to successful national marketing without significantly interfering in international activities of the TNC.

Of principal interest to any TNC looking at Yugoslavia is whether or not there is an ability to serve the Yugoslav market—import substitution—and potentially enter the COMECON through Yugoslavia. But, the regional market is cut off by the necessity to export there (as elsewhere) only for *valuta* or foreign exchange; therefore, only the Yugoslav market beckons. To get a foreign investor to enter a joint venture to serve the Yugoslav market requires some special inducement. The advantages to Yugoslavia of such inward investment are clear, but the attractions to a TNC are either a market in Yugoslavia or a source of low-cost production there (similar to a branch plant). While other countries are offering incentives to foreign investors, Yugoslavia has simply removed some old impediments. But the removal of impediments to imports of components, or to the repatriation of capital, merely reduces the disadvantages that Yugoslavia faces compared to locations in Western European or some developing countries.

**Profitability.** One of the key aspects of any foreign investment policy is whether or not a (satisfactory) profit can be expected from the operation, which does not mean that *maximum* profits have to be obtainable. Yugoslavia allows a profit, but it is controlled by cost data and price limits for a foreign investor. However, the level of profits that is deemed satisfactory will depend on the alternative opportunities that the investing company sees around the world. These opportunities are judged not solely in the short run but also over a longer period, permitting the conditions of the investment to change. Therefore, the most critical elements are the stability of the government, the certainty or credibility of its promises, and the likelihood that the underlying economic and social conditions will remain substantially the same. These were favorable to Yugoslavia until Tito's death and do not appear significantly adverse since then.

In assessing profitability, many other factors than market demand, prices, and costs are taken into account. Among these factors are the conditions under which joint-venture arrangements can be determined. Yugoslavia relaxed these conditions in 1980, but they still must meet stipulated requirements. If it is difficult to terminate an arrangement profitably, then there will be a strong desire for a fast pay back of the capital contributions by the foreigner. If it appears that the operation may be lost through expropriation, nationalization, forced sale, or simply a narrow market at the time of potential sale or termination, the foreign investor will want to recoup his capital and reasonable profit as soon as possible (within three to five years). The lack of a clear procedure for termination of joint ventures—other than abrogation of the contract by either party—will cause a reassessment of the opportunity by foreigners, making them more conservative in their estimates by profitability.

**Transfer of Technology.** Compared with 100 percent ownership, a joint venture loses some transfer of technology, some transfer of management skills, some capital contributions from abroad, and some advances in the product line, which the foreign partner might like to make but which the local partner will not accept. The first of these losses is potentially the most serious, though the others are frequently also significant. Whether they outweigh the gains of local participation is a matter for the government to decide. However, the decision will best be made for each situation rather than through an inviolable rule, such as the one Yugoslavia has applied.

No foreign investor will turn over his complete technology or the research behind it to a joint-venture partner (especially one who holds a majority ownership) to permit it to be used at the volition of the partner. Under minority- or majority-owned joint ventures, the transferor will generally carefully negotiate and restrict the technology to be supplied over the life of the partnership. The transfer of technology from a foreign investor will be freer and fuller if he owns a majority (even more if he holds 100 percent). No written contract can substitute for the freer exchange that occurs under majority or full ownership by the company transferring the technology. Technology transfers are not simply through specifications, manuals, equipment, production layout, and so on, but are much more importantly through a free movement of individuals seeking to teach and learn not only present technologies but future product and process changes.

A TNC will not want to lose any control over the use of this technology—either its application in production, its resale, or use in products sold to competitors. Technology is often too precious to permit its control by any but those directly responsible to the TNC. Therefore, insistence on joint ventures precludes in some instances the creation of high-technology branch plants. Or the parent may be unable to accept an interruption in production scheduling that might occur from the operations being under the control of local management. Thus government requirements for joint ventures with locals have persuaded many foreign investors that they should not set up high-technology projects in countries imposing them.

**Termination.** Since the Yugoslav joint venture is both an equity-capital venture and a contractual venture, termination is rather difficult. Although the Yugoslavian joint venture seems to provide the necessary property rights in the investment process, it lacks a free ability to sell the portion owned by the foreigner. Formerly it was not possible to sell off the equity without negotiating the termination of the contract, and it was not possible to negotiate termination of the contract without selling off the equity. Although newer regulations permit more ready sale, there are few opportunities for selling equity in the Yugoslav economy, and contract termination obviously involves potential losses.

To take care of the termination problem, some of the contracts in Yugoslavia have stipulated that they will endure for a specific period of years. This is certainly feasible with a manufacturing—contract relationship, but this is hardly a joint venture. Where such a contract termination is written in beforehand, the TNC, of course, expects prior repayment of its capital plus profit so that it can abandon the activity within the termination period. A variety of clauses have been written into contracts as reasons for early termination of the contract, but such arrangements are bound to make the partnership less permanent in the minds of both parties, altering their operating decisions and permitting only partial integration.

A related problem concerns the rights of the foreign investor to specific assets. For example, does the foreign partner have the right to reclaim equipment sent into Yugoslavia? technology? contributed capital? unpaid dividends? Or is the TNC permitted only to return the cash value of the assets contributed? The TNC partner presently can offer to sell its interest to the local partner, who has first refusal; it may then offer it to a third party and, if there are no takers, seek to terminate. If termination occurs, in all likelihood some of the physical assets might be returned, but this is not clear under the regulations. Some of the contracts stipulate that know-how shall be returned to the foreign supplier of the technology, while others permit the Yugoslav company to continue to use it. It is not clear what rights the foreigner would have if the contract read that the Yugoslav company could not use the know-how but in fact did so after termination.

**Export Requirement.** Yugoslav policy includes the virtual requirement that the joint venture export for the purpose of generating proceeds of foreign exchange out of which to repay the foreign partner. The foreign partner is not permitted to be paid either his earnings or his capital unless the partnership generates sufficient foreign exchange. Though there are no restrictions on the transfer of profit in local currency (*dinars*), this is hardly an attraction to the foreign investor, for without permission to transfer these earnings he can do virtually nothing with them except to reinvest in Yugoslavia. Any agreement is, of course, concluded under an expectation that foreign exchange will be earned, simply because no foreign investment contract that does not provide for exports will be approved by the authorities. However, it is not clear that there will be *sufficient* foreign exchange earnings to meet dividend remittances. Where such risks exists, the foreign partner will be even more intent on obtaining a substantial payout of his capital through prices for components or other inputs sold to the joint venture relatively higher than what he pays for items he imports from the venture. But such sales from the West often depend on an adequate level of export earnings, and materials inputs are for *all* production while exports are only a portion of total output; thus an imbalance often arises. The two claimants—imports and remittances of profits—can readily exceed total export earnings.

When exports are required by the venture, the resulting relationship will be closer to the branch plant form since it is a mixture of local-market orientation plus export. Whether the exports are similar to a branch plant or a manufacturing contract depends on who received the exports or is responsible for their sale—the foreign partner or the venture. If the foreigner is responsible, this results in a type of dependence on the part of the Yugoslav joint venture. The effort to achieve independence through increased exports produces just the opposite result. A type of interdependence results that may not have been sought by either party.

Similar questions of availability of funds arise in the repatriation of capital upon termination. Given the fact that guarantees of repatriation of capital and earnings are limited by the volume of earnings of foreign exchange and by the possibility of nationalization (which would abrogate the guarantee or repatriation) the foreign investor is not certain that his interests are adequately protected. Rather, all that the guarantees include is that if there are funds after termination, and if the joint venture has enough foreign exchange remaining, and further if the Yugoslavian government has not nationalized the assets or the company, then the foreign investor will get a return of capital and earnings on termination. Obviously, the investor might also get a return of capital and of earnings prior to termination, depending on the contractual provisions agreed upon and the availability of foreign currency to the joint venture. Contractual agreement is also necessary as to the splitting of the burden in case of devaluation of the dinar.

**Management Systems.** A further obstacle to the substantial expansion of West European integration with Yugoslavia through TNCs is that of the management system, which has three elements: (1) the management of the Yugoslav company which is a partner, (2) the management of the foreign company, and (3) the joint operations board (JOB), through which agreements have to go to the general manager, who in turn is partly subordinate to the worker's council of the joint venture. An attempt merely to describe the responsibilities, authorities, and functions of each of these would indicate the complexity of the arrangement. Although contractual agreements can modify and specify these arrangements, their negotiation adds to the likelihood of disagreements. This is not to say that complex management arrangements cannot be worked out, but it is less likely that TNCs will be willing to invest substantial amounts of money, expanding the size of the Yugoslav venture, where such complexities in management decision-making exist.

**Avoiding Competition.** A final obstacle is the desire of TNCs to avoid competition between the products exported by the joint venture enterprise and those of the Western affiliates of the foreign partner. This concern leads to contractual agreements that fill gaps and limit the market areas where the Yugoslav company can export. Although such agreements exist in many licensing contracts in Western countries, they are not necessary in affiliates wholly or majority-owned by the TNC. These provisions ensure a limited scope for exports of the enterprise and its predominant orientation to the national market, restricting also potentially integrating imports.

In sum, given the joint-venture constraints on foreign investment into Yugoslavia and the nature of other investment opportunities around the world, it appears that the government has reduced its chances of integrating with Western and worldwide markets. Whether or not the form of ownership and control is more important than the growth possibilities is a matter for governmental policy determination; but, equally, the TNCs are able to decide the way in which they will react. Tax and other incentives may ameliorate some of the disadvantages, but they are unlikely to offset the fundamental requirements of Eastern European countries as to the nature and form of organization and control, which limit market opportunities and reduce means of achieving least-cost operations.

Though the joint-venture (contractual) approach meets some of the needs of Eastern Europe, it is *not* a significant step toward an industrial integration that would produce substantial economies of scale and efficiency in specialization. It also limits integration to bilateral ties—or at least puts it on a *per country* basis from the side of Eastern Europe—rejecting the major contributions of the ME-form, which would bring a greater degree of integration through continuing flows of technology, managerial and marketing skills, and even capital. The ME-form is the one most capable of producing high levels of industrial integration, but it has not yet been permitted to function between the East and the West.

East European countries do assert that the region should not be closed, and that integration between the COMECON countries and the West is both necessary and desirable for growth in Eastern Europe and to buttress COMECON integration. Several socialist economists have asserted that both imports and exports need to be expanded with the West (they assert) to gain efficiency, better-quality products, raise living standards, reduce dependence on only Soviet goods, and provide a greater variety of products for COMECON exchange. Pursuit of new solutions to mutual international specialization and cooperation in production between East and West, plus flexible trading methods, are also seen as necessary by socialist officials. If the COMECON countries do desire industrial integration, they can have it more readily with participation of the ME-type company than with any other. Also, as with OECD integration, the ME can be guided into arrangements that provide for both efficiency and the desired sharing of benefits.

## The ME in COMECON Integration

As indicated earlier, industrial integration can occur among the Eastern European countries themselves, between Eastern and Western Europe, or between Eastern Europe and Third World countries. It is not clear that the COMECON countries are seriously interested in integration within Eastern Europe, although they continue to assert that it is their objective. If it is, they could draw on the capabilities of the MEs to achieve that goal.

The members of the COMECON assert that economic integration

*among* them is necessary in order to achieve further economic progress, since none of the smaller countries are large enough to achieve economies of scale. It is apparently now recognized in socialist circles that in order to support long-term economic plans, long-term specialization agreements in particular fields will be necessary among COMECON countries, and these specialization agreements cannot become rigid. There must be a degree of flexibility, it is argued, with wide margins of tolerance in terms of product changes and prices, so as to permit innovations to take place. But the development of cooperation in production is recognized as a particularly delicate problem. One of the basic problems in allocation of production is seen as the harmonization of prices among products within a particular industry or between components and final products. The differences in national price levels, untied to world market prices, make it difficult to achieve cooperation based on specialization. Real (world-market) prices will be necessary also if the COMECON countries are to be able to increase their share in world trade, as they desire.

It is clearly in the minds of some analysts that integration within the COMECON is part and parcel of integration between the East and the West, and solutions to integration in one would facilitate solutions in the other. Some of the basic problems standing in the way of integration *within* the COMECON and between it and the West are resolvable through the TNCs. The ME-form is capable of conducting operations in several locations within the COMECON countries and adjusting its trade patterns so as to provide some acceptable distribution of the benefits, transfer appropriate technology, and privide economies of scale through specialization that would permit it to match world-market prices and thereby ensure not only greater consumer satisfaction within the COMECON but also to make exports possible. The rigidities of the five-year plans would probably force some uneconomic and inefficient activities, which would become a reason for wider integration with the West. But, of course, such an opening is dangerous from the standpoints of external payments and internal economic control.

Western MEs would soon form close cooperation between COMECON operations and subsidiaries or parents in Europe and Japan (maybe even in the United States). To attempt to use the ME in this way, however, presupposes that the United States and its Western allies have made a policy determination that integration is a desirable objective, and of course that the USSR would be willing for its satellites to expand contacts in this market, and accept resulting interdependence. But such an integration is not inherently in the interests of the West, which can find ample trade and investment-ties in nonsocialist countries. The decision is more political than economic.

## Alternative Approaches

There are at least three different orientations that underlie policy proposals toward cooperative arrangements between East and West. First, such arrangements have been viewed as economically advantageous to the West even on terms dictated more or less by the socialist countries. Conversely, they have been seen as part of a grand Soviet design to exploit the West and to subjugate it economically, with the Soviets insisting on the games being played only by its rules. Third, cooperative arrangements have been said to be advantageous to the West, politically and economically, only if the Eastern countries were drawn into the Western orbit, thereby requiring a restructuring of the rules so that economic ties bind the Eastern economies fairly tightly to Western opportunities and growth.

Each of these alternatives leads to rather different results and therefore a different structure for world industry. The first approach would leave TNCs to negotiate the best deals they could with the socialist countries, essentially under the rules dictated by those countries. It would permit a continuation of monopsony advantages to the socialists vis-à-vis Western companies and would enhance the Soviet's capability of setting the rules for all East bloc countries. If this is the approach accepted, the Soviets gain additional influence over Eastern European countries, since few inhibitions have been shown by Western TNCs in dealing directly with the USSR and under its rules. The Eastern countries would likely be required to follow the Soviet lead rather than to make accommodations with the West. This identification of rules between the USSR and the Eastern European countries would increase the ties within COMECON, magnify the control that the USSR exercises there already, and potentially increase its influence with LDCs to trade in the same (controlled) manner with the West. Expanding this pattern would demonstrate the superiority of socialism over capitalism, which would be seen as begging for foreign markets—just as the Marxists have asserted.

The second approach, based on an assumed Soviet grand design of subjugation, would be evidenced by the USSR's preventing the Eastern European countries from adopting independent rules and requiring its approval in all negotiations with Western TNCs. This view rests on the belief that the Soviets are still trying to bury capitalism economically and that the USSR seeks a chance to disrupt world markets and to relocate industrial activity and trade patterns to its advantage. If this is its purpose and its capability, the best Western response is to seek to reduce substantially the level of economic cooperation, but Western Europe is highly unlikely to adopt such an approach. If it did, the result would be a separation of major world powers and a greater reduced level of interchange between Eastern and

Western Europe. This, of course, is a singular potential disadvantage of the creation of spheres of influence discussed in chapter 4.

The third approach redefines the present rules of cooperation so as to achieve greater East–West industrial and economic integration. This approach starts from a Western position of no fear of the economies of the USSR or Eastern Europe and seeks to persuade them to play by rules that are *mutually* beneficial to all parties. The assumptions of this approach include the view that it is possible to alter the policies of the Eastern European countries if the advantages of greater cooperation are demonstrated and if there are means of ascertaining that the distribution of the benefits is both discernible and acceptable.

U.S. policy has not been clearly moving along any one of these three approaches, nor is it evident that each has been considered and rejected. It has instead merely sought to prevent certain types of activities that were deemed threatening to U.S. national interests and to let the growth of contacts occur at the desire of the socialist countries, who have invited Western companies to respond to particular opportunities offered. The hope, undoubtedly, was that the attraction of markets in the West would gradually pull the Eastern European countries into Western modes, but the fact has been substantially the reverse. That is, Western companies have accommodated themselves more to the Soviet system than have the Soviet planners to the modes of operation of Western TNCs. Also, Eastern European countries have been caught between, unable to cut ties in the COMECON or to form strong ones with TNCs. This is hardly a picture of integration and certainly not one of interdependence.

A more positive policy on the part of the West would begin with a determination of the type of interdependence that we thought desirable—aimed at enhancing economic advantages for both sides—taking security interests into account. Within this policy, it should be determined whether the desired degree of interdependence would be achieved by stages (either sectorally or regionally) with specific industrial sectors chosen as test cases for new integration policies or specific countries (Poland? Romania?) selected as tests of interdependence.

The objectives of such a policy orientation would be to open the Eastern economies more to Western modes of operation and at the same time open the Western markets to Eastern European products. Given the planning orientation of the Eastern countries, prior determinations would have to be made of what industrial activities in the Soviet Union and Eastern Europe would be relied upon in the integration process. Similarly, in order to expand the market access of Western companies in the Eastern European economies, early discussion of the expected trade patterns would have to be undertaken before agreement could be reached on specific integration arrangements.

Both of these moves argue for a cooperative determination by OECD countries of their industrial policies and the ways in which TNCs can be brought into play both intra-OECD and between it and the COMECON. Within such policies, there would be a strengthening of the exchanges of technology (mostly toward the East, but also two-way) and increasing contacts among company officials on both sides. Once such cooperation succeeds, joint efforts could then be more readily mounted between Eastern and Western countries *in* the developing countries so as to accelerate the latter's growth and productivity. These packages of multination, joint-factor transfers could reduce LDC demands for *unbundling* of the factors of production, since they would arrive untainted (politically) by coming from a single national source and combining socialist with capitalist origins.

The strength of the Western countries in mounting a policy of closer interdependence and industrial integration lies in the ability of the TNCs to adapt to different situations (provided the same rules apply to all players), their continued dedication to innovation, and their emphasis on quality control. By raising quality and performance standards of their products, the USSR and Eastern Europe would improve their prospects for sales in Western markets.

The major obstacle is Soviet Russia, which does not understand that neither the United States nor Europe seek military solutions or have imperialist objectives; nor does it understand the benefits that 200 years of peace could bring to the evolution of mankind. If it could reduce military tensions, it might also see the advantage of tying itself closer to Western private institutions and markets, though such a move risks some upsets to the planned systems under which Eastern countries now operate. Undoubtedly, these countries are torn between wanting the advantages of innovation and flexibility and the desire to increase certainty and stability within their countries. But the trade-offs in increasing industrial integration need not be as hazardous as they have seemed in the past. Given the USSR's existing sphere of influence in Eastern Europe (save for Yugoslavia), no significant moves to integration with the West will be made without its permission; even then Eastern European leaders will probably move carefully so as not to cause a reversal. But what would make the USSR change its views? Maybe nothing on the horizon. In this case the future holds no significant East–West integration; rather, a stronger push by Soviet Russia is likely toward widening its economic and (political) sphere into South Asia and the Middle East.

But if Eastern and Western European integration could be part of a package of greater, more effective COMECON integration at the same time, some progress could be made toward East–West integration also since it could be *designed* to enhance the benefits of COMECON integration, through providing new inputs, components, techniques, raising productivity, reducing costs, and improving quality. For example, Polish metal-working equipment sold to the USSR could be improved by joint steel ventures between Poland and West Germany, which could hardly threaten Soviet interests. Also, wider markets for Czech products in Western Europe would cut costs to all COMECON members and help set more realistic prices to guide resource allocations better under the national plans.

The United States and Western European countries could take an initiative to design and explain such cooperation. Yugoslavia, Romania, and Poland are slowly realizing that the basic laws and regulations dealing with foreign investment into their countries are inadequate to stimulate the types of cooperative arrangements sought. If they could be shown that even more advantageous arrangements would be available with some policy changes but *without* serious modification of their policy *objectives,* a constructive dialogue could begin as the means to achieve closer integration. Without such an effort, continued separation appears inevitable.

## Notes

1. United Nations Economic Commission for Europe, *Analytical Report on Industrial Cooperation Among ECE Countries.* Geneva, 1973 (E.73.2.E.11) pp. 30*ff.*

2. *Ibid.,* pp. 30*ff.*

3. *Ibid.,* p. 40.

4. Even if, by the time of publication or reading, the Yugoslav policies *have been* changed, the analysis here is useful in that other countries will face decisions on similar orientations. The lack of appropriate policies for joint ventures was assessed similarly by Z. Karasznai and M. Laki, "Conditions and Possibilities of Cooperation in Production and Trade with Western Firms in Hungary." *Acta Oeconomica* 29 (1-2), 1982, pp. 149–166.

# 8

# North–South Industrial Redeployment and Interdependence

The developing countries, which are predominantly in the Southern Hemisphere, have called for an international restructuring of industry. Despite initial rejection of the idea, speeches by government and corporate officials in advanced Northern countries have referred positively to the concept. The fundamental questions are: What would a restructuring look like? How will it be achieved? What is necessary to make it acceptable?

Restructuring implies several potential changes: (1) a shift in the proportion of industry located in developing countries; (2) a redeployment of industry from advanced (ACs) to developing countries (LDCs) but serving AC markets through a new structure of integration; (3) a shift in the composition of industry within LDCs to higher technology sectors; and (4) a balancing of industrial development within LDCs (or among them) to reduce dependence on AC industry and create greater industrial integration within or among LDCs. It is not clear from most of the policy utterances which of these is sought. The first three are examined in this chapter and the fourth in the subsequent chapter—all from the standpoint of the potential role of the TNCs.

TNCs will remain a significant part of the institutional framework (despite the wishes of some critics) and they will be important contributors to industrialization in the world economy. Several questions are addressed as to their roles: What criteria will be used in determining acceptable roles for these companies? What market orientations will exist in LDC industrialization? What contributions can the TNCs make to North–South and South–South integration? Also, what policies would elicit the best use of the TNCs in achieving the types of integration desired?

## Decision Criteria on Integration

Economic integration—which involves determination of what types of industry are located where, what trade patterns will develop as a result, and what distribution of benefits occurs—raises one-sided problems of adjustment when applied to North–South relations. Industries in the North will bear nearly all the adjustments initially. LDC insistence that the present

169

location (deployment) of industry between the North and the South is unacceptable, therefore, challenges established interests in the North and the basis for location of industry there. LDCs have stated that the mechanism of the free market and long-standing comparative advantages are not acceptable as the means of determining where industry will be located and who trades what with whom. (They previously rejected the colonial decision-criteria, under which the metropolitan country determined the scope of industrial activity in the colony and the nature and direction of trade.) Further, they will not permit the TNCs to make these decisions for them. Governments and local interests in LDCs are to be the decision-makers, but they, in fact, need TNCs to implement policies of industrial integration.

One of the difficulties of determining the present role of the TNCs is that they are seen by LDCs as tools or at least representatives of foreign powers, who are seen as eager to retain an exploitative relationship. Although the TNCs do not generally carry the flag for their governments (though they are sometimes induced or forced to in specific situations), they remain suspect in the eyes of the developing countries. One of the reasons is that the decision-criteria of the foreign-owned affiliates are importantly oriented toward the goals of the parent company, which is located in an advanced country.

What are the decision-criteria by which such investment occurs? There are several different sets of criteria, depending on the group or agencies that have an input into the decision. The four groups having a part in many of the decisions on private direct investment include the parent company itself, financial institutions, government (home and host), and the private sector in the host country. The criteria of acceptability held by each are different from those of the others, requiring direct or indirect negotiations to achieve an acceptable accommodation of interests. Each seeks to maximize its benefits (including protection of its assets) and minimize its costs, within constraints set by law or custom.

The TNCs employ decision criteria that include the following: a degree of political and economic stability in the host country, a high level of certainty in governmental agreements or contracts, a sufficient market size, an adequate labor force, a cooperative government, and an opportunity to return some of the earnings back to the parent. All of these are necessary for an acceptable expectation by the TNC as to return on investment. They are also often prerequisites for a host country to be able to compete successfully for the resources of the TNC against its opportunities elsewhere in the world.

The criteria financial institutions apply to lending to TNCs for their investment abroad also include those of economic and political stability in the host country, as first-cut evidence of credit worthiness of the recipient country and therefore of its ability to repay. But some of the international financial agencies are funding infrastructure projects on terms that do not bear so heavily on the recipient's balance of payments. The debt-service criteria of these institutions then relate more to the viability of the project itself and its usefulness in the overall program of industrialization of development than to balance of payment contributions. Since these institutions are frequently concerned with building appropriate infrastructure for industry, they affect the location of industrial activity any time they choose to support a project in one industrial sector rather than another or in one country over another.

The criteria employed by LDC governments relate to their own concept of industrial development, but few of them have established a set of industrial policies out of which to guide the development of specific industries. On the contrary, they have frequently sought investment in key sectors—steel, auto, chemicals, airlines—so as to create poles of development, even if at high cost. Rather than seeking a specialized role in international industry, or even to build the domestic base for industrialization, many have focused on specific industries in order to build a superstructure even if the base for it is inadequate. In these cases, they have forced a pattern of industrialization that has not been the most attractive to foreign investors but has clearly altered the location of international production and the flow of trade.

The government of the headquarters company (the home government) also affects the location of international private investment through policies seeking to tie foreign countries into its economic influence. For example, we find that the French government promotes private foreign investment in French-speaking Africa; the Dutch in former colonies; the British in the former commonwealth; and even the Swedish government has its favorites. Over the postwar years, the U.S. government also has had a priority list of countries (based on political, economic, and military criteria) in which it wished to stimulate U.S. direct investment. Any such differential selection alters the location of industry *among* the developing countries as well as the relative positions of industry in the North and the South.

Finally, the private sector in the host country also has an interest in the reception of foreign private investment. It sometimes welcomes such investment, as a complement to its own efforts, as an investment outlet for local private funds (which find only sparse opportunities in local industry), and as a reduction of risks through joint ventures. Local industry sometimes, however, seeks to reject foreign investment in order to monopolize the opportunities in the host country for itself; at times, it seeks to force divestment of foreign ownership of industrial investment so as to be able to take over existing facilities and markets.

In the future, we can anticipate the continued application of multiple criteria in determining the acceptability of the location of specific industrial activities and their ownership and control of foreigners. These criteria shift with the growth of the country and the development of specific sectors. The criteria will be derived from the social, political, and economic goals sought by each of the interested groups, so that negotiations will involve multiple trade-offs among them.

The trade-offs will be determined by governments under the six criteria presented in chapter 4: efficiency (or effectiveness), equity, participation, creativity, stability, and autonomy. Even AC governments will apply them in determining the acceptability of any activities leading to greater North-South industrial integration and the role of the TNC therein. But neither AC nor LDC governments have yet set up decision procedures by which they can consciously make the necessary trade-offs among these.

The criterion of *effectiveness* relates to the use of resources available to the country and to problems of productivity and least cost—but not simply in a market sense. It includes the concept of what should be produced from the available resources: mass consumption goods; development of a complete transport system versus mere production of private autos; educational systems; military defense; and so on. This criterion is met by efficiency in achieving broad economic and social goals: a nebulous and shifting target.

The *equity* criterion relates to the host country's share of benefits and to the composition of its share. No longer is aid acceptable as a means of achieving equity. Rather, what is sought is an appropriate industrial base to serve all of the needs of progress through domestic production and export. If necessary, these are to be gained not simply by industrial growth in the South but also through redeployment of industry from North to South.

The criterion of *participation* means having an acceptable voice in the determination of both the size and composition of the country's share in international industrial growth and in formation of the rules of decision-making. The operations of the free market and the TNCs themselves are not seen by LDCs as providing them with an adequate voice and thereby have been rejected as the means for determining the nature and scope of industrial integration. The governments wish to have adequate ownership and control from within the country (by state or private entities) so that there is both the appearance and the fact of an active local role in decision-making, even if private nationals would not make the decisions the way the government desired!

Application of the criterion of *creativity* means to LDCs an ability to have a voice in the determination of the design of product and process technology. Developing countries will not accept continually being fed at the technological trough of the advanced countries. The idea that technology and R&D will be used to maintain technical dominance (for the sake of competition) between the North and the South will be wholly rejected by the latter, as soon as it is able to achieve a different relationship. These countries feel the same need to have pride in their culture and capabilities as any other peoples. In the industrial realm, self-respect is achieved through indigenous R&D activities.

Finally, LDCs seek *stability* and orderly international arrangements made under the above criteria, reducing international uncertainty. Yet they want a relatively high degree of continued *autonomy* so as to remain culturally diverse and distinct. They still will seek social and political nationalism, which requires (as they see it) a high degree of separation to facilitate the development of political modernization and progress toward national wealth and power. To buttress this autonomy, they seek new international law, which they help formulate and a rejection of political interference by TNCs themselves or by their home governments.

Any arrangement for greater North–South integration or restructuring must take these criteria into account, and the TNCs are capable of helping to meet many of them. To do so they will require some governmental guidance or encouragement since they are unlikely to pursue them without some persuasion, even if they would benefit thereby. Few institutions or governments like changing their behavior patterns or criteria of performance; they often have to be cajoled into doing things that they later recognize as having been beneficial.

## LDC Decisions on Industrialization and Integration

In order to determine the degree of integration between the North and the South and the precise roles that TNCs can or will play, a number of issues that have not been investigated carefully will require examination: alternative routes to industrialization; the problems of the mobile industries; and the adjustments that will be required in the advanced countries to industrialization in the developing countries. Out of such investigations would come a better appreciation of the role of the TNCs and the necessary adjustments that would have to be made to permit industrial change. The need to explore these issues gave rise in 1976 to Secretary Kissinger's call before the UN for creation of an International Industrialization Institute (in which both advanced and developing countries would participate) to examine these three problems. The need had been formally recognized earlier by a panel of international experts called by the (U.S.) National Academy of Engineering. Unfortunately, the proposal died, and no effort has been made to revive it, nor has the extensive research necessary been mounted in other fora.

Industrialization within the developing countries will require a process involving both separation from some of the existing ties to the advanced countries and creation of new ties. A major problem for the developing

countries is the selection of the industry sectors in which to permit or promote investment. A second problem is the provision of the infrastructure
necessary in LDCs to support the selected industries and the third is to ori-
ent industries toward appropriate markets (domestic, regional, or within the
advanced countries) and the use of appropriate technologies. In choosing
effectively among the alternatives available, an assessment of costs and
benefits is necessary, as well as a determination of the means through which
the benefits can be increased compared to the costs in each alternative.

*Selection of Industries*

Many developing countries have permitted industrialization to occur
through choices made by the investors themselves, based on free-market signals or company interests. Increasingly, governments have injected their
own criteria and decisions into the process. In some countries, entire industrial sectors have been reserved for governmental development, as in Mexico, Brazil, India, Venezuela, Nigeria, Indonesia, and others. In selected
sectors, the governments have established procedures for restricting entry or
guiding investment decisions.

Since the recognition of the success of the Japanese in the 1960s in
developing with governmental guidance, many LDC governments have
sought to follow the Japanese model, focusing on those sectors that were
previously supplied by imports. This import-substitution policy was aimed
at cutting off the drain on foreign exchange; it was used as a quick determination of those sectors in which there was a demand and for which local
supply was lacking. Under these criteria, TNC investment was attracted into
the developing countries when a market was large enough and sufficiently
protected. In the pre-World War II decades, the principal investors had
been engaged chiefly in the extractive sectors and infrastructure projects:
transportation and communication, port facilities, and public utilities.
Under the later import-substitution policies, a number of foreign companies
entered to serve national markets from local manufacturing facilities. But
import substitution frequently meant building capacity to serve a small
high-income market and often required larger inputs of capital goods and
materials to produce similar items.

More recently, developing countries have considered that they need to
expand the base of their domestic markets by serving the larger mass of consumers and also to increase their capabilities of supplying export markets.
The criteria for selection of industries to accomplish these goals are less
clear, since mass demand is not certain and demand abroad is served from
many competing sources. TNCs have been less eager to rush in to meet these
goals—which require low-cost products for domestic consumption and

high-quality items for export—because of political uncertainty, economic instability, uncertain quality, unstable schedules of delivery, high costs of production, and the existence of similar export capacities elsewhere. Although several companies have moved into developing countries for an export base, using low-cost labor, they have done so most frequently in order to supply captive markets for components within their own company (the branch plant form, noted in chapter 5). TNCs have seldom entered developing countries for the purpose of exporting *finished* products from them through their *worldwide* network, for the reasons noted. Although these conditions are improving in the more advanced of the developing countries, they remain as obstacles in most. Therefore, stimulation of industries for export remains a difficult problem for the developing countries.

Industrialization of developing countries has therefore tended to pull them away from the international economy (in some sectors) toward autarchy, rather than their using TNCs to help integrate with the advanced countries. As yet, there are no comprehensive policies in LDCs that would attempt to use the TNCs, and especially the ME-form, to achieve international or regional integration for the developing countries. Consequently, there is little cooperation between host countries and TNCs in the process of selection of industries to be developed. This lack is seen (if in nothing else) in the repeatedly changing rules imposed by governments on TNCs as to their entry, operations, and market orientations, and their eight-year effort to establish four international codes of behavior for TNCs through the UN, none of which will do anything to restructure LDC industrialization or integration.

### Infrastructure

The needs of the different sectors for diverse infrastructure facilities seem repeatedly to surprise governments, both in advanced and developing countries. Yet there is enough experience with the various industrial sectors to know the kinds of infrastructure required, and many companies carefully choose investment sites to make certain that appropriate infrastructure is available. Infrastructure needs range from transportation and communication facilities to public utilities and community facilities for families of workers and managers. They include a number of things in between, such as training and educational programs for all personnel.

Each industrial sector requires a different infrastructure, but only a few countries have attempted to mesh the infrastructure available with the selection of industries to be developed. Some have established industrial parks and then sought industries that would fit within them. Others have sought a particular type of industry and then tried to provide appropriate infrastructure. Others have simply left industry and host communities to struggle together. It would be better to study the capabilities of the economy, determine the types of infrastructure that can be created (with an assessment of alternative costs, tax bases, and other resources available), and match these with the kinds of industries that would best serve the markets under consideration.

The vast TNC experience with the types of infrastructure needed to support industrial activities could be drawn upon in the development of appropriate national infrastructures and government support of particular industrial sectors. Although some governments have used services of consulting firms in the development of supporting infrastructure and even in the selection of industrial sectors, they do not normally draw TNCs into the discussions of appropriate infrastructure for an industry sector, as part of a specific project.

*New Domestic Industry*

Two types of new industry have been selected to meet the demands in domestic markets in LDCs: those that produce native products, relying mainly on indigenous materials, and those that could substitute for existing imports. Where the objective has been to develop indigenous materials and products, both local and foreign investors as well as licensing of foreign technology to local companies have been attracted. Specific projects in this category range across all sectors of agriculture and industry. (Of course, some of these products are available for export.) TNCs are not likely to be helpful in handicraft sectors but TNCs would be interested in exporting to advanced-country markets tropical foods, forestry products, and materials for pharmaceuticals. Much research is yet to be done on tropical foods and drugs to demonstrate the extent to which many of the tropical flora are edible or useful for the production of pharmaceuticals. Some TNCs are engaged in this research and expect to establish production within the developing countries.

In the development of a new import-competitive industry (such as automobiles) the government needs to determine whether or not the market envisaged is wholly domestic, and if so, how it wishes it to be organized and controlled. For example, South Korea, embarking on the establishment of a domestic auto industry, faced the decision as to whether to (1) build a Korean-owned and controlled industry serving the Korean market alone under a monopoly position; (2) permit several local companies to arise in competition to serve the local market; or (3) permit foreign investors to establish operations, supplying major or minor parts from abroad. A

Korean-owned monopoly would obtain technology from a TNC, though it might be difficult to obtain the latest technology because of the potential buildup of a competitor. This may be perfectly acceptable to an LDC, but the alternatives of industrial development are limited thereby. Opening the industry to several competing national producers is likely to bring in the foreigner—either as a joint venture partner or licensor—but the contributions made by the TNCs will be limited, which shows up in the quality of the product and the service supplied to the market. TNC ownership and control of local operations would probably have cut costs initially but could have been delayed. In the event, Korea opted for the national market and a single national supplier: Hyundai. Later, two national entries were permitted, and South Korea is now exporting small volumes of its compact car to Europe and Latin America.

In the South Korean case, its decision to develop local facilities forced a relocation of industry from the former exporters to the host country, though no facilities were actually redeployed. Imports and foreign investment were prohibited, giving a monopoly to the local producers. (The government at one time tried to force a consolidation of vehicle manufacturing into one for cars and one for trucks, but the companies refused.)

When a foreign investor is brought in, he is usually offered a favored position, as under the agreement between Renault and Portugal in the late 1970s, guaranteeing 50 percent of the local market to the company, despite the existence of several other auto suppliers. Such a grant is offered to obtain greater benefits for the host country out of the TNC operations. Industrialization in this fashion relies on investment in local subsidiaries by market-seeking TNCs that will invest in a protected market fairly readily and do not expect to integrate these operations with the rest of the company, since they will be separated by high costs and sometimes different product design and standards. Yet the affiliate may constitute a market for components for a time, providing one-way integration.

*Redeployment*

In the process of industrial stimulation, there have arisen repeated cases of physical redeployment of industry—moving it *from* the advanced countries *into* the developing regions—under the aegis of the TNCs. Considerable discussion has occurred on this process, not only by the developing countries that are seeking new industry, but also in some of the advanced countries from which TNCs find it easier and less expensive to move industry to the foreign workers rather than try to import workers from the less-developed economies. With high unemployment, the problem of the guest worker is less manageable in many countries of Europe. But does the creation of adequate opportunities require the actual shift of jobs from one country to another? This is the question raised by U.S. unions. Even if so, to which countries? And in what sectors? And who is to determine when the shifts should occur and by how much and who bears the cost? There is still no agreement on the answers or even *how* they should be sought—that is, through what institutions or fora.

Some industries have already shown themselves to be fairly mobile internationally, in response to incentives for redeployment. Electronics, textiles, and cosmetics are more mobile than other industries in that they can locate operations in many different settings, even shifting locations at relatively small cost as economic or political conditions change. Others can shift product lines within existing facilities or build additional plants in response to governmental or economic incentives: textiles, shoes, rubber products. Adjustments in the advanced countries are necessitated by shifts within these mobile industries, as has been in textiles, electronics, autos, chemicals and petrochemicals, shoes, pharmaceuticals, watches, and food processing. The electronics, textile, photographic, sewing machine, earth-moving equipment, and medical instrument companies have shifted some plants into the Far East and into Mexico. Some of these shifts have been stimulated by investment incentives similar to those that are employed *within* countries to move industry from one region to another. Tariffs have long been used for the purpose of encouraging domestic production and prohibiting imports, at the cost of reduction of production in the foreign countries. Local-content requirements have been imposed by developing countries (Brazil, Argentina, Mexico, and so on) and by some advanced countries as well (Canada). These requirements not only shift production from the advanced country into the host country but also stimulate the development of local supplier and ancillary industries. Again, the location of industrial activity is altered among countries, at the initiative of TNCs or host governments.

The corporate selection of activities to be shifted to another country is done by identifying the lowest-cost factor of production found—usually labor. This is the basis for the movement of some of the electronics plants into Asia and Mexico, for they have a high labor-input and that factor is relatively low cost given the technologies supplied by the foreign company.

This redeployment of industry from the North to the South entails unwanted adjustments in the advanced countries, however. First, there is a loss of past or potential exports in the balance of payments. Second, there is an actual shift of production and loss of employment; the facilities existing in the advanced countries will now no longer be needed for the purpose for which they were built, and adjustments will have to be made. These adjustments will occur in a shift in product lines made in those facilities, if such a shift is feasible; or workers will be relocated and retrained; finally, efforts in advanced countries to maintain production will cause a shift in the direction of trade as they seek new markets. Such adjustments do not come easily, especially in time of general unemployment. Since they appear to be, or may in fact be, wasteful of capital and manpower resources, governments in advanced countries will seek to prevent or slow the adjustments to make them more palatable. This process of delay can slow the shift to LDCs, thereby impinging on its industrial development. Some accommodations appear needed at an intergovernmental level. The *principle* of interference to maintain production location has already been established, through escape clauses in tariff agreements. It was done also through the U.S.-Canadian auto agreement. The Multi-fiber Agreements have clearly indicated that redevelopment can be contained by markets allocation between advanced and developing countries. They stipulated the phasing of the expansion of LDC exports with growth of markets in the advanced countries, so as to absorb the added LDC capacity without damage to advanced-country facilities.

*International Integration*

Integration of LDC affiliates of TNCs with their *international* operations would probably generate a more efficient use of world resources than at present, but it will require intergovernmental dialogues and agreements. For example, in the auto industry, the TNC affiliates in Southeast Asia or elsewhere, would be tied to affiliates in Australia, South Africa, and probably Japan. Components would be exchanged and models swapped across national borders. The same benefits and problems of their distribution arise as discussed in chapter 6 on OECD integration.

A few individual countries—Taiwan, South Korea, and the city states of Singapore and Hong-Kong plus Mexico and Brazil—have opted for such international integration in specific sectors in specific sectors, even encouraging TNC affiliates with export subsidies or other instruments.

There are, therefore, several routes along which the LDCs can travel to use the capabilities of the TNCs. These capabilities differ according to the form and market operation of the specific companies, and they fit different industrial policies. It is up to the LDC governments to decide the policies that they wish from among the alternatives. OECD governments can decide to help (or not) through the formulation of policies that will permit the TNCs to work toward the goals adopted by the LDC government. This does not mean that the OECD governments should foster any particular policies in the LDCs nor support whatever policies LDCs promulgate. However, if the objective is to achieve international industrial integration—and it is not at all clear that nations are actually seeking, compared to verbally support-

ing, that objective—greater effort should be made to demonstrate the usefulness of guiding the industrial choices of LDCs and the responses of the
TNCs to specified goals.


## Costs and Benefits

Whatever choices are made among the alternatives for industrialization in
the LDCs, careful assessment of the cost and benefits should be undertaken
so as to obtain full acceptance and support of the alternatives chosen. Several of the criteria of acceptability noted earlier can be met from use of the
TNCs in cooperative industrial policies: (1) an increase in *efficiency,*
through achieving least-cost operations under greater economies of scale
(the extent of each depending on the size of the market, whether national,
regional, or international); through a wider product range offering greater
choice to consumers; through an increase in the skills employed, supported
by technology transfer; and through an expansion of exports and imports,
reflecting greater productivity; (2) an increase in *participation* through
greater opportunities for managers and labor; closer dialogues between
LDC and OECD governments on integration approaches by TNCs; and (3)
an increase in *creativity* through the gradual development of indigenous
R&D activities.

The value of these benefits is not necessarily adequate to gain agreement on allocation of industrial sectors or even on industrial policies, and
especially not through the TNCs. An acceptable *distribution of the benefits*
will also be required, involving some potential trade-offs in the other criteria. Again, the TNCs can be helpful in meeting this criterion of *equity*
through attention to sources and uses of funds, sources of materials and
components, export markets, technologies used, R&D projects, training
programs, and so on.

The market-seeker can raise efficiency by meeting local-market
demands and increase participation through joint ventures. The ME-form
can help achieve international integration through a structure or production, trade, and financial flows that distributes benefits among companies
and countries in a manner acceptable to participating governments. These
benefits can be most efficiently distributed if they are not allocated within
*each* separate sector among all member countries, but rather among several
industrial sectors simultaneously, so as to produce greater efficiency and
increase the possibilities of innovation. Such a wide coverage would move
toward the idealized results of international specialization in the division of
labor. However, this specialization would be different in structure and
extent from that which would have occurred under completely free markets,
reflecting intergovernmental agreement. The basis for the determination of

the distribution would be more complex than that under free markets, the latter supposedly reflecting only supply and demand in a market. The distribution of benefits under negotiated allocations would reflect the negotiating strength and multiple political positions of the negotiating governments.

This procedure may seem to be an inefficient way of determining the allocation of industry leading to an inefficient pattern of production. But it is less inefficient than moves to mercantilism and is, therefore, a second-best solution. Though we have little experience in witnessing the effects of greater international industrial coordination on efficiency, we can discern many examples (vide, Japan) of close community coordination raising efficiency. The procedures do not require a loss of efficiency in order to achieve equity or the other criteria of acceptability. Rather, efficiency is first a matter of getting a job done, and to insist that it not be done if it can't be done by first-best methods is itself inefficient. Finally, it is not true that achieving equity always leads to inefficiency; equity and efficiency are synergistic in many situations, and keeping the pursuit of both in mind can minimize the costs in each.

# 9

# LDC Restructuring through National and Regional Integration

Another objective of industrial restructuring sought by LDCs is the reduction of dependence on advanced countries. This can be done by greater *internal* industrial integration and by more intensive and extensive *regional* integration among LDCs themselves. In each case, different types of TNCs can be effectively employed to achieve the desired goals.

## National Sectoral Integration

Although much of the prior discussion has been on means of achieving international industrial integration so as to avoid the more difficult conflicts arising from national industrial policies, there are justifications for focusing development efforts on specific sectors from a national-market viewpoint. In many LDCs, especially those of large economic size with potentially wide markets, there are sufficient economies of scale in various industries to permit producers to be competitively successful even against imports. And there may be no need at all for export markets, in order to achieve adequate economies. These industries comprise what have been called in the literature the domestic sector as distinct from the export sector and the import-competing sector. In fact, development of a given sector has often been stimulated by import-substitution policies that seek to reduce drains on foreign exchange reserves.

To achieve the most rapid and extensive strengthening of the competitive position in a given sector, attention needs to be paid not only to the major elements of the sector but also a variety of ancillary, secondary, and tertiary components related to the sector, including infrastructure support, so that the most efficient production and distribution is made possible. It is proposed here that the developing countries can accelerate development of national-market oriented sectors through a systematic approach to sectoral development and that this approach itself can be implemented in conjunction with capabilities of TNCs. The proposal involves contracting the entire system-development of the selected industrial sector in a host country; a contractor would be a single TNC or consortium of TNCs, responding to bid specifications laid down by the host goverment. This approach offers to governments the opportunity to select the priority sectors and to gain the advantages of drawing on the resources of TNCs while remaining in complete control of their own national industrial development.

The need for the transnationals arises from the fact that developing countries require assistance in several areas: in the planning of particular projects or sectoral development; in the administration of project plans; in the transfer and adaptation of technology; in the establishment of production facilities; in the training of workers; in the creation of linkages into supplier facilities and technology sources; and, finally, in the development of distribution facilities (both domestic and foreign). All of this requires management, which is the resource most widely stockpiled by transnationals. Beyond this, however, transnationals are also a source for each of the types of assistance needed by the developing countries in their industrialization process, including (critically) their ability to tie that industrial development to sources of supply and markets in other countries, thereby reducing costs and expanding opportunities.

The proposal for systemic development of industrial sectors in developing countries made here relies on a new *use* of the capabilities of transnationals—one which they have not themselves initiated nor have governments called upon them to perform. However, transnationals are capable of responding to it effectively if they are willing; and governments can employ the technique without losing critical elements of control.


*Role of Transnationals*

The transnationals have continued to play several roles in the developing countries, and although their activities and relationships have changed over the past two decades, they are still welcomed and considered necessary for the pursuit of national objectives in most of these countries.

Their contributions range from a variety of contractual relationships—franchising, management assistance, know-how agreements, licensing of patents and trademarks, natural resource development, and turn-key projects—through joint ventures to wholly owned operations that are either virtually independent or dovetailed with parent-company or affiliate operations elsewhere in the world. One objective of a systems approach would be to mix and match these various roles in a total system so that they provided precisely what the host country needed and desired for sectoral integration and did not require more resources than necessary.

One of the concerns of host countries in the past about the incursion of the transnationals has been the inability to know the effect of the entry of the corporation on the domestic economy and its foreign economic relations. Considerable fear of the transnationals has arisen in a number of countries and is waning currently only because governments have begun to realize that they are more powerful than the transnationals, if they wish to exercise their ability to control. To date, that control has been exercised on an ad hoc basis (that is, project-by-project and company-by-company) rather than on a sufficiently coordinated basis to prevent duplication and waste of resources. In addition, the ability to control what the various transnationals do has been generally limited to a set of restrictions on licensing provisions, profit remittances, local-content requirements, personnel transfers—all related to the internal operations of the company. Some constraints have also been imposed on ownership, relative to formation of local partnerships or sale of shares to the public. But little effort has been made to use the transnationals to pursue a balanced development plan for any industrial sector.

This can be done by the judicious choice of the sectors in which to employ the proposal made herein for a more systemic approach to industrial development. Three sectors with reduced ties to international markets include agribusiness, transportation, and energy. Other sectors can be largely nationally oriented while remaining reliant on significant foreign inputs, such as petrochemicals or pharmaceuticals. Others are also largely national but with a significant foreign component in potential exports, such as textiles, shoes, toys, plastics, and so on. A fourth, more complex group is made up of high-technology sectors or those requiring world markets to achieve economies of scale, thus leading to problems of international integration.

The proposal involves contracting the entire systems development of a selected industrial sector in a host country; the contractor would be a single company or consortium, responding to bid specifications laid down by the host government. This approach offers governments the opportunity to select the priority sectors and to minimize conflicts with the interests of other nations, while at the same time opening up opportunities both for national and international integration through the linkages of the transnational enterprises involved in the total project.

## Use of Prime Contractors

The technique proposed is an extension of contracting procedures used in engineering/construction, in the NATO co-production arrangements, and with the petroleum and petrochemical companies during the last decade. Each of these requires that the purchaser (government or intergovernmental consortium) determine the nature of the project, its objectives, and the basic specifications, and put the project out for bids. In each case a prime contractor is eventually awarded the contract, after substantial negotiation in the process of bidding and confirming the contract. The prime contractor is responsible for collecting and meshing the work of subcontractors and demonstrating that all aspects of the bid can and will be fulfilled by specific companies. The final responsibility lies with the prime contractor, who must make certain that each subcontractor does comply, or if not, that other subcontractors are found who will do so.

Either in the statement of the bid itself, or in negotiations thereafter, the government indicates what kind of support facilities will be provided; or they also can become the responsibility of the prime contract, such as the provision of training or some parts of the infrastructure. The government can even stipulate the roles that existing local companies shall play, particularly where there are state enterprises.

This procedure, when directed at the problem of systemic development of an industrial sector, would open the opportunity for the government to receive diverse proposals for meeting the goals specified. A bid could be received from a consortium of companies wholly within a single foreign country or from countries mixed and matched across international boundaries by a single prime contractor. This procedure would open opportunities for small- and medium-sized firms to participate in international production in ways from which they now feel excluded, simply because of the uncertainty of their roles and the lack of familiarity with procedures. They would in a sense piggy-back in international production, just as many have done in serving export markets.

The responsibility of the prime contractor would involve making the initial bid proposal (after bringing the subcontractors together in a total package), overseeing the implementation of the construction of the various units of the system and their linkages, and directing negotiations with the government through the process. Once all aspects of the project were in place, responsibility of the prime contractor would cease as far as the total project goes (though this company might have taken a specific portion of the project for its own continuing operations). The individual companies would then operate separately, but with the continuing support of the entire system which would have established appropriate suppliers and vendors for each major company component.

The problem of selecting company participation can be resolved by the government as a part of the bid specifications: It can stipulate a proportion or a number of local enterprises that are to be involved as well as specific state enterprises, or the company participants can be left to negotiation between the government and specific bidders. In any case, any desire to assure local participation becomes part of the specification *or* negotiation, rather than relying on a *general* rule of ownership and control that is often inappropriate. Obviously, if there are only a few local enterprises that can be involved or are specified, the bidding procedure becomes difficult in that several different competing bidders will have to negotiate with the same companies in the host country.

Similarly, the government could specify the extent of local production that would be required in the total system—that is, limitations on imports at various phases of the system, including a gradual diminution of such imports. But this provides much greater flexibility than local-content requirements in autos, for example. At one extreme, all production could be required within the host country, and the prime contractor merely be asked to provide the management, administration, and coordination for putting the pieces together. Only a small inflow of capital might be required; however, the prime contractor could have increased responsibilities through the requirement to bring technology in on an independent basis (that is, untied through capital ownership) from a variety of sources outside the host country. In essence, such a system would merely supply the managerial and technical skills necessary to make certain that the host countries' existing facilities or resources were integrated effectively on a national basis.

It is not necessary in this scheme, therefore, that the host country be without *any* facilities in the sector that is the subject of the contracting. On the contrary, the work could be facilitated if some of the sector is already in existence. However, if there is overcapacity in any one phase of the sector, delicate problems of removal of redundancy would be raised and conceivably become part of the contract, leaving the TNC the responsibility to determine which are the most efficient and likely to remain competitive in a revitalized sector. *How* the redundant companies would be moved would also be part of the contract.

The system design could also extend to the infrastructure required to make the sector more effective. Each sector—textiles, steel, automobiles, energy, pharmaceuticals, petrochemicals, and so on—requires a different kind of infrastructure to support it. Thus the requirements for electricity, commuting facilities, training schools, movement of materials and product, health services, and so on, differ from sector to sector. Again, not to waste resources, and to phase their availability in with the creation of the industrial sector desired, it would be appropriate to place some of these responsibilities on the prime contractor as well. If this is not desired, then a close coordination of government activities to supply the appropriate infrastructure and the activities of the prime contractor is required, leading to the question of how the system is administered, as discussed later.

In some instances, the host country would require some preliminary assistance even in design of the sector to be promoted and the scope of the responsibilities of the prime contractor. Since there is little experience in designing such complex bid specifications, consultation would probably be sought with international institutions that had some experience (such as NATO). What must be avoided above all is the attempt to redesign the wheel in every instance. However, it also must be cautioned that there is no set way of accomplishing the goals sought in this proposal; no one given set of rules is required in all cases or even in the majority of cases. What worked in one co-production arrangement did not work in another, even with a substantial duplication of the countries participating; they had widely divergent arrangements and procedures, and most were relatively successful. What is required is that adequate consideration be given to the various elements of the system: the specific phases that are to be covered in the prime contractor's responsibility, the precise functions that he and subcontractors are to undertake, and the duration of those responsibilities.

*Examples of Sectoral Systems*

There are obviously many ways to conceptualize a system, delineate it, or define its scope for the purposes of efficient integration of its parts. Every system has a set of inputs that are processed through a set of procedures, leading to the outputs. These outputs are themselves the objective or they are used directly in pursuing the goal of the system. There is, in addition, an evaluation or feedbck system that determines whether, in fact, the goals have been met and, if not, how to adjust the rest of the system to do so or to modify in the event that the goals themselves change.

For our present purpose, we consider the system that is to be the subject of contracting to extend from the infrastructure surrounding it, to the direct inputs, the throughout processes, and the outputs, plus their distribution to a final user. The evaluation and feedback system is presumably the market itself or some other appropriate decision system already in existence in the host country. There is no necessity to design the *entire* sector, meeting all conceivable demands in projected volume; rather, what would be feasible is a set of linked functions assuring that all necessary elements of a system would be in place and functioning at minimal levels at least. These would constitute a model for others; and, as demand grew and altered, the system parts would respond as signaled by the market. Presently, sectors are often not responsive in many LDCs for lack of an adequate signaling. In many instances, the recipient of signals is state enterprise, which is unresponsive because of various bureaucratic inflexibilities.

Three sectors—agribusiness, transportation, and petrochemicals—are potential subjects for systemic industrial sectoral integration.

**Agribusiness System.** To integrate the agribusiness sector, the host government would design bid specifications that required the prime contractor to determine the following:

products that were most suitable for production in the various regions of the country;

the necessary procedures for preparing the land (fertilization, irrigation, rotation, etc.);

the infrastructure required for settling the land;

transport facilities from farm to market (either directly to consumers or to intermediate processors);

the necessary preservation procedures (refrigeration, freezing, canning, etc.);

the provision of appropriate facilities for these processes;

the determination of facilities needed in supplying processors with packaging materials, labels, cartons, etc.;

the necessary distribution facilities from processors to retailers;

the required retailing network; and

the provision of products to customers for final preservation and use of the products (household refrigeration, potable water, etc.).

The prime contractor would, in addition, be required to determine the supporting infrastructure, such as educational training, extension services, production facilities for fertilizer, provision of seeds, pesticides, trucking facilities, supermarket design, and so on.

The bid specifications would require that the prime contractor be responsible for obtaining the cooperation of specific investors, licensors, or joint-venture partners who would, together with local enterprises, establish the required network within a specified period of time. Priorities to certain export commodities, fruits and vegetables, or even development of under-utilized native products (e.g., the winged bean) could be assigned.

The bid specifications could include also the requirement that the prime contractor be responsible for developing the financial package for each of the constituent parts, even including the financing of transport facilities although probably excluding the construction of farm to market roads and the construction of educational facilities. However, the prime contractor could be requested to provide necessary assistance for development of educational curricula and appropriate ties to agricultural and technical universities in other countries.

The prime contractor would be responsible for proper phasing of development of each of these elements of the system, for providing necessary management and technical assistance to local enterprises, and for the formation of the necessary linkages among the various elements of the system.

This is nothing more in concept (less technically complex, but probably more complex organizationally) than is required of NASA in developing through contractors any one of its space exploration projects. The responsibilities would continue until the completion of the final set of facilities and a proving-out period to make certain that all were in communication and fitting together as effectively as feasible.

The prime contractor would be responsible further for determining the extent to which the system required governmental incentives, support, or protection and a time frame within which this would likely be required, leading eventually to a removal of such support so as to make certain that the system achieved the levels of efficiency that would make it competitive.

In responding to such a bid request, any potential prime contractor would have to obtain sufficient consultation to make certain that he could supply the appropriate solutions as well as facilities in the form of managerial and technical know-how and these specific operating capabilities required—either through local of foreign enterprises. He would also have to determine the financial needs and the probable sources.

The prime contractor would probably find it desirable to arrange for subcontracting with a large number of smaller companies who would feel comfortable working with him on such an affiliated basis. The larger transnationals might find it difficult to work together under the guidance of one of them because of their own decision-making, quasibureaucratic procedures, and existing antitrust implications. From the standpoint of U.S. policy, this would be one of the major benefits of the system approach because it would involve a large number of enterprises that are normally not brought into the process of assistance to developing countries, despite the fact that the modes of operation of small and medium firms are more appropriate to those countries. Particularly in the agricultural field, the services of private voluntary organizations dealing with sanitation, rural housing, facilities for ditributing urban products to rural areas could be appropriately included (thereby encouraging greater productivity on the farm so as to be able to afford the improved living standards available through industrial products brought out from the cities). Connections into the local banking system and procedures for makings small farm loans available; credit for small truckers might also be part of the system's specifications. The absence of such credit in the past has been due to perceptions of high risks facing small firms or farms, reflecting the absence of ties with a functioning production system with assured roles.

In many instances in developing countries, an initiative fails because of the lack of appropriate linkages with other activities that are necessary to make it profitable. These linkages include not only the transport of goods, but the communication of ideas and product changes, credit facilities, phasing or schedules of production in different stages of the activities of the sector, and so on. The systems approach has as its prime advantage the design of all of the pieces necessary to come to a particular industrial advance in a type of PERT analysis. Each link and cog is therefore identified, sized and sequenced as necessary to make the system work effectively.

This is not to say that activities other than those designed into the system are not feasible or desirable. This system design is principally to make certain that all of the necessary pieces are there, and the rest of the activities in this sector can be developed in response to market changes as the economy develops. It is not a locked-in system; it is simply the assurance that all that is required in a minimum system is available and linked up effectively. For example, such an approach would close the gap of appropriate fertilizer production and distribution, which slowed agricultural output in India for so long.

The return to the prime contractor would arise not only from his particular role in the continuing system but also from payment for the management of the system during the time in which he was held responsible. This fee itself would be negotiable under the initial contract.

**Transportation System.** Similarly, if what was desired was the formation of a transportation system, the government involved would request bids under specifications stipulating that transport of goods and people was to be provided through multimedia, and the initial bid would include a proposal as to the distribution of transport facilities among air, water and land; the land aspect would cover common carriers, automobiles, long and short transport, including extremely short transport of people and goods by advanced technology. The system would stop at the entrance to buildings, excluding the movement of goods and people within particular edifices.

The prime contractor would have to respond with a system proposal that would include the supply of necessary equipment, the design of the networks, both urban and interurban, indicating the extent to which local production could be drawn on for the equipment, the flexibility of the system in expansion, the costs, and those sources of equipment and assistance that stood ready to put the system into effect. Included in the specifications would be recommendations on the types of automotive vehicles that would be needed and the extent to which they could and should be produced locally.

Obviously, one of the more difficult aspects would be to adjust the ideal system to what was feasible, given the existence of various components of the system already in the given country.

This type of approach is not one that any of the present elements of transport systems have noticed. For example, automotive companies are really not transport-system companies; neither are shipping companies or shipbuilding companies, airplane or airline companies, road builders, or railroad companies. Therefore, a new team of experienced individuals would have to be brought together, with considerable accommodations made to the interests of each in favor of building an effective integrated system for the purchaser. The duration of such a commitment would likely be quite long term, but one of the things that developing countries need most is an efficient transport system, taking it out of state management (though not control) and eliminating the featherbedding of workers and redundancy of equipment and supply that occurs because of political pressures.

**Petrochemicals.** Petrochemical complexes are already developed under procedures similar to those suggested here. The government decides first the products that it wants to come out of the sector and what use it will have for joint products coming out of aparticular process or by-products that also arise during the manufacturing processes. Bid procedures require a prime contractor to specify the minimum levels of feedstocks needed to sustain an integrated petrochemical complex, and the particular stages that would rely on imported products, if found too expensive or scarce domestically; the minimum scale of output for specific products and the minimum market to be served; and the extent to which a given process could be separated from others and become a specialty to be served by a single company.

The prime contractor helps determine the particular stage in the processes at which the host country would enter: for example, begin at the fabrication stage in plastics and move back to molding, production of polystyrene or PVCs, and eventually back up the processes as far as it could go economically, given the origin of the feedstocks.

TNCs bidding also identify the capabilities of local enterprise and those foreign companies willing to help in the development through provision of technical and managerial assistance at various stages or through joint ventures.

Where the state already holds a monopoly in the production of oil and gas, the major responsibility of the prime contractor is to set up the most effective use of these feedstocks for local needs, undertaking the phased establishment of all of the downstream activities, and sometime providing entree into foreign markets through the various members of the contract team. Once having set up the system, however, the contractor may stay as part of a joint venture or turn the operation over to the purchaser.

*Procedures*

As seen from the viewpoint of the developing country itself, there are several steps necessary in pursuing a system approach with contracting in order to achieve balanced growth in a specific industrial sector. They include the definition of the sector itself; determination of the objectives, specification of the bid requirements to be met by the prime contractor; assessment of the bids and negotiation of final terms with the selected contractor; determination of the acceptable impacts on the balance of payments; determination of any taxes and duties imposed on participants or specific activities; the desired organizational and administrative structure to protect the interests of the government; any legal immunities to be provided; and the projected duration of the contract as well as procedures for early termination or longer continuation. On its part, the prime contractor would be responsible for the design of the system that responded to the government's requirements, presentation of a proposal, including a commitment from subcontractors in specific parts of the system as well as any financial commitments required, the technologies to be included, the cost and pricing criteria, the proposed organizational structure and management, and procedures for modification of any of the terms of the contract in the event of changed conditions.

**Definition of Project Scope.** The definition of the project to be undertaken depends on the resources and condition of the country and its ability to undertake some aspects of the system development on its own—that is, without the help of the foreign contractor or subcontractors. The entire system required to establish balanced growth within a sector involves all of the supporting infrastructure, the physical and organizational structure of the sector itself, the financial and technical contributions necessary, and the existence of a user community to effectively receive and employ the output of the sector.

The process for designing project requirements would involve the developing country in a much more specific iteration of its goals than is done normally in five-year planning. But this is the purpose of a systems approach in that it seeks balanced industrial growth, fit rather precisely into larger economic objectives. What must be avoided in the system requirements is such a high degree of specification that rigidity results; the system is then not flexible enough to meet changes in the economic environment or markets or to adapt to technological changes once the system is in place and the prime contractor has withdrawn.

In serving a national market, the bidding contractors will be particularly interested in the guarantee of security of that market, particularly in terms of foreign competition. The extent and duration of such protection would be a part of the terms of reference for negotiation between the host country and the prime contractor. In addition, the legal parameters are important: for example, the extent of immunity from antitrust laws that might conceivably be violated through initial arrangements among the participants in the system. Such immunity could be granted for a specified time, to be removed as the system evolved.

One of the problems in the design of the scope of the project is that it will likely be found to be inadequate in one respect or another as the project becomes implemented. Therefore a process is needed for the renegotiation of the responsibilities of the prime contractor as the project proceeds. This requires careful thought in the structure of the administration and also consideration of some means of arbitration of differences.

The difficulties of designing such a system, with so little experience among developing countries and potential prime contractors, means that considerable care and consultation will be required to proceed successfully. Several different groups—particularly some of the more systems-oriented consulting ones that exist primarily in advanced countries—should be drawn on. It is conceivable that a combination of groups such as A.D. Little and Bechtel would be required to assist even in this first step. They should work with local governmental agencies and private engineering–consulting groups to help them learn how to proceed.

**Bid Preparation.** For a company that has been selected as one to prepare a final bid, the first steps are the organization of a team to prepare the system design and to put the various participating companies together through subcontracting. From the standpoint of early and continuing cooperation among the parties to the contract, it would obviously be important to get the subcontracting companies active in the design phase as well. Each needs to provide detailed information as to how it would carry out its part of the system and the linkages that are required with other subcontractors as well as into the infrastructure in the host country. This step is easier if all of the participating companies are in the same country, but for most of the developing countries this would not be permitted. Local companies in the host country will be required to be included, and particularly some state enterprises will be involved. A difficult process of negotiation even in the formation of the consortium arises, but these groupings have been established in the past successfully and can be formed much more readily among enterprises than among governments. In fact, it is a major purpose of the proposed procedure to circumvent the sticky political negotiations that would become involved in detailed aspects of the system if it were undertaken among government agencies.

Each of the subcontracting units will be required to indicate the precise nature and extent of their contribution in technical assistance, licensing of patents or trademarks, managerial assistance, joint-venture relationships, or the creating of a wholly owned subsidiary. Where some of the parties already have affiliates in the host country, the contribution may arise only in the form of expansion of existing activities or the addition of new ones.

The capacity of the facilities projected as well as the preferred location within the host country would be specified. Each company would be required further to stipulate the infrastructure needed to make his operation successful and, in response to the bid specifications, which of these they would be ready to provide and at what cost. Each would specify the origin of the inputs required, outlining whether they would be local or foreign, the kinds of materials needed, the methods of supply and handling, materials testing procedures, and so on. Each would specify the training programs that it would be able to offer and what were considered necessary and appropriate for the needs of the particular host country, at all levels of the operation. Each would specify further the types of distribution facilities that were needed and would be provided stipulating which markets were to be served and specifically where, if this is requested in the bid requirements. Finally, the financial package would be put together from a combination of the equity contributions of each of the parties, their projected borrowing (both locally and internationally), and assistance to be obtained from any governmental agencies (for example, for infrastructure needs).

Each participant would be required to stipulate the projected extent and degree of their participation beyond the contract itself; that is, whether licensing of technology would continue beyond the four- or five-year contract and whether it would be willing to sell out the local facilities to local investors.

The bid should also include a description of the management and organizational structure and the administrative procedures for the project, showing the links between the consortium management and the government administrative unit.

**Administration.** The administrative structure for the system is eased by the existence of the prime contractor's sole responsibility (compared to a consortium) in that it would be the key element to forming the organization and staffing it. It would probably use some of its own management in order to be able to draw on internal experience as well as avoid the problems of how to fit the system management back into the company at the end of the contract. The necessity to transfer management from the subcontractors into the system team will raise some problems of lack of expertise or capability, as is often the case when personnel are moved out of headquarters into a temporary assignment; but, again, responsibility for accepting such individuals rests with the prime contractor.

The composition of this administrative structure is not dictated by any particular form; many different forms have been shown to be effective in diverse situations. What is required is a strong liaison group with the government administrative unit. The government itself would require a surveillance and negotiating unit to keep tabs on what the consortium was doing, its scheduled performance, and to be familiar enough with what is going on and the changed conditions so that it could renegotiate the contract effectively if this were necessary. It must also be sufficiently aware that it can defend criticism from within the country as to what is going on.

Finally, procedures for the settlement of disputes between the prime contractor and the contracting body in the host country will be required; this could be done through an arbitration mechanism or established within the administrative units themselves.

*Benefits of the Systems Approach*

A number of benefits would result from successful implementation of a system approach to sectoral industrial development. One would be a reduction in the waste of resources and in the cost of achieving particular rates of growth. This result would also be obtained through a reduction in the time required to get to a certain level of capability, again reducing costs and accelerating the benefits of higher standards of living.

For most developing countries an effective participation by government in the process, without stifling entrepreneurial orientations, is critical. Many LDCs do not have managerial or planning capabilities nor sufficient ability to implement their plans and to provide adequate evaluation of what is being done. To pass some of these responsibilities to companies (under procedures for adequate surveillance and consultation) would improve efficiency considerably and remove much of the deadening weight of governmental bureaucratic decision-making.

From the standpoint of advanced and developing countries, the procedures outlined here would open avenues for small- and medium-sized companies in advanced countries to join in international activities, which they have been reluctant to do to date. The formation of the total system would indicate a greater security for the smaller company, providing better information as to what was expected and the opportunities for success. It would also make it easier for the smaller company to know exactly what contribution it could make.

The formation of such a system with greater reliability in the roles played by companies at each stage would entice local investors into joint ventures. Such participation might begin with very small levels of equity, growing as the success of the firm permitted.

The fact that the total system is designed also would lead to a greater understanding of the precise behavior patterns of transnational companies and their affiliates within the system. In fact, the concern of each party for the role of others would provide a constraint on aberrant behavior. This constraint, plus the constant surveillance by the government itself, should be much more effective in guiding corporate behavior than any code espoused by the UN or any other international body. Experience under such a system would also lead governments to better legislation regarding business behavior than it might otherwise arrive at.

Roles for state enterprises would be designed into the system, and pressure would therefore be applied to make such enterprises more efficient and less politicized, both of which have burdened the developing countries seriously. The existence of the newly stimulated sector would also provide some employment opportunities, which should relieve the burden of such underemployment in the state enterprises.

Finally, a major benefit is the establishment of appropriate and effective linkages not only among suppliers and intermediate producers but from the technology and component R&D sources into the user community and back from it into the supplier network. In many developing countries, one of the more difficult gaps to fill is the lack of linkages between science and technology and stage of commercialization. Other linkages are with infrastructures, such as those between the educational system and the needs of industry. Each of these would be designed into the system so that these critical gaps would be filled.

*** 

During the 1970s over 1500 major industrial projects (macro-projects) were undertaken in LDCs by TNCs under contract with governments. They involved consortia (at times) and cost on the average over $600 million. There is, therefore, experience in such contracting procedures.

What is proposed here is a substantial expansion of the concept—even as compared to $1 billion petrochemical complexes—to encompass all phases of an integrated industrial sector. Whether governments in LDCs are capable of playing their role is as doubtful as whether TNCs are able to expand their preview beyond mere products and processes to sectoral systems. If both are ready, the dialing should start for the economic and political benefits are substantial.

## South-South Regional Integration

A second means of reducing dependence on the advanced countries is for several LDCs to form associations for economic integration among themselves. Several attempts have been made, including countries within Latin America, the Andean region as well, members of the Association of the Southeast Asian Nations (ASEAN), the West African and East African Unions, the Caribbean Free Trade Area, the Central American Common

Market, and so on. But all of them have found it difficult to integrate their industrial structures to increase efficiency through widening the market while achieving equity in the benefits. Some have attempted to form their own multinational enterprises for the purpose of such integration, but these efforts have not been notably successful. Although it was suggested to several of them that they could rely effectively on foreign transnationals, they have been unwilling to do so. Several TNCs (notably in automobiles, heavy equipment, and electronics) have in the past proposed integration schemes covering their own activities in several countries of a region, and a few of these have been accepted. But in general they have not, because governments did not see them as effectively integrating the industrial sector as a whole, because the governments could not see how the distribution of the benefits would take place and because existing local companies were opposed. Any new initiatives, therefore, should be set within policies for an entire industrial sector and should contain sufficient government–business coordination so that government officials consider that they are continuously aware of what is taking place under the arrangement and that it is equitable.

*Past Efforts at Sectoral Integration*

Within the LDCs, various sectors face similar demand patterns and sales can be oriented to LDC regional markets under agreements for industrial integration. Many of these products will be of types and qualities not necessarily available from or suitable to the advanced countries. Others will be similar—as with steel, autos, and machinery—though sometimes at higher costs of production in LDCs than world prices. Among those suitable only for LDC regional markets are rudimentary vehicles and farm equipment, indigenous drugs, clothing, food, construction materials, furniture, and cosmetics.

Regional industrial integration, for example, is most attractive to developing countries (as in ASEAN and the Andean region) that require a larger protected market than that within their national boundaries but cannot yet stand the heat of international competition. To help shut out imports, several groups of countries have sought to develop LDC-oriented products in sectors such as automobiles, metal working, pharmaceuticals, chemicals, petrochemicals, rubber, and others. Products distinct from those in the advanced countries will require less advanced production techniques and processes than would be used by TNCs in their home countries, thus making technology transfers easier.

The development of intra-LDC exports also raises the question of whether exports of advanced countries will be displaced. The result will depend on the products, markets, trade arrangements, and balance of payments of the countries involved. In some instances, however, differentiated markets will be served by local and foreign products because the quality and even the price are likely to be different among similar items supplied by both advanced countries and LDCs (for example, autos from South Korea going into the Philippines alongside of U.S. autos). However, a regional arrangement will certainly require protection against some products of the advanced countries, thereby diverting trade, altering production locations, and forcing adjustments in advanced countries.

International specialization among the developing countries could also be achieved through trade with other LDCs—not necessarily in the same region—either by exports directly from local companies or through international trading companies, such as have long been operating out of Japan. Introducing the trading companies of advanced countries into LDC trade brings the TNCs into the picture; in time, as partners in joint ventures, they could be a channel for closer ties in production among the LDCs.

**ASEAN Efforts.** A U.S. auto company offered to the ASEAN countries to establish an integrated auto and truck operation locating some of the component production in each of the five member countries and assembling different models in different countries so that each obtains experience in a number of the production aspects of the automotive industry. It proposed further to balance the value of exports and imports among the various members so as not to put a significant drain on any one of them. The models would even be developed within the ASEAN market; and the distribution of tax revenues would be agreed upon in the initial arrangement. The company made the offer with the stipulation that it would have unrestricted access to the markets in the five countries and unrestricted movement of components in the manufacturing process. It also agreed to minimize and eventually eliminate all imports of components from outside of the region. Obviously, given the likelihood that some of the component production would be high cost in the country selected for its location, some protection was involved. In this particular case, the governments were unsure how the various existing component manufacturers would fit into the scheme, and several were not happy with the specific manufacturing activity proposed for their countries.

In an effort to work out the structure of the auto industry in the region, the ASEAN governments decided to leave the negotiations to representatives of the locally owned components and accessory manufacturers, leaving out of the discussions the international companies. These representatives soon found that efforts at complementation should have been started twenty years earlier, before the local manufacturers got started, for they constitute a sizeable obstacle to rationalization of the industry; yet there are too many of them to achieve economies of scale. To achieve low-cost production, they must reduce the number of cars and the models that are presently assembled within the region out of knocked-down components brought in from advanced countries and assembled with some locally made parts. One of the objectives is to increase the share of local production compared to the imported components. Many of these local component manufacturers are themselves either licensees or affiliates of international companies; thus, three Japanese companies control all of the shock-absorber market in the ASEAN region.

Given the national aspirations and existing structure of component manufacture, the five countries decided to attempt to use industrial complementation agreements as a means of expanding local production and reaching economies of scale that would permit a reduction in auto costs. The reduced prices of the autos should then expand the market, permitting additional producers to enter the region and thereby eventually develop full-scale *national* industries.

The objective of the complementation agreements, therefore, is a disintegration of this sector, eventually, although integration will be used initially to expand economies of scale and reduce cost. Ten major component lines, in which member countries do not have production facilities at present, will be set aside for industrial complementation. Under these procedures, the foreign company would be invited to join with ASEAN companies or capital to form a producer of an item, such as carburetors (or drive chains, or engines of a particular size), to serve the five-country market. Being designated a complementation item, the five countries agree to let the component in at preferential rates compared to supply from outside of the region. This preference is granted for a period of four years after start-up in one of these new categories of components. Each of these complementation companies will be a multi-joint venture composed of either government or private companies or banks (lending the capital) plus the foreign company. The foreign company is permitted to own 15 percent of the enterprise, with the remainder divided equally among the ASEAN countries, unless one of them desires to have a smaller percentage, in which case others might pick it up. In principle, a foreign company can own as much as 49 percent of a complementation enterprise, but that level should be reduced to 15 percent as soon as practicable.

Once the four years of monopoly status is through, any other country can build facilities that would compete with the initial enterprise. Automotive officials in the region have argued that the decision would be based on competitiveness and the size of the market; but U.S. company representatives have feared that the interest of governments in having full-scale national operations in autos would induce them to force new local joint ventures in a particular component, especially if that component appeared vital for military vehicles as well. Each government could add a component manufacturer as it deemed appropriate after the four-year grace period. Given the military concerns in the region, more than one additional country is likely to seek production of critical components. Their entry would likely reduce the sales of the first company, despite its commercial ties; therefore, the company must assess carefully whether it wishes to go in for a period of four years certain, with the possibility of damaging competition from sub-sidized quasigovernment-owned activities after the four years.

It is questionable whether the ASEAN countries can sustain five separate national producers by 1990, given the experience in Argentina and Brazil on the necessity to reduce the number of companies and models in order to gain lower costs.

Further evidence that industrial dis-integration is sought within the ASEAN region (at least with reference to automobiles) is that each nation has a different list of components that will make up local content, and the percentage of local content required differs. One advantage for the comple-mentation enterprise is that its products are counted as local content in any of the other four countries in the region.

Consequently, the offer to the international companies is to come in as a minority joint-venture partner or licensee (with the trademark given up or one substituted by the local manufacturer) in an enterprise whose partners have been selected by either government or the auto federation of the host country. This procedure is not likely to bind the various elements of the auto industry closer together, nor does it utilize the specialized capacities of the various parts of an international enterprise.

Given the problems of the auto industry around the world and the likelihood that the number of major companies will be reduced to eight over the next ten years, it seems likely that the long-term objective of the ASEAN group will be frustrating if not frustrated. With each country having a na-tional producer, it would be difficult even to trade among the ASEAN countries. Japan would be pushed out of its 80 percent dominance of the total ASEAN vehicle market (of which the motorcycle market is 100 percent Japanese).

To save their position and provide continuing outlets for production in Japan, the Japanese companies (Nissan and Toyota) have offered company complementation agreements. But the ASEAN governments do not want to rely either on single companies or on a single country, such as Japan. They seek to induce U.S. and European companies to come in, but the pattern of short-term integration and later dis-integration is not attractive to some of the international companies. Some companies will undoubtedly come in as licensors to a regionally integrated component manufacturer, but even these will not be able to make the contribution they could if tied into a total system of component manufacturer and final product assembly. Thus the

ASEAN countries are missing a significant opportunity to integrate their auto industry and produce an inexpensive set of vehicles.

**Latin American Efforts.** Similar proposals were made during the 1970s to Latin-American governments for the purpose of integrating operations of single auto companies throughout the region, but similar objections were raised by several of the countries; thus each of the major countries wanted the more sophisticated technology and more valuable components such as the motors or transmissions. In the case of both Brazil and Argentina, the governments insisted on the higher technologies in order to support their military vehicle production. The need to balance off the technologies employed in each country indicates the necessity to have several major companies involved in these integration schemes simultaneously. With this expansion of participants, each company could locate different components in the various countries, providing each with experience in production of the entire range of products in industry. Where six to twelve auto companies exist already within a region, it would not be difficult to conceive of a dispersion of production that satisfies the requirements for technical experience in each country. This is not to say that the countries would be readily satisfied with the bargains but rather that the objections would then rest on concerns other than those over the location of technologies.

The Andean countries attempted such a dispersion of different activities within an industrial sector in their industrial complementation agreements. Fourteen sectors were slated for repartition among members, and three major sectors were finally agreed upon—automotives, metal working, and pharmaceuticals. But there were no ready mechanisms for implementation of the various investment requirements in the member countries since the Pact Junta decided that foreign enterprises would not be permitted to invest on a cross-national basis to achieve the integration. Rather, Andean multinational enterprises were supposed to be set up, but these were not yet formed or readily formed. The TNCs, employing an ME-form of organization, would have been able to make the appropriate distribution of activities, although they certainly would have insisted on location also in the profitable national markets in order to sustain the operations in the less-profitable or high-cost locations. Being unwilling to work with the TNCs and unable to form their own regional companies, the Andean complementation agreements have produced little integration. The inclusion of *several* TNCs would have answered some of the concerns over competitive structure, prices, and profitability. But concerns related to power and influence on the part of the TNCs remain; and, of course, they can be resolved only in terms of developing government officials who are competent enough to examine what the companies are doing and assess their impacts on an *ex ante* basis.

*Proposed Complementation*

In anticipation of the future need to mesh diverse production facilities more closely, several TNCs have begun to design product lines and individual products in such a way that it is economical to separate production operations in different locations and to bring the components together in different places for assembly. Such dispersion was not considered economical previously because products had been designed so that people working on different parts were in close contact and could make quick adjustments through their ready communication and an ability to see first-hand the problems of interfacing components. Tolerances, therefore, were sometimes finer than necessary for product performance, simply because they could be achieved through a production process located in a single place. With products now designed from the outset to have their components manufactured in distant locations, demands on the part of governments that some part of production be located within their boundaries are more easily met. This is not to say that *any* demand can be acceded to, but that the TNC will have greater flexibility in responding to governmental requests.

Consequently, we can conceptualize a model of cooperative industrialization beginning with regional agreement to coordinate industrial development. The particular sectors to be organized in this fashion would be selected: for example, automobiles, chemicals, petrochemicals, electronics, metal working, and rubber products. Offers by TNCs within each sector would be requested specifying how they would set up cooperative arrangements, balancing the various interests and meeting the particular criteria laid down within the agreement, and following the contracting procedures discussed in National Sectoral Integration above in the sense that bid specifications would be carefully stipulated.

Only a limited number of integration arrangements would be accepted, determined by the size of the estimated market within the region, so as to not create excess capacity and raise problems of redundancy. Each of the TNCs making a proposal would be informed that the market structure would be competitive once the structures were established; that is, each would be expected to compete in the market with others, thus inducing overall efficiency in the system and encouraging innovation. Innovation and competitive response would occur within the structure proposed and established by each company, but any major shift would have to be agreed to with the governments involved; and some governments might feel it necessary to support and maintain activities within their borders in order to prevent their being altered unfavorably to its interests.

In order to meet national objectives, local-content requirements could be set by each of the countries in a region (such as ASEAN) at whatever level a national government wishes. These different content requirements would have to be taken into account by the separate TNC bidders, and each would make its own representations as to how successfully it could comply with the different regulations. The result would probably be that the governments would find it desirable to harmonize their local-content requirements, permitting more efficient complementation by each of the companies involved. For the ASEAN region, three different auto producers could be given complementation status throughout the region (and three different motorcycle producers could also be given complementation status), thereby achieving competitive efficiency as well as ties into international markets once the affiliates in the ASEAN region reached international cost levels. A number of different companies could be requested to bid—one chosen from the United States, Europe, and Japan respectively so as to avoid dependence on any particular country or region. The governments of the ASEAN countries could take small minority positions in the companies set up by the TNCs so as to have an entry into their day-to-day operations—if this were found necessary or desirable.

*Effects of Complementation*

With agreements to restructure industry in this fashion, a number of present constraints and regulations would be alleviated. For example, the trade patterns would already be established within the arrangements, and trade restrictions would likely be removed. Employment arrangements and obligations would be stipulated in the offers of the companies, removing thereby many of the present employment constraints. Technology flows would be agreed upon by each of the country participants, thereby removing present restrictions over such transfers. Given a substantially competitive structure in the market, price regulations would be less necessary. Transfer pricing would also be agreed to within the arrangement, particularly as necessary to meet the agreements on the distribution of tax revenue. Investment regulations would be unnecessary in terms of entry negotiations since they would be done as a package; and concerns over restrictive business practices or illicit payments would be neither more nor less than at present.

Therefore, the companies would face no greater regulation than they do now, though they would be expected to be in continuous dialogue with the governments showing that in fact the arrangements were working out as planned. Nor would the companies be put at any competitive disadvantages, since all other TNCs in the industry would operate under the same arrangements. Whether or not each operation was profitable would depend on the ability of the company to make a reasonable proposal and to carry it out efficiently in terms of the initial investment, technical training of the workers, effective distribution, and marketing. But if the numbers of entrants were appropriately limited to fit the size of the regional market, there should be no additional constraint on profitability.

The major difference that arises from this type of cooperation and what exists today is a recognition of cross-impacts of the various regulations in the negotiation of a single package and a comprehensive treatment of TNCs within governmental industrial strategies. Given the fact that some TNCs have initiated talks along this line indicates that they would not be reluctant to engage in dialogues to this end.

It is really governments who are presently reluctant, despite the fact that they are calling for a restructuring of industrial patterns in North–South and South–South economic relations.

For the companies, inclusion of the home countries in the arrangements would make adjustments easier, since more product lines could be included. Also, a widening of the market in this fashion would increase efficiency for the LDC economies as well. However, a continuing fear of dominance is likely to prevent acceptance of inclusion of the advanced countries. Still, Brazil and Mexico are beginning to feel that they are able to merge some activities with the United States and might well be persuaded to consider such sectoral arrangements.

Though it complicates the negotiation process, the simultaneous consideration of several industry sectors provides some leeway in balancing the interests of various countries. For example, if it were not possible for exports and imports to be balanced appropriately within one sector among all of the countries, a different and offsetting balancing could be arranged in other industrial sectors, satisfying the requirements to maintain relatively balanced trade patterns. Multisector negotiations would also permit greater specialization among the sectors rather than within them, thereby increasing overall efficiency for the region as a whole. Still, this would not sacrifice equity or participation, and the various sectors in which creativity would be exercised could themselves be negotiated and agreed upon.

**Role of TNCs**

When the focus of complementation is one of the more sophisticated industries, which are the subjects generally of regional integration among developing countries, the potentially key role of the ME-form of TNC becomes apparent. What is sought in such integration is a binding together of industrial segments across national boundaries to serve the entire regional market. Of considerable concern to groups such as the Andean Pact countries is the question of the distribution of benefits of industrialization, which ensure that no one country can gain advantage over others and the benefits are not siphoned out of the region by TNCs. The Andean Pact adopted provisions which, in effect, prohibit the TNCs from making a substantial contribution to regional integration in an effort to prevent the gains from integration from accruing to the TNCs.

The Andean Pact has decreed that any company serving the *regional* market from within a member country (and thereby not paying import duties) should become *majority-owned* by nationals within the Andean countries. In other words, no TNC can retain a majority in any Andean affiliate company if it benefits from the removal of duties among the Andean Pact countries. (Contrarily, if the TNC's affiliate sold only within a single host country, it could remain 100 percent owned by the parent company.[1]

Given the unwillingness of TNCs to divest themselves of important affiliates, they have generally restricted Andean affiliates to selling wholly within their national markets. This means that the reduction of costs that would be possible through integration is lost in the Andean countries.

In addition, it is unlikely that any TNC will bear the investment cost required to establish specialized production among its affiliates, if it knows that it has to give up ownership of the newly combined affiliates. Participation by locals would mean conflicts of interest not only among the various partners but between the partners and the parent company abroad, simply because of the fact that integration and specialization were taking place and altering the flow of profits and the structure of the product lines and the pattern of trade *among* affiliates. Such conflicts would destroy the ability of the company to achieve the objectives of economic integration.

The Andean Pact, therefore, should have reversed the provisions if integration is its goal. It should have required any company selling only in a single market to become majority-owned by local entrepreneurs while permitting affiliates of TNCs to remain 100 percent owned if each specialized so as to integrate the regional market. This would have accelerated rapidly the progress of integration at virtually no cost to the Andean countries. The Andean Pact is perfectly designed to reject the major contributions of the MEs in fostering integration across national boundaries. Contrarily, they have (unwillingly) fostered investment in local markets, keeping them separate and high-cost.

A different example is provided by the auto industry in Taiwan. The Taiwan auto industry has been developed through joint ventures and licensing with TNCs, but the small volume of sales is divided among four companies, preventing low-cost production. Further, there is little chance of export because of protection throughout the regional market. Consequently, the choices that Taiwan has made leave it with a high-cost local industry, unable to move into regional or international integration under the existing structure. If it wishes to move into regional specialization, agreements would be required with countries such as Indonesia, Malyasia, Philippines, Japan, and South Korea so as to design the components supply and its allocation among various countries, with TNCs participating as indicated in the model above. Such arrangements wait only on the agreement of governments, who need to be persuaded that the benefits of integration are greater than the independence that allegedly arises from economic autarchy. As presently structured, the ASEAN group *can* use the capabilities of the ME, for its seeks integration and will allow 100-percent affiliates at times, but it has precluded TNCs from negotiations on integration industries for fear that they will gain the major benefits, leaving little for local companies.

How can governments prevent the benefits of international or regional integrations from accruing to the TNCs? After setting the guidelines for balancing of benefits among the countries (as noted earlier) governments would need a means of surveillance over each of the affiliates operating in their country or region. The necessary information could be obtained after the fact through reporting on changes in product line, trade patterns, and so on; or, it could be gathered *ex ante* by locating a government official within the offices of the affiliate companies.

To raise the possibility of using the TNCs in these ways implies that there is already an understanding of the desirability of such integration— leading to interdependence rather than independence—and the recognition of the undesirability of maintaining *dependencia* of either the old or new colonial form. The removal of any threat of *dependencia* would be achieved through establishing the rules of behavior on the part of the international companies through specific arrangements (*not* through a broad code) and then detailing the proper people for surveillance of the activities so that compliance could be confirmed before the fact rather than afterward. Such control mechanisms can more readily be established and result in greater efficiency in resource use than the pervasive entrance of governments into enterprise as has occurred in many of the developing countries.

## Note

1. But where there is a substantial need for foreign capital and a need to begin the management learning process at an early stage, the reception of foreign investment under wholly owned arrangements is more attractive to both the foreigner and the host country. This is the reason that the Mexican government accepted 100-percent-owned arrangements for many years and then fluctuated between 100 percent and minority partnerships from one year to the next during the 1960s and early 1970s before deciding that the country was able to carry out a majority Mexican-owned relationship successfully.

Its initial interest was in import substitution, which meant serving the national market. It has become increasingly concerned to stimulate exports; but now that it is requiring foreigners to accept minority positions, it is facing the likelihood of losing some opportunities to sell in the world markets through the lack of interest on the part of the U.S. partner in promoting Mexican sales through its other affiliates. Mexico has, therefore, made some policy changes that will stimulate exports out of the joint ventures, indicating a recognition that requirements of joint ventures are likely to be costly in some sense to the Mexican economy.

# 10 Restructuring Petroleum Extractive and Processing Sectors

Restructuring of the petroleum and petrochemical sectors has been going on at least since the Arab states took over greater ownership of operations in their countries in the 1960s. The form of TNC that was active in the early development of Arab petroleum resources was similar to the resource-seeker, which was discussed in chapter 5. If closer international integration is desired a different structure will arise, and the Arab moves are continuing to a type of interdependence to which Europe is not accustomed. Integration formerly existed internationally *within* TNCs through their ownership and control of exploration, development, shipping, refining, and petrochemical production and distribution across several national borders. Although there are a few instances in which an international company explores, develops, and exploits natural resources in a foreign country, bringing the resources into the metropolitan country (or others) for processing and eventual distribution and sale, this pattern has radically changed as governments have taken over the ownership and control of natural resources. In most countries, this form of integration has been fractured by governments taking over the stages of exploration and development of their resources, adding refining in some cases (and buying technology as needed form TNCs related to these three stages), but leaving transport, some refining, and marketing to the TNCs. The new arrangements involve concession agreements between host governments and TNCs (for exploration and development) and some buying of equity by Arabs in processing companies in Europe.

These new arrangements have led to a type of contractual integration. Integrative ties between independent buyers and sellers throughout the natural resource sectors rely principally on bids and offers in the market or longer-term bilateral negotiations between governmental or corporate buyers and sellers. But new forms are emerging with participation of Arabs in downstream activities of European companies, European participation in petrochemical production in Arab countries, bilateral deals involving oil prices and industrial development assistance, and cooperation by Europeans in selling Arab products as an inducement to Arabs to supply oil. The patterns are in flux, and the debate continues over extent and nature of competition, cooperation, and integration and over the threats to security

209

arising from the potential dependence of Europe on Arab supplies. Interdependence is mandated; what is not certain is the form and extent of integration and whether the resolution of the latter can mitigate undesirable levels of dependence.

Since the issue of dependence encroaches on national security as well as economic interests, the resolution will be by political criteria, rather than by market signals. However much TNC executives call for nonintervention by governments in new forms of industrial cooperation, corporate interests are not paramount. Governments will, therefore, set the stage, produce the play, direct it, and, at times, assume the leading role. TNCs did not act with much foresight and will, thereby, be relegated to implementors of policy rather than to policy formulators. They can regain some of the decision-making roles only by taking initiatives now that respond to the forces currently in play. In this they can expect little help from the present U.S. administration.

## Lessons of Dis-Integration

Because of their concern over the power of TNCs in their control over natural resources, and the consideration that the distribution of the benefits was greatly one-sided, governments have significantly altered the organizational and operational relationships of TNCs in the natural resource sectors. These companies have become contractors, providers of technical and managerial skills, traders, and shippers, but with significantly less ownership and control over the development and exportation of the resources themselves. These shifts have occurred principally in petroleum, copper, and bauxite (aluminum).

To attempt to produce order in a constantly shifting set of relationships, a number of proposals for cooperation have been made: the formation of multilateral negotiating groups of buyers and sellers to establish long-term contractual relationships; the formation of long-term bilateral contracts between buyers and sellers, including swaps; the formation of an international energy monopoly to buy all petroleum from anywhere in the world and to be the single seller to all customers; the formation of international agreements concerning the roles of negotiation among buyers and sellers; the formation of international commodity agreements to regulate the ranges of prices and to conduct buffer stock operations; international mergers; joint production facilities; and others. A singular characteristic of all such proposals is that they virtually void competition among companies involved in the natural resource sectors by placing the control of the market in governments or TNCs either directly or through agreements. Yet one of the prime objectives of restructuring should be to stimulate the efficiencies of intercorporate competition, not to rigidify their activities under tight governmental operational controls. There should be as much leeway in determination of product mixes, technologies employed, and sale as is feasible within the larger socio-political-economic objectives.

A singular opportunity was missed in the mid-1970s to restructure the organizational and institutional relationships in the petroleum and petrochemical sectors (as well as other extractive sectors) when governments in developing countries began to request increasing percentages of ownership in the exploration and development within their countries. In the main, the TNCs responded that they did not wish to give up such ownership and negotiated reluctantly (and under duress) to increase the gains received by the host countries. Unwilling to take any initiative or to see the potential long-run gains from a more cooperative structure, they eventually lost ownership and control of the developmental phases in some countries. They have been increasingly pressed to establish downstream facilities for processing and manufacturing in the producing countries so that the latter can share even more in the benefits of employment and income from higher-valued products.

The negotiating position of the TNCs remains buttressed by their widespread marketing capabilities, their technology, their shipping and transport facilities, and their refining capacities. But their abilities to determine the volumes of crude oil to be processed have been greatly attenuated by governmental agreements. Restructuring of this sector remains high on the agenda of producing countries, and TNCs will have to respond. New arrangements will seek not only desired levels of efficiency, but also a more equitable distribution of benefits, greater participation of all who are legitimately involved, a diffusion of creativity, and some stability in these sectors. Each party will also seek to guard his independence (or autonomy).

**Concerns over Cooperation**

To achieve these criteria means, again, that cooperative approaches rather than adversarial or conflict postures) must be sought. Europe will not only have to accept greater competition from the Mideast but also closer cooperation; the latter appears harder. But there are ways of melding the interests and abilities of the various groups so as to encourage a cooperative orientation at both policy and operational levels. To approach such a solution, it is desirable to look specifically at what the various groups seek. Overriding the interests of each of these groups is a worldwide concern over the uses to which the natural resources are to be put, by whom, and with what concern for future needs.

Presently, responses to these concerns are not considered acceptable to governments if derived from market forces alone, or made by managers of TNCs. Nor, of course, do governments of either producing or consuming countries consider that the appropriate answers are dictated by the other— the positions of both being affected by the extent and fear of dependence and costs/benefits. Unfortunately, there is no constituency to represent the interests of the future, but it is feasible to organize the ownership and control of natural resources so that some consideration of the future is elicited. The governments of producing countries are more likely to represent the concerns of the future, given their interest in conservation of their resources for future wealth creation. But consuming governments also can be induced to consider conservation measures through careful assessment of all alternative energy resources and uses.

TNCs have shown themselves less interested than producing countries in long-run problems of supply and demand, but their interest in serving markets in an efficient manner should be drawn into any institutional structure for the development and use of natural resources. The increasing concern of both producing and consuming governments for future energy requirements is a significant addition to the other forces drawing governments directly into ownership and control of these resources. But to leave governments alone to negotiate the development and use of natural resources is to play down the interests of the private consumers and to weaken the contribution of the private enterprises and the efficiencies of competition. Consumer interest can be met by maintaining an acceptable level of competition in these sectors, and the efficiency orientations of the companies can be included by their direct participation in policy and operational activities in these sectors.

Governmental concerns over the use of energy in the consuming countries extend beyond conservation for the future to questions of the competing uses of energy within the economy; the forms of energy generation (hydroelectric, wind, tidal, hydrogen, nuclear, thermal, coal, etc.); the pollution effects of different sources of energy both in production and in use, the mixing of different energy sources or fuels (e.g., gasohol); and even the level of prices (given the high inflation stimulus of energy prices). Finally, governments are directly concerned in the R&D activities of natural resource companies, related not only to alternative sources of new products but also to conservation efforts and depollution objectives.

A further concern of the consuming-country government is continued dependence on politically uncertain external sources of supply. They would like to establish a just cause for protection of these sources in the event of a threat to their continued flow. With increasing scarcities (compared to demand) governments will also be more concerned over the allocation of natural resources to competing uses (e.g., fuel versus plastics). Given the increased governmental concern over maintaining the key industrial sectors within their economies, and the reliance of these sectors (steel, autos, chemicals, etc.) on petroleum and other natural resources, a strong tendency to governmental interference will arise. The move to industrial policies therefore will extend backward into natural resource sectors as well.

## A Restructured Partnership

In considering how to restructure the petroleum extractive and processing sectors, we obviously do not start with a tabula rasa. Rather, there is already a complex network of intracorporate affiliates among the consuming countries (both advanced and developing) and some in the producing countries. U.S., European, Canadian, and Mideast companies have affiliates in each other and throughout the rest of the world. This network of companies provides the base for continued competition as well as the attraction for a more cooperative orientation through governmental participation in the companies themselves in areas of their most critical interests.

The Mideast producing countries, for example, have their most critical interest in the exploration and development of petroleum; the consumer countries have their most critical interest in the phase of distribution and consumption; and the most critical interest of TNCs lies in the refining and manufacturing stages, where their technology is most in demand and where transport facilities are important. Unless these interests are woven together in a more stable pattern of cooperative competition, the world will be continuously faced with disputes among producers and among consumers as well as between them, leading to continued instability, lack of order, and opportunism. This situation will guarantee neither efficiency nor equity and reflects little concern for the future.

The pressures arise from the fact that there is a high level of dependence and yet significant conflict of interests. The objective, therefore, should be to organize the dependence and to increase the mutuality of interests. Proposals to date do not achieve these objectives. On the contrary, suggestions for multilateral negotiations between producers and consumers (each coalesced into bargaining groups) lead to a type of bilateral monopoly in which the division of revenue and responsibilities is impossible to determine with any sort of certainty. The agreement is likely to fall apart repeatedly, and there is nothing the other party could do about it. Each party obviously would seek to maximize his share of the benefits, but since the situation is neither that of pure conflict nor pure cooperation, there is pressure toward a process of joint maximizing in a wholly uninstitutionalized manner. If the process could be institutionalized to ensure clear agreement on *how* the gains are to be distributed, much less concern over the level of gain at any

*one* time to any one of the parties would result for each party could anticipate a later improvement or balancing. Although conflicts may remain in
the working of the process, if the agreement on the process is so clearly to
the interests of all, it is less likely to fail. In any event, procedures for settlement of disputes and even for automatic renegotiation can be built into the
agreements.

One way to give all parties an interest in the *total* process of natural
resource exploration, development, refining, manufacturing, and distribution, is to provide for participation of all in each activity. The companies
want assurance of continued supplies of petroleum and raw materials; governments want dependable supplies also; oil-producing governments want
markets and some downstream activities, including inflow of technologies
and foreign exchange; processing countries want employment and dependable supplies; and all want an acceptable share of the revenue. These desires
can be satisfied only by a long-run and stable solution that each party finds
equitable.

The objective of close institutional ties is to satisfy major interests of
each party, provide continuity of supply and demand, and thereby to reduce
the use of threats, sanctions, or embargoes in periods of tension. Obviously,
where governments are concerned, extreme measures are always available,
but a system of cooperation with competition would significantly reduce the
likelihood of their use. This result assumes, however, that there is a high
degree of rationality among the parties in their pursuit of mutually agreed
goals and that acceptable shares of resource use will not be subordinated to
geopolitical strategies.

To accomplish this degree of cooperation and mutuality requires that
each of the major parties have a direct interest in all phases of the process of
development and use of the natural resources. The Middle East countries
(and other raw-material-producing countries) desire participation in downstream activities. But the European governments could not permit this ownership to arise without their own direct participation in both production
processing and distribution facilities. Otherwise, the private companies
would be subject to being held up periodically by the producing-country
partner.

To achieve a mutual balancing of interests and benefits would require
the restructuring of relatively equal shares in the *total* process, with each of
the three parties dominant in the sector of its major interest but in partnership with the other two. In order to achieve equal ownership and control
(and thereby equitable distribution of benefits throughout all phases of the
industry) and to establish a pattern of responsibility and administration that
would be effective and efficient, the distribution of ownership in the petroleum sector might work out as follows with control in each segment falling
to the majority owner:

| | |
|---|---|
| *Development and production* | 51 percent owned by producing governments; 29 percent processing TNCs; 20 percent consuming-country governments |
| *Processing* | 51 percent TNCs; 29 percent consuming-country governments; 20 percent producing-country governments |
| *Distribution* | 51 percent consuming-country government; 29 percent producing-country government; 20 percent TNCs |

Given that several countries (United States, United Kingdom, Canada, Norway, Soviet Union, Mexico, Venezuela, and others) are engaged in all three activities, the interests merge more closely. To balance these interests, present sole-producers and sole-consumers will want to enlarge their interests by establishing processing facilities, which can be accommodated readily if only growth-capacity is added. The consuming-country governments have less direct interest in the exploration and development of petroleum than producing governments and they have little to contribute (save through state-owned TNCs). The TNCs, on the other hand, have experience in exploration and development, and they generate technology and provide distribution facilities. They therefore merit a larger portion of the minority shares than do the consumer governments. In the processing phase, the companies have the shipping facilities, the refineries, the technology for processing as well as experience about the product-mix demanded by markets. The consumer governments are more directly concerned in this phase than the producing-country governments, since they will be involved in the determination of the product mix and total volumes of throughput. In the distribution phase, the consumer-country governments (especially the European) are already significant partners in the revenue through high tax rates on distributed products, and they might as well have a large direct share in the revenue (which should reduce tax rates). The TNCs would have 20 percent of this last stage and the producing-country governments 29 percent, to balance out the equality of shares in all three phases. This distribution would give all of them a third of the total and thereby an equal standing in final stages and in the distribution of revenue. What would remain is a determination of the distribution of revenues among the processes themselves, requiring negotiation of transfer pricing.

The criteria of acceptability sought in this distribution of ownership and control are those of *efficiency, equity, participation,* and *stability* in the industry; a dynamic equilibrium is likely to be reached only with a balancing of these benefits. Such a balance would significantly reduce the dominance of any one party, but it assures the continued participation of all. Compared to the situation in early 1980s, the role of the TNCs would be enhanced, but this is highly desirable in a rational world in that it reduces government confrontations that would arise through their bilateral or even multilateral negotiations. Leaving the processing facilities in the control of TNCs would place the responsibility squarely on them for technological advance, and they are the ones most likely to develop new technologies. Although the TNC's role would be less in the operation of distribution facilities, governments could let them carry out the activities under management contracts, or they could concentrate or disperse national distribution facilities, developing the level of competition at the pump to whatever was desired. The management of distribution facilities could then be regionally integrated or left wholly local within each country.

The role of the companies could also be increased at the production phase if the host government wished to contract out the management and operations of exploration and development. Given the interest of the TNCs in the entire process, they would have a greater desire to work closely with the producer governments to achieve greater efficiency at the production stage.

Such a three-way partnership could well bring stability to the petroleum industry and reduce some of the pressures on consumer governments to find substitute energy sources. However, continued search for alternative sources of energy or alternative sources of petroleum would also prevent the OPEC countries from being able to exercise any threat of a cutoff. In the final analysis, the potential long-range effects of a disruption of the triangular arrangements by any one of the three parties would be a strong deterrent to the use of their position for political or strategic ends.

## Remaining Problems

Such an equilibrium arrangement as discussed earlier would not remove all frictions, however. There would still be problems of intercompany pricing, dividend policies, and investment locations. But each would have full information *ex ante* on all policies and operations, and no one of the partners could operate at the particular stage that is under its majority ownership without regard to the interests of the others. Each segment could, however, expand its operations beyond the ability of the others to accommodate, but this would not make much sense. For example, the Arab countries could produce more than the downstream facilities could accommodate or customers would buy. If they did so, they would obviously be seeking new arrangements or outlets with other customer. Nothing would prevent such an initiative, so long as the resources used were not previously dedicated to these triangular arrangements. Also, the processing companies could buy crude elsewhere (if need to be) to utilize their total facilities and serve the markets outside the triangular arrangements. Similarly, the distributors could obtain products from other processing sources if demand was greater than that which could be supplied through these interdependent arrangements.

To arrive at such a triangulated solution would be a complex undertaking since a substantial number of companies could be set up with tripartite ownership, given that there are a dozen major producing countries, a dozen major international petroleum companies, and a dozen or more major advanced consuming countries, to say nothing of the interests of the LDC consumer countries. But not all arrangements need to be negotiated at once, and some parties might opt out. The resulting arrangement must maintain some elements of competition, however, or else it would result in one grand international cartel, dominated by governments. (Cartelization by governments is the actual result of a number of proposals extant on cooperation in the petroleum field.)

A further difficulty arises in setting the valuation of existing facilities in each of the three phases, but similar problems are met daily in the merger and purchase of companies. Even more difficult, however, is the determination of the principle of sharing on which to base the acceptable distribution of revenue among the parties involved. Negotiations of this sort would be more complex than bilateral monopoly, joint profit-maximization, or any two-party, zero-sum game, since there is no convergent solution that would fall out of the interests of all of the parties. But complex multilateral negotiations have succeeded under the GATT, NATO co-production, and the European Community; they are obviously feasible if the will exists.

A further complication is the fact that there are possible trade-offs among negotiations for the establishment of different triangular agreements in which some players are the same and others different. Frequently, two of the parties will have simultaneous negotiations going on with a different third party and could balance off a less desirable share between them in one negotiation with a more desirable situation in another. This would make the negotiations similar to the multilateral trade negotiations under the GATT.

If everything had to be negotiated at once, the procedures would probably break down because there are too many established facilities and inter-company ties to be covered under new agreements all at once. Fortunately, the process can begin slowly, and some experience can be gained before embarking on a complete restructuring.

One of the reasons for taking the matter slowly is to determine the good faith negotiating positions of each of the parties. It is conceptually possible for two of the parties to combine against a third: for example, a European government and one of its major companies against one of the Mideast suppliers. Obviously, such a coalition would be dangerous given the negotiating strength of the supplier country; unless the OPEC arrangements were dismantled prior to the restructuring of the business relationships. Even so, such coalitions make the negotiations into a bilateral monopoly, again making an efficiency solution less determinant than if each of the three parties negotiates in its own best interests.

The different viewpoints can be readily illustrated: Take European consuming governments and Arab producing countries. The European governments have an interest in dependable supplies at low cost, which could lead to requests for faster development and a larger flow of fuel supplies than the Arab countries might wish. The Arab countries would have an interest in maximum revenue, leading to a smaller flow of oil and a higher price, determined by a trade-off of present versus future revenue. Companies would have an interest in large throughput at the refineries, since costs of crude and gasoline prices would be determined in the other two stages. These differences exist in addition to those over the division of the total revenue among the three parties. All three would be constrained by availability of substitutes and elasticities of final demand in any individual effort to raise costs and prices in order to gain a greater return.

**Pressures for Restructuring**

No such complex changes will be undertaken unless some strong pressures or imperatives arise. What would impel an Arab supplying country to seek such a triangular arrangement? Given the willingness of the consuming countries to buy from any sources or virtually any terms, there is no such imperative. However, if the companies and governments determined that they needed more certain supplies and made offers of the type proposed here, there are reasons why the Arab countries might be induced to enter such negotiations. These factors are related to their interest in downstream facilities, stability of earnings, continuity of employment and production, and conservation of supply.

The European governments, on their part, are impelled by a desire to obtain certainty in supplies and in prices as well as a participation in the revenue. If the initiative for a restructuring were taken by the Arab countries, the European governments would be strongly impelled in that direction. The imperative is mitigated only by the existence of alternative supplies in Europe itself and alternative sources of energy, but these will apparently remain an inadequate substitute for some time. Also, the European producers can be brought into the same arrangements.

The companies would be interested in such stable arrangements (particularly if their returns were acceptable), and they would not like to be bypassed by the two sets of governments establishing their own facilities or taking over the companies' refining and distribution facilities. At the limit, this is possible; therefore the companies are likely to be rather amenable to new arrangements. In fact, the TNCs have the most urgent need to start negotiations of this type. They are the most vulnerable to threats from either set of governments, despite the fact that they are the major source of technology.

As a consequence of the limits on their bargaining positions, the TNCs probably have the weakest ground to negotiate from and are more likely to seek agreement avidly than the others if such a restructuring began to take place. The companies will have to give up more than will governments unless they are protected by the governments themselves. The position of the private companies would be strengthened only if the two sets of governments agreed that the companies should remain partners. Still, such a guarantee of participation would say nothing of the division of responsibilities or revenue.

Under present institutional relationships, the TNCs are also in a weak position in that both sets of governments have the possibility of negotiating collectively through established organizational structures: the European Community and OPEC. It is conceivable that these two groups coordinate their policies and interests internally, with OPEC merging its supplies and the European Community merging its processing facilities and demands. If so, the companies would be used merely as contract suppliers of management, technology, refining capacity, and distribution facilities.

However, the European Community has not yet achieved an energy policy for its members, and present orientations indicate that each of the major countries will negotiate for itself with Arab countries. On its part, OPEC has had difficulty agreeing on prices, and each country has set its own production schedules based on the revenue it wants at that price. Even prices are not uniform among OPEC members, indicating that it may well be possible to negotiate separate arrangements with them rather than having to deal collectively through OPEC. On their part, the TNCs have no present way of combining to negotiate their interests in such triangulated arrangements.

If the European governments did move to a concerted policy on energy and petrochemicals, the structure of company relationships would likely change significantly within Europe, with state enterprises becoming more important in these sectors. It is conceivable that half a dozen companies would be left operating competitively (under close governmental supervision), with most of the foreign companies being squeezed out of Europe. In fact, it is arguable that there can be little stability in the energy picture within Europe until the industry is rationalized to the point where it can be guided more readily by European governments. Such a rationalization is likely to diminish the role of foreign TNCs in the European picture except through merger or joint ventures. (The only mitigating factor against a squeeze-out is that European petroleum companies also operate significantly in other advanced countries and would like to retain some reciprocal privileges.)

Obviously, a variety of scenarios are conceivable, changing with the hypotheses as to the degree of consolidation among company interests, the nature and extent of cooperative arrangements within OPEC, the pattern of concentration among European governments, the coordination of energy policies within the European Community, the extent and nature of integration and dependence accepted, and the reactions of such governments as those of the United States, Canada, Brazil, Mexico, and Venezuela. What the precise outcome would be, however, is less significant than the realization that the petroleum and petrochemical sectors can be restructured so as to achieve some of the criteria of acceptability set out in chapter 4.

Without some move toward a more participative restructuring of the industry, the Mideast countries and other oil producers will increase the pressure for building downstream facilities within their own countries or for buying operations in Europe that they can eventually control. They can then even press for participation in distribution outlets and the transport systems. As with Iranian plans under the Shah, moves would follow into the production of semirefined and refined products and into exports of these in order to raise the value-added in earnings of foreign exchange. Though economies of scale do not support refining at great distances from large consumer markets, the economics of the situation may not be the basis of the decision by the producing countries. It behooves the consumer governments and the companies to examine their diminishing influence in the structure of the industry if they do not take the initiative to form a more cooperative arrangement.

Still another alternative is for both sets of governments simply to buy shares of the international companies, letting them reenter all stages of petroleum exploration, development, refining, and distribution, with the coordination occurring through the ownership and control of the policies of the boards of the various companies. Obviously, if the same governments owned similar shares in a number of companies, the competitive structure of the industry could move fairly quickly into monopoly as long as the governments attempted to exercise their ownership in the companies in a coordinated fashion.

The precise forms that cooperative solutions take is less important than the policy determination to find *some* such solution. The extent to which interdependent and cooperative sections are built will be determined by the ability to see new ways of arranging the ownership and control of industrial activities, leading to a more acceptable structure of industrial activity—one that does not destroy the advantages of economic integration and specialization but reflects the legitimate interests of all involved.

**Selected Readings for Part III**

Behrman, J.N. *Multinational Production Consortia.* Washington, D.C.: U.S. Dept. of State, 1971.

Behrman, J.N. *The Role of International Companies in Latin American Integration.* Lexington, Mass.: D.C. Heath, Lexington Books, 1972.

Behrman, J.N. *U.S. International Business and Governments.* New York: McGraw-Hill, 1971.

Ettinger, J. van. *The Need for Industrial Restructuring by Industrialized Countries.* New York: United Nations Development Program, 1980.

Herman, B. *The Optimal International Division of Labour.* Geneva: International Labour Office, 1975.

Lauter, G.P., and Dickie, P.M. *Multinational Companies and East European Socialist Economies.* New York: Praeger, 1975.

Levcik, F., and Stankovsky, J. *Industrial Cooperation between East and West.* White Plains, N.Y.: M.E. Sharpe, Inc., 1979.

Murphy, K.J. *Macroproject Development in the Third World.* Boulder, Colo.: Westview Press, 1983.

Zurawicki, L. *Multinational Enterprise in the West and East.* Netherlands: Sijthoff & Noordhoff, 1979.

# Part IV
# Conclusions

Although there are no *conclusions* (as such) to the proposals in the foregoing chapters, *process* remains, and embarking on the process requires an act of will that involves some basic decisions on where we want to go with the world economy. *If* we wish to move toward international industrial integration, it is apparent that the neoclassical prescription is not acceptable, since it does not encompass acceptable modes for the distributions of benefits. Continuing involvement in decisions on structure and location of economic activity will be required. The proposals here show one mode of doing so.

There remain many obstacles to such a process, despite the opportunities that it offers to resolve some of the continuing, intransigent problems we face. A further cost-benefit analysis is required.

# 11 Obstacles and Opportunities

The proposals herein for restructuring several industrial sectors toward greater national and international integration by using the special characteristics of TNCs are one means of institutionalizing nonadversarial relations among governments and between business and governments. If a wider community of interest is to be built among nations, small but significant steps such as these can pave the way. Each such successful arrangement will lead to more cooperative solutions within larger economic communities and easier trade-offs of narrow national interest. Although accommodations as proposed are difficult, similar trade-offs occur repeatedly in ad hoc situations and have been accomplished in several longer-run agreements establishing the rules of cooperative competition in specific areas of trade, in restrictive business practices, in exchange rates, in defense, space exploration, power development, and so on.

If governments were wholly accommodating to the interests of all others, classical competitive market mechanisms might be acceptable, for they are based on an assumption of peace. Thus the complete ethical foundations under that system would also be acceptable and the rules would be followed. But given their concern for power and wealth, governments will continue to limit the free market and underlying comparative advantages as the bases for determining the location of economic activity and the distribution of benefits. They are presently unwilling to redesign the entire system in a more cooperative manner to form a new international economic order. Yet the system *will* change, for no government can avoid completely the constraints of its country's resource endowment or the shifting market conditions of supply and demand in making determinations as to its role in international production. Governments continue to interfere, however, in an effort to change factor endowments, market conditions, and benefits received. Contrarily, they recognize that this continued intervention is unlikely to redound to their welfare in the long run.

Both business and government express concern over the increased role of government, adversarial positions adopted between business and government (at least in the United States), and the need for a more cooperative relationship in which greater efforts are made to define mutual goals and the means of achieving mutual benefits. Although there are moves in this

225

last direction, a firm shift in orientation (evidenced by some specific steps) is required. One such step is the formation and implementation of regional sectoral policies. The restructuring of industry must facilitate moves toward international production under cooperative competition. (This is essentially Japan's internal system: a national system based on fundamental agreement on the necessity to achieve harmony through cooperation, with strong competition among individual units or companies in the pursuit of the agreed goals.) The precise form of such cooperation is unimportant and will undoubtedly change as we shift the goals and the means of achieving them. The form of company structure or the form of intergovernmental agreements should themselves be by-products of the objectives sought and the means employed. What is important is cooperation for equity, a coordinated use of resources efficiently allocated to achieve the objectives, and a participatory role for all countries in the design of the objectives sought.

Although completely free international trade under a worldwide free-market competitive system would generate an efficient structure of the location of economic activity, it is clear that this structure is not perceived as equitable. The rise of international production has demonstrated the inadequacies of the present system in the competitive efforts to shift the location of activity. International production is, therefore, a key to melding of national interests in both efficiency and equity. The mere shifting of industry will not be enough, however; even that could produce inequitable results in terms of the distribution of income and control. To be *given* an equitable share is not the same thing as to participate in the decisions and in the creativity that lead to equitable distribution.

Therefore, a series of other fundamental questions are involved in the question of how to structure international production:

1. the degree and extent of integration necessary to achieve acceptable efficiency;
2. the degree of dependence or interdependence acceptable in view of the desire for national security;
3. the nature and extent of adjustments necessary to the restructuring of industry internationally and the determination of who bears these adjustments;
4. the distribution of benefits and the methods of determining that distribution; and
5. finally, the means of merging worldwide interests of harmony and cooperation with individual drives and responsibilities.

The breadth of these related issues indicates that their resolution should not be attempted at once. We must only understand that these issues are affected each time we make decisions as to the structure of international production. Given these complex issues, it is hardly appropriate to insist that any *one* business form should be the sole means of accomplishing any particular goal or that it should be protected in any way. The TNCs are relatively new on the scene (at least the ME-form) and they will undoubtedly change in structure and significance, as have others in the past. In fact, corporations will take virtually any structural or organizational form dictated by external forces (such as market shifts, governmental constraints, and technological innovations) because survival is the key objective of a business entity. The TNC therefore should be encouraged by the rules of the game to maintain organizational flexibility and capabilities but also be given a clear set of guidelines and constraints.

Although it will be difficult to proceed with proposals for restructuring, the primary question is not *whether* to permit a restructuring, for it will occur. Rather, the important issues are *how* the restructuring is to occur, whether it will be integrating or dis-integrating industrially among nations, and whether the process is to be cooperative or adversarial: That is, is it a step in the direction of mankind's evolution to a recognition of interdependence with each other and his habitat or yet another human effort to assert an egotistic will over others and over his environment to the detriment of the full development of all human and natural resources? There is clearly enough in the world to satisfy mankind's largest visions of (inner and outer) progress if we only seek internal sources of power and help each other to seek the goals obtainable by learning how to live *together*, economically and spiritually, while *separated* physically, geographically, culturally, and politically. Togetherness and separation are inherent conditions of mankind, but a question remains of the realms and extent of each. Resolution is necessary; we grow by finding new and better means of association.

### Obstacles

Five sets of obstacles stand in the way of restructuring through the use of TNCs: one set relates to present principles underlying *policy* prescriptions, which are grounded in history, theory, sentiment, and diverse practices (often in violation of the policies); the second set relates to the difficulties of *negotiation;* the third to the problems arising in *implementation;* the fourth relates to our *perception,* and the fifth to our confusion of managament and leadership.

### *Policy Principles*

One of the major policy obstacles to a restructuring of the world economy toward closer industrial integration is the absence of a theoretical model showing how it might be done and therefore the continued adherence (at least in principle) to decision criteria that have predominated since World War II and before. The gap in theory is largest in the critical issue of the distribution of the benefits in world economic growth. There is no explanation or mechanism for achieving the application of the Pareto optimum so that all participants are in fact better off. There is also no criterion of equity in the distribution of benefits; even if all are better off they are likely to be better off to different degrees, but *relative* wealth and power are important. To resolve this problem of equity will require governmental coordination, guidelines, rules, and agreements that are difficult to achieve even within a nation, not to mention internationally.

The policy of the U.S. government downgrades all criteria of acceptability other than efficiency—as expressed in the concept of undistorted market decisions[1]—not sufficiently (or explicitly) recognizing that there are multiple goals, some of which are conflicting. But even the pursuit of efficiency requires multiple trade-offs as to level and conditions of employment, use of specific resources, markets to be served, and so on. These also are not always left by governments to the free play of market forces when key sectors are involved. Further, the other criteria such as order and stability do not come out of efficiency. Rather, they emerge from perceived equity, which requires changes in benefit relationships compared to what has occurred under (distorted) market determinations. Thus, a long-standing policy orientation will have to be modified if a goal of the United States is also to gain greater international economic integration, as is frequently asserted. The U.S. government is reluctant, at best, to discuss modes of restructuring international industry since it still hopes that the present trend toward the new protectionism is a short-term aberration. Its view is that departures from this policy are *exceptions* to be abhorred and corrected rather than forming a basis for new policy orientations. Consequently, even its aberrations have no consistency and abide by no rules, and the feasibility of establishing *rules* for the so-called exceptions, leading to a new rule system, is not recognized. Further, the United States retains a strong bias toward a legal orientation, based on adversary relationships, and a historical orientation of business away from sociopolitical problems to purely commercial ones.

Its adherence to the Bretton Woods concepts (as discussed earlier) thwarts any move to examine segmented (functional or sectoral) problems. But only such specific issues are likely to be encompassed in policy discussions at present.

The TNC is paramountly a creation of U.S. business, being the U.S. multilocation, multidivisional, multiproduct corporation writ large upon the world economy. Per se it has neither been supported, understood, nor utilized by the U.S. government for policy purposes since U.S. policy has stuck to the principle of nondiscrimination among sectors, companies, or types or sizes of companies, except when it saw fit to select one or more for special treatment.

As TNCs are being formed in other countries, they are being supported by and dovetailed on occasion with their government's policies. State-owned TNCs have already entered this realm of cooperation, as have some national champions in the private sector.

The role of TNCs in international economic integration is simultaneously a narrower (functional) issue (when treated sectorally) than a new world economic order and a broader issue than encompassed in the Bretton Woods Agreements, since both trade and investment are included. Future steps require focus on *specific* issues, since an inadequate community of interests exists to undertake a reordering of the world economy, thereby denying the ready identification of mutual goals that would be required to formulate an ordering principle by which an entire new system could be formed.

Even the rather broad approach of giving attention to specific *worldwide* problems (such as energy, hunger, population, environmental protection, renewable resource development, and science and technology in development) is on too grand a scale. Also, no significant progress has come out of the several UN conferences on these problems. Even the attention given to the role of TNCs has resulted in little constructive effort, and attempts to set the limits of TNC behavior through codes of behavior are too grandiose and general.

Attempts to negotiate codes of behavior constitute a *second* policy obstacle to the proposals made here, since they imply that such codes are adequate and effective means of defining the TNC's role within a new international economic order (NIEO). There are the following: an OECD code on foreign investments; an International Labour Organization (ILO) code on social policies of TNCs; a UN code on direct investments in process; a recently agreed UN code on restrictive business practices; two UN codes on investment and technology transfers in negotiation; and a UN code on corrupt business practices in disagreement. These are being supplemented by work on codes for transborder information flow and information policies and an agreement on standardization of accounting practices. Each of these codes is seen by the developing countries as a step in the formation of new international low, guiding worldwide TNC behavior. However, many advanced countries see the codes as political concessions that are likely to have little economic effect; and many LDCs are now recognized that they are essentially irrelevant for their own national interests. These codes will not help in addressing the fundamental (priority) issue of industrial restructuring. Mere alterations in the behavior of TNCs, unrelated to the location or balancing of economic activity, will not satisfy governments that they have in fact achieved the desired restructuring of industrial production and balancing of benefits.

At present, the advanced countries do not see instituting new modes of industrial coordination for development as a priority. Instead (like the TNCs themselves), they are seeking to prevent erosion of their positions in the world economy. The orientations of the advanced countries are grounded in a concept of world economic order (how it *is* functioning and *should* function) that does not include the acceptance of significant changes in underlying economic relations or the creation of new international institutions. The orientation of the developing countries, on the contrary, includes a continued fear of dealing with existing institutions: It prevents some of them from understanding the potental contributions of private enterprise and induces others to impose numerous constraints on TNCs to gain some progress toward their industrial goals.

A major obstacle even in a sectoral approach to restructuring and the use of the TNC is the continuing fear in LDCs of the power of the TNCs themselves. Any new institution (such as the TNC) is seen as disturbing existing relationships, and complaints have been readily directed at the TNCs. These complaints are followed by restraints that seek to rebalance power relationships and redistribute the benefits of TNC activities. The problem of making appropriate adjustments for the TNCs is exacerbated by the fact that they have operated in numerous political jurisdictions and are not the creatures of the governments responsible for the welfare of these political units. It is crucial, therefore, to assess carefully the contributions that TNCs can make to the restructuring of the world economy and to the particular interest of nations involved. If the desired contributions are not forthcoming, constraints will be imposed on the TNCs (as through the codes), resulting in their integrative capabilities being destroyed.

A third policy obstacle arises from the fact that the TNCs themselves have done little to allay the fears and concerns of LDC (and some AC) governments over their competitive power and lack of accord with governmental socioeconomic objectives. Therefore many LDCs have adopted policies of permitting TNC entry only under multiple constraints. Though constraints would exist under the proposed sectoral restructuring, they would be negotiated multilaterally and free of full control of any one government. TNCs have shown greater responsiveness of late, and governments have greater confidence in dealing with them; but an attitudinal obstacle remains. If we are to take advantage of the capabilities of large private institutions, however, government participation will be mandated to reduce concern over unbridled power.

Finally, the proposals herein will appear to many as being a giant step toward international economic planning, which meets opposition from a variety of directions. However, there is no implication here of worldwide or macro planning; rather a step-by-step approach to coordination of sectoral industrial development aimed toward removing inefficiencies in the use of world resources (overcapacities and misuse) and reducing conflicts in the patterns of investment and trade is recommended. Planning is required to determine where we want to go collectively, but the agreements should also include wide discretion for participation to avoid rigidities and to promote innovation. Competition should be promoted within a set of cooperatively determined rules. Setting of sectoral rules will require considerable cooperation among business (industry and banking), labor, government, and various concerned groups, including international organizations.

To use TNCs effectively to achieve such equitable arrangements will require a significant shift in underlying economic orientations and institutions. This is a substantial challenge to U.S. policies. But the United States is presently an unlikely leader in moving the world toward such cooperative approaches because of its dedication to unrequited policy positions. U.S. policy remains so far out of touch with the fundamental movement and issues in international trade and investment that it has lost the chance to lead. The United States can inveigh and cajole, but it presently can lead neither from a position of economic dominance (as in 1945–1950) nor from one of reasoned policy prescriptions. Its policies remain tied to the assumptions and conditions of Bretton Woods despite its own abandonment of those conditions and prerequisites. Its leadership role is handicapped by the decline in the relative economic significance of the United States on the world scene, the continued lack of personal leadership by its top officials within the OECD nations, and an unwillingness or inability to accept the role of burden-bearer and to make necessary internal adjustments. Whether there are other countries more suited to the role, whether an initiative waits on a strengthened European Community, or whether the private sector can take a significant initiative is unclear; but the answer lies in the *will* to act responsibly.

The options appear to be leadership to international integration of drift to dis-integration. Dis-integration, in the sense of duplicated facilities and reduced sectoral trade, is acceptable within desired worldwide goals if national markets become sufficient in size to permit economies of scale. But many countries do not have the opportunity to gain that optimum size, and for several sectors only a *few* countries can do so. Even these would find infrasectoral specialization more efficient than sectoral self-sufficiency. Therefore, to use the world's resources more effectively will require closer international integration.

A restructuring toward closer industrial integration is virtually mandated for the world, given the interdependence that has already arisen. Guided integration would permit achieving several of the criteria of acceptability of a new order: greater efficiency, greater equity (by techniques explained earlier), protection of bio-resources and attention to a variety of externalities, greater participation of all nations, and greater recognition of socioeconomic costs of industrial progress (through better information, *ex ante,* on corporate decisions and industrial directions; closer interaction of interest groups; faster feedback, etc.). The benefits are too great not to seek them assiduously. To accept the challenge will require strong initiatives in both the private sector and governments.


*Negotiation*

Even if the United States and other OECD governments can make necessary shifts in policy orientations and the LDCs could accept a key role for TNCs, several obstacles remain to *negotiating* the kinds of arrangements discussed in the previous chapters. One such obstacle is the very complexity of the agreements requiring the accession of at least two governments and one or more TNCs in any given sectoral arrangement. The preliminary decision as to which countries will negotiate is an obstacle, in that participation itself is negotiable: Will the members belong to a given region or be scattered worldwide, and how many will participate? Only if the negotiation is sought among members of an established group (OECD, for example) is this obstacle mitigated.

Evidence as to the difficulties of negotiating NATO, Andean, and other such cooperative industrial arrangements indicate that there are a number of trade-offs to be taken into account with reference to each of the criteria of acceptability. These trade-offs will differ among country priorities and shift from one sectoral arrangement to another. Thus, the efficiency criterion will be sought by achieving economies of scale, selecting the best technology, employing the most capable management (from whatever country), and marketing effectively. But the most efficient arrangements must be balanced against the equity criterion, which will be met by decisions on the flow of funds, the pattern and volume of imports and exports, the application of technologies in given countries, the distribution of employment, the acquisition of worker skills, division of product lines among countries, effects of transfer pricing, and tax revenues. These, in turn, will be modified by the desire to gain effective *participation* on the part of all nations involved in negotiations through employment of their managers, creation of joint ventures, and worker training. Decisions on *creativity* will affect the prior selections through the support of the local science community, the development and utilization of R&D institutions, participation in design functions, desire for local innovation of inventions, and efforts to diffuse technology within member countries (as well as among them). The criterion of *stability* will be affected by the extent to which the markets of countries are tied together in the restructured sector, which determines the nature and extent of transmission of economic fluctuations through the sector. Each of these criteria is potentially tradable against another, although some are additive; for example, greater perceived equity has led to greater productivity (and efficiency) rather than reducing it. The result is greatly dependent on motivation, which we still understand inadequately.

Despite the complexity of the trade-offs, such negotiations can be successful. Success simply depends upon the *will* to do so, which probably needs strengthening by pressure groups and by high priorities among governmental policies. In any case, the negotiations for such restructuring would involve fewer nations than those engaged in the tariff negotiations, which have succeeded periodically.

A second obstacle in negotiation lies in the selection of the various industrial sectors to be integrated and which to start with. Several industrial sectors are in sufficient difficulty to place them on a priority list. Given the desirability of getting a good model for subsequent agreements, the priority should be given to the one in which success is most likely to be achieved with the least difficulties. The automotive industry seems to be a prime candidate, given its extensive location of operations, the pervasive interest in that sector in a number of countries, current pressures on supply and demand, the expectations of declining demand in advanced countries, and the slow rate of technological change in the sector. Another is heavy electrical machinery. Governmental attention to any industrial sector with the purpose of enhancing its competitiveness has tended to move toward protectionism. Apart from protectionist moves, only international cooperation remains; and intergovernmental agreement will be required on which sectors are to be first and whether they are to be taken singly (seriatim or simultaneously) or collectively with trade-offs *among* different sectors. A collective approach increases the complexity but also increases the ability to make trade-offs through having more elements to bargain over, and it raises efficiency by (potentially) increasing specialization as between and among rather than only within sectors.

A third difficulty is that of deciding the division of specific activities: that is, the degree and extent of specialization among the member countries, which is itself related to the decision as to the countries to be included in any arrangement. Related to the matter of responsibilities is, of course, that of returns; some principles as to the division of participation in each aspect of operations and the rewards for participation in each aspect of operations and the rewards for participation will be required. Returns would also be related to initial contributions to any consortium (capital, equipment, technology, patents, going conern value, etc.) and are tied to the decision of whether to undertake two or three agreements simultaneously in order to have the possibility of offering one party more in one sector and one less in another.

One of the most difficult obstacles in negotiation, however, is that of meshing regional industrial integration arrangements with cross-regional ties or bilateral ties between nations (with shifting alliances). What will emerge from such agreements would be a new structure of industry and trade, with additional sets of rules affecting competition among the parties to the agreement. The necessity to mesh various forthcoming agreements argues for an international umbrella agreement to coordinate national and regional industrial policies and to avoid reinventing the wheel for each new agreement.

*Implementation*

Such complex arrangement are not carried into implementation without difficulty—however complete and satisfactory the underlying policies and the negotiations.

A priority problem in daily administration is the selection of personnel to oversee the implementation of the agreement. Surveillance is needed even for the OECD and UN codes of behavior; closer scrutiny will be required over these arrangements even if the application of the rules will be largely through competition among the TNCs or national companies participating. If personnel assignments in an administrative oversight group are made on a quota basis, the problem of obtaining the best individuals for the positions arises. Further, the acts under surveillance will become a subject of discussion and the information needed will require new decisions. Surveillance itself opens opportunities for corruption, in addition to those in the process of negotiation. Such surveillance is less significant if there is a reasonable degree of competition in the market among the various entities (industrial consortia or TNCs). But even with competition, the national members may wish to be assured through surveillance that the competitive structure remains as desired.

Apart from the day-to-day problems that arise in any organization, such cooperative new structures will involve some difficult decisions as to control, dispute settlement, and duration of the arrangements. The problems of control include those relating to formation of overall operating policies, the maintenance of desired competition, and shifting objectives of national participants.

Duration issues relate to the causes and procedures for either renegotiation or termination of the arrangement. Termination could be prompt if the project only involved a turn-key operation, but what is envisaged here is more complex. Procedures for renegotiation of such agreements will also be required since conditions within a given sector will change. Within the original negotiations, therefore, provisions should exist indicating the agreed causes for renegotiation or termination and the procedures for accomplishing each. Obviously, national governments can break even these agreements, but the multiplicity of parties would tend to dampen an irresponsible pullout by a single country.

A procedure for settlement of disputes is required, whether over activities of the company participants or over policy positions taken by government officials. Complaints will arise, and procedures for a reconciliation are needed. Some facilities exist in the International Center for the Settlement of Investment Disputes, but a few countries are reluctant to put any disputes before that body. New procedures may have to be formed; NATO consortia experience can be instructive here.

These difficulties are no different in kind than exist at present in various efforts throughout the international economy. But the new element will be the degree and extent of prior and continuing agreement among nations aimed at a significant restructuring of industry under mutually acceptable criteria.

To reduce the likelihood of failure through inability to surmount some of these obstacles and to prevent surprise failures in implementation, it is highly desirable to examine *all* aspects of the restructuring prior to agreement. The Andean Pact countries got through the first two sets of obstacles: the policy shift to integrated industries was easiest in that although the negotiation was difficult it was accomplished for three sectors; but implementation was not adequately conceptualized or thought through for any of them. Consequently, only one of the fourteen sectors selected for complementation arrangements has even begun the process of implementation. Also, it is hampered by the inability to make cross-national operational trade-offs, which could have been offered through the use of the TNCs to integrate cross-national activities efficiently and equitably.

*Perceptions*

The *fourth* obstacle to international restructuring on a cooperative basis is our *perception* of the world. The Western view of the world and its modes of living has been fundamentally based on a concept of separation and differentiation. Rather than seeing the world and its inhabitants as a single entity intimately interdependent, we have sought our knowledge and our modes of life through a process of distinguishing differences and through classification (in science) of these differences and in eulogizing (in lifestyles) modes of differentiation. There is obviously nothing inherently wrong in making distinctions. What is flawed is a reliance on that approach as opposed to an attempt to balance it with an understanding of the differences' purpose, which is to supplement and complement the others, making up a whole. This approach has placed strong emphasis on the individual, unbalanced by a similar emphasis on individual responsibility to others or on formation of community orientations. It has permitted and encouraged the separation of academic disciplines so that each feels its area is unique and autonomous, rather than professors or students visualizing it as part of a totality in which all things mesh together. It has permitted us to carve out territory both nationally and individually and to disregard the fact that its use affects all others. It has supported our desire to discriminate against others on a number of bases (race, creed, color, weight, club, talents, place of birth, family, etc.). It has encouraged a cultural egotism that at the extreme sees others as barbarians or nonpersons.

Even in our individual lives, we have been able to separate the various facets, rather than seeing them as part of the same essential I. Thus we develop our intellectual life in one way and employ it in isolated activities; we develop our physical life separately from our intellect; both of these areas are from emotional development and stability; and spiritual development is kept still further isolated.

This concept of separation has continued to feed three of the most insidious passions of mankind—greed, power, and sex.[2] *Greed* is fed by the concept of separation through the belief that it is appropriate for us to remove resources from the use of others to our own pleasure and that there is no limit to the process. The idea that such a continued accumulation would never adversely affect the resources of the world or their development simply did not seep into the collective consciousness. The concept of *power* also developed in the direction of individuals having power over other individuals or entire nations, to the point that several individuals have sought to rule the world. Power will always exist, since it is an expression of energy or force, but the comprehension of power as a balanced system of forces would alter our perceptions significantly. Even the fundamental emotional, spiritual, and physical union in *sexual relations* has been misused and misapplied through the concept of separation, rather than its being seen as an act of complete unification. Acts of unification represent surrender and merging, whereas we eulogize sexual relations as conquest and sensual pleasure, reflecting both power and greed.

Finally, our concept of separation has committed us to believe that we can command nature to do our bidding without adverse effect on the development of nature itself. This has led to considerable wastefulness and destruction, so that we have, in fact, been fouling our nest without perceiving the consequences and even destroying our sustaining sources.

Once again, there is nothing wrong with distinctions and differentiation that help us perceive and understand the many manifestations of the One Cause; but when they are relied on solely or in such a way as to deny the extent to which we are in fact interdependent and reliant upon the environment within which we live, this perception of differences becomes destructive. Reliance upon our environment does not imply stagnation or lack of use of that environment; nature itself has not been stagnant. Evolution is the process of nature, and ours is the same. What we need is a new perception of our own role and our relationship to each other and to our environment.

The introduction of international production in the world economy also requires a new perception and a more holistic approach. A world under free trade itself involves a number of interdependent relationships since it requires shifts in market penetration, product lines, wages, capacity utilization, location of production, trade of intermediate as well as final goods, and a number of adjustments in the distribution of benefits. When movements in the factors of production (including management and technology) are added to the movement of goods, interdependence increases significantly, with much of the trade resulting directly from the shifts in the production factors, thus giving rise to new patterns of comparative advantage. Yet we seem unwilling to change our perception of the world economy to see its interdependence and to understand that we must relate to one another in more complex and cooperative ways than a merely commercial fashion.

We even continue to try to treat international monetary problems as distinct from the issues of international trade or international production and clearly distinct from issues of international equity. Yet they are all intimately related.

To change our perception is not easy, but it can be done. It will be achieved more quickly when we see that what we are doing has not acquired the efficiency that we wish and that there must be some better way.

*Management versus Leadership*

The *fifth* obstacle to effective international restructuring is the gap in the United States (and other advanced countries) between management and leadership within and by TNCs. This gap is itself partially a result of the separation of academic disciplines and areas of knowledge mentioned above. Management has increasingly been perceived as a means of controlling situations, markets, production processes, resource development, and even people through the manipulation of workers and other managers. Leadership involves marching with, rather than commanding, others; it certainly does not include manipulating them. Manipulation is an expression of greed and power; its use exacerbates the fundamental problems.

Management seeks a more certain environment and means to minimize risk, since specific performance is expected (under the false presumption that control is possible), and the manager is to be held responsible for that performance. Leadership is required because of the uncertainty that exists (which is full of risks for the participants) and coordinated responses are necessary in order to achieve collective goals. The assumption of the responsibility of leadership implies not acting *ir*responsibly in terms of the interest of the group.

Leadership does not mean that we are responsible for those who follow; they have their own decisions to make as to whether and how they follow. But it does mean that the leader is responsible to others to maintain the values of the group, to serve the larger society, and to help the group act within the society's ethical constraints. These orientations will help in the development of the individuals themselves, which is the high purpose for which any group ought to act. Management, on the other hand, has frequently avoided the ethical issues, often preferring to see corporate organization as a mechanism itself, without ethics or morals. Many managers have not felt any responsibility for encouraging members of the organization to behave ethically or even to set ethical standards for the group. A number have even found it convenient or desirable to flout the legal constraints that society has imposed in order to reach social goals.

Leadership, therefore, is an exercise of will in the pursuit of high purpose. (The concept of leadership does not apply if the pursuit is of *low* purpose.) Leadership by its nature should elevate both the leader and the led, with mutual responsibilities fully accepted and acted upon. The leader, therefore, should build bridges for others to cross, destroying them as soon as they have served their purpose, and should help each of the followers learn how to build their own bridges. Such leadership relies on the power of purpose, which means that there must be a vision that catalyzes the followers, and the vision needed now is one of greater cooperation in meeting the problems of a disturbed world economy. Such leadership and new perceptions would help in the reformation of policies, in the necessary intergovernmental negotiations, and in the process of implementation with the abilities of the TNCs.

## Alternatives

Turbulent and stressful times offer the opportunity for building new institutions and new modes of international cooperation. The frequent calls for new institutional arrangements indicate that perceptions are changing and that the groundwork is being laid for such changes even if they are not yet wholly visible. Change does not always occur step-by-step, for even in evolutionary theory we are now contemplating that changes have occurred by leaps or by structural shifts for which we lack evidence of sequential linkages. Man has the ability to change his view quickly and radically and to alter his behavior equally radically, and a minority group forming a critical mass can bring change acceptable to all. This does not mean, however, that we are likely to form a world federation of states overnight. But it does imply that we can readily conceptualize that nation-states should be the building blocks for the next stage of international cooperation rather than the stones in the path. We need not operate everything multilaterally on a worldwide scale, but we can proceed through bilateral cooperation among nations on specific functional issues or sectoral problems. Even these are sufficient to require a shift of perception—or, in the current usage, a paradigm shift.

One of the required shifts is that we recognize the significance of the problem of the distribution of benefits, which is a problem of *political* economy that exists in both market and socialist economies. A secondary shift is recognition that protection is not the means of coming to an acceptable accommodation on this issue. There appears to be a sufficient recognition that existing institutional arrangements are not working, but the idea that they have to be altered to become more cooperative among a significant number of nations has not yet been put into policy deliberations. In order to get movement along these lines, small steps will probably be necessary but with an eye on the overall vision to be pursued.

In taking such steps, business managers need to become leaders within the international community, identifying themselves with high purposes, just as the classical economists sought to mitigate the passions of man in their support of the capitalist system: the containment of the drive to power, the mitigation of licentiousness, and the channeling and constraining of individual greed to the service of others. These system objectives have been too readily forgotten by both economists and corporate managers. One of the first steps to the leadership required of business is a recognition of the unity of the work in which the company is engaged with the evolution of the individuals who are participating so that motivation is channeled into service to the larger society.[3] Recent literature on successful management has emphasized the values, high purpose, and spiritual or superordinate goals whch distinguish such managers from others.[4] These managers fare leaders and developers of *persons* and not merely operators or manipulators. They see their people and the company as evolving and they provide a *vision* of that evolution.

The exercise of such business leadership leads also to an *acceptance of responsibility* to address the socioeconomic problems of the system, rather than having that responsibility taken over or assigned by government fiat. It remains difficult for many U.S. businesses to accept responsibilities other than the pursuit of profit through the production and delivery of goods and services. But there are evidence of an emerging shift in its orientations in the direction of greater corporate responsibility for both internal and external personal relations and community impacts.

The assumption of such a responsibility implies that these companies and their managers recognize that business is but one part of a complex whole within which mankind is evolving. This recognition will lead further to acceptance of an holistic orientation (a systemic understanding of everything being related significantly to everything else), as expressed in an old American Indian cosmology that "Everything is alive; and everything is related." This is a sharp departure from the particularist or extreme individualist view of "I'm OK, Jack," or "Viva Yo!" Rather than focusing only on individual wealth and the carving of one's individual niche in society, a careful and judicious mixture of individual roles and communal belonging would be formed, helping each individual to gain and hold a place for growth within society. This concept of place (so strong in Japan), would be added to that of individual achievement, and objectives of sharing and equity would be consciously added to those of acquisition and efficiency for the society as a whole. The process and concept of achievement would be modified to encompass other than material goals and rewards, leading to a sharing of both opportunities and benefits with others in the system.[5]

Systems of sharing exist now within and among the national economies of the world, starting with the family, extending to various (more or less formal) grous within each society, to the nation as a whole through welfare programs and transfer payments, and internationally through aid (and even extortion). Not all of this sharing is moving toward an expansion of the concept of community to encompass the world. It appears exceedingly difficult to move toward a wider community given the large number of countries involved in the "worldwide" problems and given present concepts of identity and institutional loyalty. Currently, as we try to extend our reach to encompass global problems, the mechanism used is the governmental bureaucracy, which increases the likelihood of central control and diminishes the feeling of individual (personal or corporate) responsibility.

The alternatives we face, therefore, are greater individual responsibility and greater individual freedom leading to greater corporate (and TNC) responsibility, including the protection of individual freedom *or* greater government control and corporate authority (whether or not used responsibly).

However, no *national* economy is wholly structured on a concept of place or community roles and many small community groups have failed in attempting to apply such a structure and still retain individual freedom. The primary obstacle, of course, is motivation—that is, acceptance of a system of sharing and a willingness to commit oneself to the pattern of behavior necessary for such a system to work. Japan has come closest to it among nations, although it is now moving significantly toward the economic and social patterns of Western industrialization (rapid consumption, urbanization, individualism, and alienation) and appears to be losing its vision.

Unwillingness of peoples to play by the rules of economic sharing, social place, and political equality is matched only by their unwillingness to play by the rules of economic competition and free enterprise. A competitive system is itself a means of cooperation in the processes of production and distribution, but it requires a set of agreed rules, constantly and pervasively applied. The game, as we have played it, has come under criticism through the fact that the major league players (TNCs and AC governments) will not themselves abide by the rules, and consequently the (self-appointed) umpires and both major and minor league players (labor, consumers, small companies, and LDCs) do not find the results acceptable. Even if the system of competition worked as in theory, it would not be acceptable unless certain ethical conditions or constraints such as equality of opportunity, individual self-discipline, acceptance of certain communal obligations (stewardship of property and wealth) and social values (honesty), and protection of the environment and growth opportunities for future progress also existed.

Both competition and cooperative systems, if they are to permit individual freedom, require mutual obligations. What is different in these two systems are the specific ways in which rights and obligations are formed and to what extent. Unless competition is to lead to annihilation of opposing players, it must be conducted so that the players (and future players) return to the game, or at least to *some* game. (Thus we can understand the concern even in a competitive society to provide full employment opportunities.) The competitive system also requires constraints in that competition cannot be so successful that it ends in monopoly. With such constraints, the competitive system takes on some of the characteristics of a place society, for there are obligations to know and stay within the limits set by the rules of behavior. Even though the limits change over time, it behooves the players to follow the rules so that the system's goals are achieved and the players can remain free to cooperate in each play and each game.

A problem arises, of course, with the types of constraints imposed to achieve the right place orientation. The competitive place is more open, mobile, flexible and changing—or is supposed to be—in responding readily to shifts in market conditions and demands, to technologies leading to new products and processes, and to shifts in resource availabilities. In fact, none of these responses has been *readily* accomplished in the United States or world economies over the past decades, demonstrating to many observers that something is wrong with the system. At root, rigidities introduced by the dominant players' unwillingness to abide by the rules, eagerness to take or receive without commensurate production, and reluctance to pursue goals higher that material ones have contributed to the breakdown of the postwar international economic order.

The rigidities have arisen for good and sufficient reasons in the eyes of the policymakers, but the results of the new, undesigned system have not been desirable or fully acceptable in the eyes of those affected in advanced, developing, socialist, or capitalist countries. This lack of acceptance reflects an assessment by the LDCs that they have not been dealt an equitable share or appropriate role, as a consequence of Colonialism (past present, though the form is different). They now have the power to change their position. The unease also reflects an assessment by many observers and officials that in a *finite* world, with resources increasingly scarce (relatively), *relative* shares become more important and the advanced countries (particularly the United States) are unacceptably wasteful. Finally, the assessment that the situation is unacceptable is based also on the view of Mahatma Gandhi that, "The earth produces sufficient resources for everybody's need but not for everybody's greed." Consequently, greater attention needs to be paid to the *content* of production, toward mass consumption goods or basic human needs. Yet if growth is not to be stifled, the motivation for excellence and creativity must be nurtured and differentials of abilities recognized in differential material and other rewards.

Fundamentally, what is required in both competitive or cooperative systems (if also politically free) is a shift in attitude toward acceptance of a responsibility for our acts—jointly and severally. We are no longer in a position in which we can impose our will on others, or on nature, and expect the errors to be simply absorbed in adjustments elsewhere at little cost to ourselves or others. The costs are becoming greater and more apparent and the benefits more frequently questioned. Accepting the responsibility for our acts means that we accept individually our responsibilities for what we do within local, state, and national communities; that national governments accept the responsibility for their impacts on the world community; and that the world community accepts responsibility for the effects of its acts on the future development of mankind and our habitat.

To accept these responsibilities means setting agreed rules for production and distribution (constraining greed) and for the diffusion of authority (constraining concentration of power) and encouragng creativity and the search for individual evolution toward personal perfection (constraining or sublimating within ourselves the sensual drives). National and international responsibilities and authorities would then reflect rights and obligations of individuals—protecting and nurturing their freedom—and thereby promoting the evolution of mankind as a whole. But these goals cannot be reached presently through intergovernmental efforts to set rules for macro, aggregate or global problems. It is too difficult to assess potential results and, therefore, to design equitable rules.

The more practical approach is functional, micro, or sectoral. Integration should focus on *activities* that can be done cooperatively and be seen as equitable, and, *full* reliance on governmental negation should be avoided. Once again, a start in this direction could be made by the managers of TNCs independently initiating the kinds of cooperation suggested in the preceding chapters, thereby requiring less governmental negotiation and involvement but necessitating greater corporate self-discipline and responsibility. If we are unwilling to accept responsibilities, it means that we are still hoping to *take* from the society or the environment rather than recognizing our place within it and our destiny to grow together with the changing ecological system. Accepting such responsibility does not mean the absence of change; on the contrary, it means recognition of the continued evolution of mankind and the planet on which we live toward higher goals and achievements. It means further that any destruction be justified by its moving mankind and the environment forward in this evolution, and it means understanding that a price must be paid for errors in decision-making, both in effect and intent.

It behooves us, therefore, to know the price of continuing to place material acquisition ahead of the fulfillment of the higher purposes of mankind and its evolution to higher capabilities, both individually and collectively; material advance is but a means to evolution and, only partly, an evidence of it. Holding material advance as the primary systems (or personal) objective was apparently a goal we had to pursue for several centuries in order to learn how to meet material needs and express ourselves creatively in production. But such an objective is clearly not wholly satisfying, nor does it resolve basic world socioeconomic problems of ignorance, disease, squalor, and poverty.

A dedication to applying material progress to the continued evolution of mankind would make any given industrial structure or pattern of business and economic decision-making work more effectively to the agreed ends. Integration of interdependence in production is only *one* step toward future modes of production, distribution, and participatory decision-making. If the future modes are to help us achieve higher levels of development, they need to be accompanied by self-imposed constraints on concentration of power; encouragements of individual and collective creativity; and greater opportunities for the development of each individual. This may be too much to expect even by the year 2000, but it is a vision, and we can begin. Industrial restructuring, whereby we seek to build relationships and institutions that help elicit acceptable behavior to promote individual freedom and the assumption of a responsible concern for the roles of other national and the development of other peoples and individuals, is a beginning.

## Notes

1. The concept of an undistorted market is the figment of theoretical economists' imaginary model-building. *No* market has ever been *un*distorted in the minds of all players in the market (even the so-called highly competitive commodity or auction markets). To be *un*distorted, a market requires a *number* of conditions, beginning with a peaceful world and pro-

ceeding through requirements of large numbers of buyers and sellers, fully, freely, and equally informed, without duress (or persuasion) or government intervention of any kind, under conditions of constant costs of supply (otherwise power adheres to some), with purchasers having acquired their income in equitable and just pursuits, and under the (correct) expectation that all parties will fulfill their promises. There is a further assumption that all parties will accept the distribution of income that occurs from such market decisions.

To pin U.S. policy on such a concept is to be willfully ostrichlike. Reality is both less and more complex.

2. See A.O. Hirschman, *The Passions and the Interests,* (Princeton, N.J.: Princeton University Press, 1977), for an assessment of the efforts by the eighteenth and nineteenth century social philosophers to meet these ills.

3. Coincident with the shift in perceptions and roles of managers, business schools also must shift to an understanding of management as an activity encompassing all of the separatist disciplines now existing within such schools (rather than a continuation of disciplines that cannot communicate with each other or with corporate executives) and must focus on leadership through developing the whole person. (See Behrman, J.N. and Levin, R.I., "Are Business Schools Doing Their Job?" *Harvard Business Review,* January–February 1984, v. 62, no. 1, pp. 140–147.)

4. Peters, T.J. and Waterman, R.H., Jr., *In Search of Excellence,* New York: Harper & Row, 1982; and Pascale, R.T. and Athos, A.G., *The Art of Japanese Management,* New York: Simon & Schuster, 1981.

5. Sharing does not, of course, merely mean giving to others, it is not always a good thing for another to be given things or even opportunities; for individual evolution, there is a need to struggle and work for results. What can and should be given or shared, therefore, is help for those who *ask* for it and will commit themselves to help others in turn. The objective of sharing should be in helping ourselves and others learn how to progress, both individually and collectively.

**Selected Readings for Part IV**

Behrman, J.N. *Toward a New International Economic Order.* Paris: Atlantic Institute Study, 1974.

Coolidge, P.; Spina, G.D.; and Wallace, D. (eds). *The OECD Guidelines for Multinational Enterprise: A Business Appraisal.* Washington, D.C.: Institute for International and Foreign Trade Law, 1977.

Geirsch, H. (ed.). *Reshaping the World Economic Order.* Tubingen: J.R. Mohr, 1976.

Joint Economic Committee. *The Mercantilist Challenge to the Liberal International Trade Order.* Committee Print, 97th Congress, 2nd Session December 29, 1982.

Pentland, Chas. *International Theory and European Integration.* New York: The Free Press, 1973.

Waldmann, R. *Regulating International Business through Codes of Conduct.* Washington, D.C.: American Enterprise Institute, 1980.

Wallace, Don, Jr. (ed.). *International Regulation of Multinational Corporations.* New York: Praeger, 1976.

# Index

# About the Author

**Jack N. Behrman** is Luther Hodges Distinguished Professor at the University of North Carolina Graduate School of Business Administration, where he teaches courses in business ethics, business roles in society, and international business. He is also associate dean of academic programs for the school.

Dr. Behrman received his B.S. in economics from Davidson College, an M.A. from the University of North Carolina, and an M.A. and a Ph.D. from Princeton University. He has held faculty positions at Davidson College, Washington and Lee University, and the University of Delaware; he has also held visiting professorships at George Washington University and the Harvard Business School.

From 1961 to 1964, Dr. Behrman served as assistant secretary of commerce for domestic and international business in the Kennedy and Johnson Administrations.

He has written over twenty books, including *Some Patterns in the Rise of the Multinational Enterprise* (1969); *National Interests and the Multinational Enterprise* (1970); *U.S. International Business and Governments* (1971); *The Role of International Companies in Latin American Integration* (1972); *International Business–Government Communications* (1975); *Transfers of Manufacturing Technology within Multinational Enterprises* (1976); *Discourses on Ethics in Business* (1980); *Overseas R&D Activities of Transnational Companies* (1980); and *Industry Ties with Science and Technology Policies of Developing Countries* (1980).